SECURITY PATCH MANAGEMENT
Second Edition

SECURITY PATCH MANAGEMENT
Second Edition

Felicia M. Nicastro

CRC Press
Taylor & Francis Group
Boca Raton London New York

CRC Press is an imprint of the
Taylor & Francis Group, an **informa** business

AN AUERBACH BOOK

CRC Press
Taylor & Francis Group
6000 Broken Sound Parkway NW, Suite 300
Boca Raton, FL 33487-2742

First issued in paperback 2019

© 2011 by Taylor & Francis Group, LLC
CRC Press is an imprint of Taylor & Francis Group, an Informa business

No claim to original U.S. Government works

ISBN-13: 978-1-4398-2499-3 (hbk)
ISBN-13: 978-0-367-38288-9 (pbk)

Visit the Taylor & Francis Web site at
http://www.taylorandfrancis.com

and the CRC Press Web site at
http://www.crcpress.com

Contents

Foreword

I feel as if it was many years ago in security terms, since I wrote this book for the first time. Information security continuously evolves and develops sometimes at a lightning speed.

As a security practitioner now for over 12 years, I can honestly say that I have seen wonderful and worrisome changes come about in the information security arena. While organizations feel they are more secure today than ever, the security risks we all incur on a daily basis are continuing to increase and in the long run, in my opinion, are making us even worse off than we were 12 years ago.

As with many of us, our roles in information security change over time, and the part we play in protecting an organization continues to evolve with new technologies and new threats. Information security is not a field for the lazy or for those averse to change. We must continue to change over time; there is no opportunity for a break. We must always strive to stay one step ahead of those who plot malicious attacks on organizations or individuals so we can remain safe.

This book is not full of pretty graphs, ugly statistics, or a one-size-fits-all solution. The purpose of this book is to provide individuals and organizations with a guideline for establishing a patch management process within their organization not only to protect them against zero-day attacks but also to be proactive instead of reactive when it comes to just one facet of information security.

It is imperative that organizations implement this process, though it is simple, to ensure their security is taken as a proactive measure and not a reactive one. You may find a plethora of useful information or just one juicy nugget in the following chapters; either way, I hope you find this book useful as a guideline for establishing one of the many processes required to ensure a successful information security program.

About the Author

Felicia M. Nicastro is managing director of the Ethical Hacking Center of Excellence (EHCOE) of BT Global Services. Felicia is responsible for managing the delivery of ethical hacking projects throughout North and South America. With a team of over 40 testers and managers, Felicia interacts with multiple types of clients on a regular basis to ensure that the penetration testing they are having performed provides them with the guidance and information they need to protect themselves from a malicious attack.

With more than 12 years in the information security field, Felicia has covered almost every aspect of information security throughout her tenure, including developing and providing an organization with the policies and procedures required to maintain an appropriate security posture. Because of her experience, Felicia clearly understands the needs of an organization, from both a security and an end-user perspective and thus can provide solutions for her customers that allow them to accomplish the needs of the business and to obtain the security posture they desire.

In March 2003, Felicia authored a white paper for International Network Services (INS) titled "Security Patch Management—High-Level Overview of the Patch Management Process." Her article also was published in the November–December 2003 issue of *Information Systems Security Journal*. Although the importance of the process has remained the same, there have been some major accomplishments in patch management as well as the process, which are changed and expanded on in this book. Felicia earned a bachelor of science in management information systems from Stockton College in New Jersey. She is also trained as a Certified Information Systems Security Professional (CISSP), a Certified Information Systems Auditor (CISA), and as a Certified Health Insurance Portability and Accountability Act Security Professional (CHSP).

1
INTRODUCTION

The patch management process is a critical element in protecting any organization against the emerging risks of exploited vulnerabilities. It protects the organization by ensuring that all vulnerable systems within the organization's environment are being patched appropriately, long before an exploit is released in the wild.

A comprehensive security patch management process is a fundamental security requirement for any organization that uses computers, networks, or applications for doing business today. Such a process ensures that the security vulnerabilities of a company's information systems are addressed in an efficient and effective manner when the need to deploy patches is the remediation measure required. The patch management process introduces a high degree of accountability and discipline to the task of discovering, analyzing, and correcting security weaknesses. Considering the Blaster, Nimda, and SQL Slammer issues that have occurred in the past, this book will arm the information technology (IT) staff with a method for combating these situations, ultimately saving the organization both time and money.

The intentions of this book are not deeply technical. An extensive knowledge of technical jargon is not needed. It is easy enough to click on Windows Update and get the system updated with the appropriate patches as needed. Microsoft makes this function easy for the unskilled user. Instead, this book is geared toward the CISO, C*, director, and management levels within an organization. This book will provide them with the support and guidance they need to ensure that the appropriate patch management process has been integrated into their environment. It will also provide a level of understanding on the importance of patch management and on why having their support in the process will drive the establishment of it in the organization.

One important item to note up front is that patch management is just a process—one that is neither exceedingly technical nor extremely complicated. However, many organizations have a difficult time establishing a patch management process because it overlays all of the groups and departments in a company. For this reason, patch management is perceived as a complex issue that organizations try to resolve through the use of products that automate the task itself. If an organization is large or dispersed or has multiple locations spanning various countries, patch management can be difficult to establish effectively. This can make it a complex process that organizations tend to throw tools at, hoping to alleviate some of the issues. Whether the organization is large or small, centralized or decentralized, patch management should integrate into a company's other operational processes through successful planning and design. How an organization gets this done is not solely from a technical view; it must be seen from a process perspective, with the people and technology tied into it.

Patch management is not about technology; it is about the process and getting patches deployed onto the vulnerable systems in a fast and efficient manner. Patch management is not about patching 50 systems in 2 weeks; it is about distributing a new patch to protect 10,000-plus systems in a period of time acceptable to the organization. This does not mean that an organization with only 50 systems should not implement a patch management process; it means that the larger the organization, the more quickly it needs to deploy the patches to the vulnerable systems. An organization cannot just push out patches to a large number of systems at one time (e.g., 10,000-plus at once). This can have a dramatic effect on the organization's network, which can be even worse than if an exploit were running through it. Pushing out patches to multiple systems at the same time will result in a loss of business operations. Instead, having the patch management process fully defined will ensure that the patches are deployed in a staged manner, having little to no effect on the organization's network infrastructure and meeting acceptable time frames to do so.

With the following goals in mind, the security team within the organization should develop a formal patch management process. This formal process is then used to address the increased threats represented by known and addressable security vulnerabilities that are remediated through the deployment of a patch to the vulnerable systems. Following is a list of the goals behind implementing a patch management process:

- It positions the patch management process within the larger problem space, vulnerability management.
- It improves the way the organization is protected from current vulnerabilities and the threat that a vulnerability can be exploited before a patch is deployed on the vulnerable system.
- It improves the dissemination of information to the user community, the people responsible for the systems, and the people responsible for making sure the affected systems are patched properly.
- It formalizes record keeping in the form of tracking and reporting.
- It introduces discipline, an automated discipline that can be easily adapted once a process is in place.
- It also can allow a company to deal with security vulnerabilities as they are released, using a reduced amount of resources, and to prioritize effectively.
- It improves accountability within the organization for the roles directly responsible for security and systems.

How to Use This Book

The purpose of this book is to provide readers with a detailed explanation for implementing a patch management process within their organizations. When the first edition of this book was published there were not many patch management process books available. The majority of the information that was available was created and published by vendors. Now that this second edition is being released, the necessity and implementation of the process has not changed. While security has obviously evolved, the need for a defined process has not. The fundamentals of this book have not changed. However, it has been updated to reflect changes that have occurred within security since the first writing.

Organizations are feeling a great deal of pain when it comes to managing vulnerabilities and to ensuring the appropriate patches are installed on affected systems. This book was set up to walk the reader through how the patches should be implemented on devices and systems within an infrastructure and how to distribute them in a timely manner, and to discuss the patch management process in detail. The reader will gain an understanding of the various pieces within a patch management process and the other processes that go along with patch management.

The book is arranged in a top-down approach, encompassing all the topics that pertain to patch management directly and indirectly. This chapter provides the introduction and background to patch management and some of the next steps to take into consideration while reading this book. This chapter also provides information on the different types of patches. Although the process includes only security-related patches, it is important to understand the other types of patches released by vendors. This chapter also discusses what a product vendor's responsibilities are in regard to patch management. In addition, it raises questions such as: What is the vendor's role in the process, and what must it do to ensure its customers are protected in the event of an exploit that is a direct result of a vulnerability in one of its software products?

Chapter 2 provides an understanding of the background behind the release of a patch. It discusses how a vulnerability is turned into a patch and then how a vulnerability is turned into an exploit. It also talks about the *who, when, why,* and *how* of a patch—from who identifies the vulnerability, which gets turned into a patch, to an explanation of what makes up a security announcement that is released by a third party. Chapter 2 also provides information on how to track new patch releases.

Chapter 3 provides an understanding of what to patch. Because an organization's patch management process will include a group of systems within an environment or the routers and switches and all other aspects of the infrastructure, it is important to provide background on the various system groupings. They are broken down into desktops, servers, and network devices, with an explanation on how to treat them. This chapter also discusses dealing with remote users when it comes to ensuring that they have been patched appropriately.

Chapter 4 begins to tie in the processes surrounding patch management, such as the Information Technology Infrastructure Library (ITIL) standard, which includes change, configuration, asset, and release management. It begins with a discussion of network and systems management and then moves onto the widely known ITIL standard and its various subparts. Finally, this chapter provides an understanding of how to assess and implement IT operations into an organization. This includes assessing the current capabilities, designing the operations that will be used, implementing those operational processes, and then finally putting the IT operations into action.

Once the network and systems management (NSM) and ITIL processes have been discussed, Chapter 5 provides details surrounding security management. This starts with an overview of security management and then considers gathering the requirements, planning, and implementing security operations into an organization. Although some of the ITIL processes intersect with security management, it is important for an organization to understand what security management includes and how patch management is tied into it as well. This chapter concludes with a couple of examples on how the security management processes work.

Chapter 6 aims to close the gap in the operational processes that are discussed. After providing details on network and systems management, ITIL, and security management, it is important to touch upon vulnerability management. Because patch management is one output in vulnerability management as well as a stand-alone process, it is discussed in detail so the reader will have the tools necessary to combat these vulnerabilities on a regular basis. While vulnerability management can be vast and complex in nature, a simplified version has been provided to show where patch management is involved. To avoid repetition in future chapters, there is a high-level walk-through on how to establish the vulnerability management process within the organization. Some next steps are provided at the conclusion of the chapter to give additional background on establishing this process along with other processes within the organization.

Chapter 7 is dedicated to discussing tools and how they can be implemented into an organization's environment to assist with the patch management process. The truth is difficult to take: the tools are there to assist in the process, not to eliminate the need for the process. This will be articulated by discussing in detail process versus tools and where the tools play a major role. A tool or software product can be used to perform inventory management, to deploy the patches to vulnerable systems, and to report and track the status of the patches. When an organization decides to use a tool to assist with patch management, certain criteria should be used to determine which tool would best meet its needs and requirements. The final section in this chapter provides details on various tools and how organizations can complete a comparison on their own, determining which tool is right for them.

Following the discussion on tools, Chapter 8 provides information on how an organization should conduct proper testing of a patch prior to implementing it on the production systems. Included in this chapter are discussions on some common issues with testing and the testing process itself. Providing a rating to the patch when it is decided the organization is impacted will assist the organization in determining how to prioritize the patch. Both of these aspects are discussed as well as what a test lab would entail. This is followed by a discussion on virtual machines and their role in the patch management process.

Chapter 9 digs into the details and provides an organization with a clear understanding of the patch management process. This chapter is the heart of the entire book. The first section provides details surrounding the roles and responsibilities of the individuals who are part of the process. While each organization is different, these are described in a manner in which an organization can apply them to its own environment, regardless of size and structure. The four phases of the patch management process are then provided. The first phase, the *analysis* phase, includes monitoring for the release of patches and completing the initial assessment to determine whether the patch impacts the organization. Once the initial assessment is complete, the organization will conduct an *impact assessment* to determine its level of risk due to this vulnerability. Following the analysis phase is the *remediation* phase. Some of the tasks in this phase include developing the course of action for how the organization is going to address the patch. Testing the patch and ensuring that the patch has been integrated into the standard build are two other tasks within the remediation phase. The next phase is *updating* the operational environment. This phase includes distributing and implementing the patch within the organization. While these are two important steps in the patch management process, setting a time frame and an exception process must also be a part of this phase.

In many organizations today, there are a growing number of remote or mobile users, who can be more difficult to patch on a consistent basis, especially if they are not connecting to an organization's network on a regular basis. A task established in the update operational environment phase has been set up to detail addressing these mobile users. This will ensure that they are patched in the required time frame, even if an alternative method for updating is used. The final phase of the patch management process is *tracking*. While tracking and documentation occur throughout the patch management process, it is an important phase and one that is ongoing. An organization must meet tracking and reporting requirements. Each organization will approach patch management in a different manner; thus, these differences are detailed throughout this chapter so an organization can apply whatever is relevant.

Now that the process has been described, an organization will need to take the necessary steps to establish this process. This is detailed in Chapter 10. Establishing the patch management process follows the same concept as with any new initiative: the standard plan, design, implement, operate, and maintain. Each of the steps of putting the process in place gives guidance on either modifying an existing patch management process or establishing a new one. As with any process, a defined and documented policy must also be implemented. The final section in Chapter 10 provides an organization with details about what the patch management policy should include. It also includes a sample policy that can be modified to meet the needs of an organization.

Chapter 11 provides the conclusion to this book. Organizations face hurdles and challenges with patch management. This chapter outlines the challenges and provides potential solutions to address them. Recommended next steps are then discussed, which will assist organizations with what they need to do now that the patch management process has been detailed.

Background

Information security advisory services and technology vendors routinely report new defects in software. In many cases, these defects provide opportunities for knowledgeable people to obtain unauthorized access to systems. Information about security exposures often receives widespread publicity across the Internet, spotlighting the awareness of software weaknesses and increasing the risk that cyber criminals will attempt to use this knowledge to exploit vulnerable systems. This widespread awareness leads vendors to quickly provide patches so they can show a response to a vulnerability that has been publicized and avoid erosion of customer confidence in their products.

Historically, most organizations tend to tolerate the existence of security vulnerabilities, and, as a result, deployment of important security-related patches is often delayed. Most attention is usually directed toward patching Internet-facing systems, like firewalls and servers, all of which are involved in data communications with business partners and customers. These preferences resulted from two fundamental past assumptions:

1. The threat of attack from insiders is less likely and more tolerable than the threat of an attack from outsiders.
2. A high degree of technical skill is required to successfully exploit vulnerabilities, making the probability of attack unlikely.

In the past, these assumptions made good, practical sense and were cost-effective, given the limited scope of systems. The sophistication of threats in the past was also low, and the degree of difficulty required to exploit vulnerabilities required a knowledgeable and dedicated hacker. However, both the threat profile and potential risks to an organization have changed considerably over time. Worms can now be delivered through common entry points, such as e-mail attachments, which are automatically executed and then search for exploitable vulnerabilities on other platforms inside the network.

Getting Started

Over the past year, organizations have taken various steps to improve the way they install patches in their environment. In some cases, organizations may have had a patch management process in place. In other situations, patches were installed on an ad hoc basis. Regardless of the state they were in, and given the enormous impact of exploits in recent history, organizations are scrambling to organize their patch management processes so they are not as exposed to future exploitations.

While a future chapter will provide a detailed description of putting the patch management process in place, this section aims to provide some initial insight into getting started. First, the organization must determine who will own the process, meaning who will ensure that it is established appropriately. The group to which ownership is assigned is also held responsible for ensuring the process is being followed properly, as defined. The next step in getting started is for an organization to fully understand that patch management requires an equal combination of people, processes, and technology. While organizations typically use the combination of some or all three of these pieces, everyone involved must also understand the seriousness of the patch management process. Everyone needs to buy into the process, and, once it is in place, the organization needs to implement a mechanism to measure its success. During the patch management planning and implementation phases, the organization should provide to executive management a business plan, which will provide management with a return on security investment (ROSI) for implementing the process. The organization should also establish a mechanism to measure the ongoing success of the process itself. The final part of the next-steps section provides some additional background on the patch management process and how to get started.

Who Owns the Process?

One of the first questions an organization needs to sort out is where the patch management process will reside in the organization. That is, who will own the process? If the organization has already established a patch management process and is looking to modify it, or if the organization is looking to implement a new process, this question must be answered before anything can proceed. Depending on the size of the organization, multiple departments and groups may play direct and indirect roles in the patch management process. Because patch management really overlays multiple groups, departments, and locations, it is best to have the process owned by a centrally located unit that is responsible for regular communication with the rest of the organization. To be more specific, patch management affects each group, department, and location that has systems that are chosen for inclusion in the process. Therefore, a centralized group that can have an impact on all of these groups must be chosen to own the process.

Figure 1.1 shows an example of the old way and the new way that a security group would report to management. In the old way, and even in a lot of organizations today, it is common to see the security group

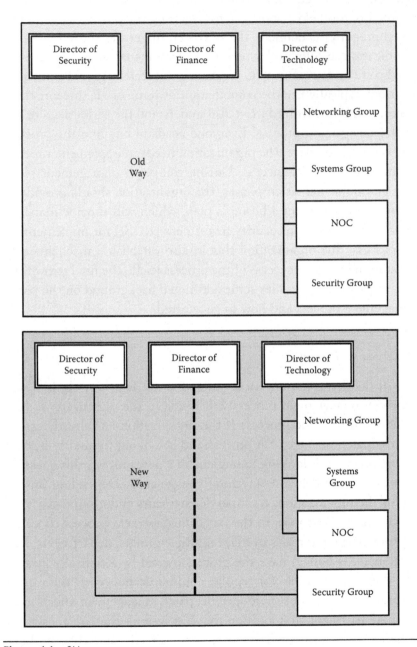

Figure 1.1   Old way versus new way.

report to the director of technology. As more and more organizations are moving toward a better overall security posture, they are seeing the need to expand this group into a separately staffed and funded group. The bottom portion of Figure 1.1 shows the new way an organization is established; it has the security group reporting to the director of security. This allows the security group to drive the overall security posture within the organization and gain the executive management support required to do so effectively. This organizational structure is used as the overall reference throughout the book when any examples or details are provided about the overall organizational structure.

While examples and suggestions for deviations are provided, using the same structure throughout will assist the organization in tailoring the process to meet its own needs. If the organization has not established this separately staffed and funded group, an immediate recommendation would be to do so to ensure that the patch management process receives the support it needs—not only from executive management but also from the other groups involved in the process. This applies to the entire security posture of the organization, not just for the purposes of implementing a patch management process.

Before the recommendation on who should own the patch management process is provided, an explanation of what the group must be ready to do should be described. First, let us take a step back and provide some insight into what is going to be explained in grave detail later. For any patch management process to be successful, regardless of the size of the organization, a *security committee* must be established that is ultimately responsible for overseeing the process and ensuring each patch has gone through this course of action appropriately. This committee does not have ownership of the process; instead, it consists of individuals from other groups. A separate, established, formal group will have the ultimate ownership of the process and will lead the effort to establish the patch management process in the organization. The group that has ownership of the process must have a level of communication with all the groups that will be affected. The group with ownership of the process must have a clear understanding of its internal roles and responsibilities, not just currently but also as the process moves forward. The group that obtains ownership must have the resources and manpower required to ensure that the process functions as it was defined. If any discrepancies are identified, this group will bring these to the attention of the security committee to ensure that the process is reviewed and revised as necessary to eliminate these questions. Because the patch management process will eventually become an established, standard operating procedure, the group identified to own the process must have assured future stability. A group that will be dismembered cannot be used. A temporary group must not be established to own the process only for the purpose of establishing it in the organization and then to be disbanded once the process is in production. The group must be in place today and moving forward.

The ownership is determined through various means. Chances are that the organization will want to assign ownership to the group having the least amount of responsibilities. This decision is not recommended. It should be owned by the group that is most capable and that has the most overall security-based impact on the organization. The group must be able to drive the process and to gain the executive support required to sustain it. The operations group should not own patch management, even though it is part of operations and the patch will affect its systems. This group is responsible for the systems that will be included in the patch management process; therefore, it is responsible for ensuring that these vulnerable systems are patched appropriately. It is the "fox watching the henhouse" scenario.

The ownership group should not have responsibility for the systems that will be included in the process, because this will influence the decisions on whether to deploy the patch on vulnerable systems. Other vectors into patch management include IT, the operations group, and the network operations center (NOC). Putting the ownership of the patch management process on any of these three groups brings back the "fox and the henhouse" situation once again. The security group is the driving force in putting a patch management process in place. The security group has the overall responsibility of ensuring that the entire organization is protected against threats, risks, and vulnerabilities. A patch is a method to mitigate against a known vulnerability; therefore, it is a security measure that must be implemented to make certain that the organization maintains the confidentiality, integrity, and availability of all organizational assets.

The security group is then the group that should have ownership of the patch management process—regardless of the size of the organization. Even if a security group is minimal in size or if the organization does not warrant a large security group, additional staff may be required to offset some of the group's current responsibilities. Any additional measures, such as manpower, must be put in place prior to establishing the process within the organization's environment.

People, Process, and Technology

People, process, and technology are all common aspects to any management process implemented within an organization. As depicted in Figure 1.2, the three aspects can be thought of as gears, all required to work together to accomplish the task successfully. They must also be aligned properly within the organization when it comes to the patch management process. Of course, this can be applied to all the processes within an organization and not just to patch management. An explanation of each of these aspects is required to provide background on what each entails.

Figure 1.2 People, process, and technology.

The *people* aspect is self-explanatory; it is the individuals responsible for confirming that a task has been completed. They may be management providing the support required to ensure that the process is established and adhered to properly by all individuals required. The operational personnel provide input and guidance into the process. They may be the ones driving the process or seeing the need to create one. The operational personnel may provide the rest of the group with guidance on how the process should be designed or some of the requirements that the process must meet. The technical personnel are the ones who may complete an actual task. They may be the ones following the procedures established within the process, such as deploying the patch to the vulnerable systems. People come into play at various intervals within a process through the ownership, establishment, and day-to-day operations of the process itself.

The *process* aspect is the predefined and documented procedures that make up the process itself. The process defines what the organization is trying to achieve and what it must do to achieve its goal. Some procedures also roll up into the process; they are the detailed steps that must be taken to complete a course of action that is ultimately a part of the overall process. This then becomes part of the policy, process, and procedure documents that an organization creates. The policy provides a high-level overview of what the organization is achieving—in this case, patch management. By including the roles and responsibilities in patch management, the process depicts how the organization will complete it. The procedures then provide the detailed steps that must be taken to ensure that what the policy and process are dictating is completed within the organization.

Technology provides assistance in the completion of the task at hand. It supports the process, enabling people to finish the task in a timely and effective manner. The technology aspect is the tool the organization uses to achieve its task as it is defined in the process. Technology can include something as simple as a server that provides authentication for remote users ranging to a network management console that gives the operations group the up-to-date status of the organization's infrastructure. In the area of patch management, technology can assist the organization in many different areas, including notification of patches as they are released from a third-party vendor or the actual deployment of the patches onto vulnerable systems.

Technology can play a role in the patch management process in various areas, although it does not always take care of the overall patch management problem.

In some instances, organizations look toward people to complete a task, and, for various reasons, the accurate completion of this task is not possible because there is no process or technology to support it. For example, if an organization requires that backups be completed on its critical servers on a nightly basis, the personnel responsible for these servers may be expected to complete the backup steps. Nevertheless, if a process is not defined and documented, these personnel may not know how to back up the systems properly. They may be backing up the wrong drives on the server each evening, skipping over the more critical drives.

Without a predefined and documented process, the staff will not fully understand how to complete this task on a nightly basis. Maybe the servers do not have a tape drive connected directly to them. How will the data be transferred from the hard drive to the tape for storage and, potentially, restoration? A level of technology must be implemented to provide the operations staff with the tools required to carry out this task. Perhaps a removable tape drive will be used, or perhaps there is a backup tape library that multiple servers use to store multiple backups. Regardless of the technology that will be used, a tool will be required to complete these backups according to the schedule. While this is a simplistic example, it is easy to understand why the combination of people, processes, and technology must be used when implementing an operational-based process. Once these three aspects are aligned, they come together to provide the total solution.

This same mind-set holds true for patch management. It is through the healthy combination of people, process, and technology that a patch management process can be established within an organization. With these three aspects in place, the patch management process can accurately, efficiently, and effectively protect the organization by deploying the appropriate patches to vulnerable systems. Now that the importance of all three aspects has been detailed, one additional item must be noted. This is the overriding importance of the process aspect. Having the people and technology to complete a task, like patch management, for example, are critical to its success. However, without a solid predefined and documented process, patch management cannot be successful. Even with a staff of 20 people and a solid tool to deploy the patches, the process must be accurately defined to ensure that it can be properly completed. With the rush for organizations to address patching issues today, the tendency is to look toward technology to assist in easing the pain. Often, it is only after an organization realizes that it is not combating patch management appropriately, even with the tools deployed, that it reviews and attempts to redesign the process.

Establishing a patch management process and putting it in place are not easy tasks to accomplish. Still to be considered is the step of communicating the process to the appropriate staff and getting the message out to the user community about their responsibilities in ensuring vulnerable systems are patched appropriately. An entire chapter is dedicated to putting the patch management process in place. Here we align the people, process, and technology required for success. Completing the task of establishing the patch management process accurately will not only improve the operational flow of updating vulnerable systems but will also reduce operational costs for deploying patches within an organization's responsible environment. Any organization that takes a proactive approach to patch management will operate at a lower cost than an organization that waits to react to an exploit, which affects an unpatched system.

Measuring Success

Once the patch management process is in place within an organization, a mechanism for measuring the success of the process should be defined. An organization needs to track and maintain status reports on the number of systems susceptible to a vulnerability versus the number of systems patched and the number of systems unpatched. This arms the organization with the information required to determine how successful the patch management process has been. This should be done on an ongoing basis. While it may not be feasible to measure the success with each instance of the process or with each patch deployed, it needs to be done regularly and in a predefined manner.

When the organization assigns the roles and responsibilities for the patch management process, the security committee will be defined. It will receive the summarized report containing the status of each patch install and then will be informed of the percentage (or number) of systems that have gone through the patch management process successfully. For example, if 90 systems are vulnerable and need to be patched, and after 2 weeks 75 have been updated and plans are in place to update 10 more in the next 7 days, an organization can monitor how the process is being integrated into its standard operating procedures. Based on these numbers, the priority level given to each patch itself will dictate the minimum and maximum lengths of time before all vulnerable systems are updated appropriately

There is also an exception process explained in a future chapter. This provides an organization with an alternative to implementing the patch if the department or business unit decides it is unnecessary. Based on the previous example, if five systems have been given an exception and then in 3 weeks' time the patch management process is 100% complete for that patch, this is a great achievement, and the organization should consider the patch management process successful. Of course, the more systems that are vulnerable will increase the chance of systems not being patched.

Another example would be if 400 desktops are susceptible to a vulnerability and need to be patched. This patch is given a priority level of urgent, and all desktops need to be patched within a minimum time frame of 1 week and a maximum time frame of 2 weeks. The tracking method would be used to measure how many desktops have been patched, with a report provided to the security committee each week. If the report at the end of Week 1 shows that only 100 desktops have been updated, the staff is left with 300 to be completed during Week 2. If only 150 desktops can be patched in Week 2, then there are still 150 vulnerable desktops left wide open within the environment. In the case of desktops, there should be only a rare exception to updating the system, especially if standard builds are deployed on these desktops. Therefore, at the end of 2 weeks, the organization should see a 100% completion rate. In this example, however, 37.5% (i.e., 150) of the desktops still needed to be updated. While 62.5% have been patched, the organization must determine the appropriate percentage that must be achieved within the defined time frames. At a minimum, 75% of the vulnerable systems must be patched in the established time frame, with outstanding systems to be patched within the next 5 days. This can put additional pressure on the group responsible for deploying the patch, but it also holds them accountable for ensuring that the process is being followed accurately.

If an issue has come about that prevents the organization from meeting these time frames, the patch management process should be reevaluated to determine what the achievable time frames should be. If it is not the process but instead the groups or departments within the organization that are causing systems to remain unpatched, then the importance of complying with this process must be communicated down to these groups by executive management. If they are not going to be held accountable for making certain that their vulnerable systems are patched, the company may take drastic measures (e.g., placing them on a completely different network segment) to ensure that the remainder of the organization is protected.

Next Steps

There is a common set of terms discussed when talking about patch management. Are we addressing *vulnerabilities, patches,* or *exploits?* The answer is clear: patch management is about the patches. The vulnerability within an operating system, application, or piece of software drives the need for the vendor to issue a patch. The vendor, in turn, releases the patch to the user community, explaining that it eliminates a known vulnerability within its software or product. Hackers turn this vulnerability into an exploit by using it to cause malicious activity. Of course, exploits are not always released for every patch. If that were the case, organizations would have deployed a patch management process years ago. The fact is that these exploits are becoming more common and damaging as time goes on, forcing organizations to establish this process now.

It is the effect the exploit has on the organization when it is released into the wild that drives the organization to establish the process. Therefore, organizations must protect themselves from the threat of an exploit by deploying all patches that affect systems within their infrastructure. For the purpose of this book, patches, vulnerabilities, and exploits are seen as three different entities, each having their own function and purpose. The reader will get a clear understanding of the differences among the three in the following chapters. Sometimes, there are also workarounds (or fixes) that are released in place of a patch to protect an organization from a particular vulnerability. We discuss patches only, not workarounds. However, workarounds can be deployed through the organization by following the patch management process. So, regardless of whether a patch or workaround has been released to address a vulnerability, either will follow the organization's patch management process to offer protection from the exploit that is soon to follow.

Types of Patches

Over the past couple of years, a lot of attention and publicity have been given to patches, including how to manage their installation on the vulnerable systems within the organization. This management has become the topic of numerous articles, white papers, and even Web-based seminars. In each scenario, only one of the three types of patches is discussed: the security patch, which addresses a vulnerability that has been identified in a software product. The other two types of patches are *functionality* patches and *feature* patches. While the common term *patch* is the same, the deployment of these patches occurs at other stages in the life cycle of the system itself. Feature and functionality patches are typically deployed in the development phases of a system's life cycle, whereas security patches are deployed while the system is already in development, testing, and production. Figure 1.3 shows the three different types of patches released to organizations today.

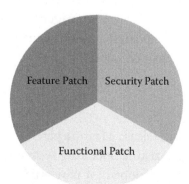

Figure 1.3   Different types of patches.

In the following chapters the patch management process is built around ensuring that organizations are deploying security patches on all vulnerable systems in a realistic time frame. The other two types of patches are not directly addressed in these chapters. Keep in mind, however, that the patch management process can be modified to fit these needs as well. The following sections detail the three types of patches released by vendors and their different deployment roles.

Functionality Patches

When a vendor releases a functionality patch, its intentions are to fix a known functional issue within the software itself. Functional issues are not related to security but instead deal with the functionality of an operating system, application, or other type of software program. The cases where functionality patches are most common are usually where a vendor is releasing a new product, updating a beta release of a product, or providing a service pack. If a vendor went public with a new software product, a bug or functionality issue may have surfaced after its release. To fix this issue, the vendor will release a functionality patch, sometimes called a "bug fix." These are very common and can be seen in Service Packs or version releases or through bug IDs that product vendors provide for their customers.

The process for functionality patches is different from that for security-related patches. The organization typically installs them during development or testing of a new software product prior to placing it in production. If the software product has already been placed in production and a functionality patch is released, the patch would go through the organization's release management process to establish that affected systems are updated appropriately. Release management is discussed in a subsequent chapter.

Feature Patches

Sometimes, a vendor will release a feature patch to introduce a new feature or function into an existing operating system or application. These types of patches can be developed for new software products or products that have been updated, usually to support a new option. While they seem to be similar to functionality patches, they are different in that they introduce a new feature into something that already exists. If a vendor adds a new aspect to its product line, then that vendor would issue a feature patch for its customers to install and use. Feature patches are not the result of a vulnerability or a functionality flaw.

Feature patches typically follow the same path as functionality patches when it comes to installation on affected systems. As with functionality patches, feature patches are usually integrated and tested during the development or testing phases of a new system prior to placing it into production. If the software product has already been placed in production and the feature patch is provided by the vendor, then the update would go through the organization's release management processes. As discussed in the previous section, details surrounding release management are provided in a later chapter.

Security Patches

Security patches are the driving force behind implementing the patch management process. These patches cause the most difficulty when it comes to ensuring that all the vulnerable systems have been patched appropriately. Security patches correct a known vulnerability and are released by the vendor. Though functionality and feature patches are important, security patches are the ones that can have an impact on business operations. This book was written to discuss security patches and how to implement a patch management process to make certain that the organization is protected in the event of an exploit or malicious activity due to a vulnerability.

In most cases, a patch management process concerns itself only with security patches versus the functionality and feature patches. As previously discussed, functionality and feature patches follow the release management process, and although patch management ties into release management a separate process is established to address them specifically. Subsequent chapters provide an organization with not only an understanding of the patch management process but also guidance in how to establish a patch management process within the organization.

Product Vendor's Responsibility

The reasoning behind the patch management process lies in protecting the organization against vulnerabilities that are a result of faulty or improperly programmed software. Whatever the case may be, a vulnerability within a piece of software is the vendor's responsibility. Patch management is thus an effort to protect the organization against these vulnerabilities by deploying the vendor-provided patch onto the vulnerable systems. Product vendors have a certain level of responsibility when it comes to the software or hardware they develop, create, and sell to customers. A vulnerability can exist that affects software and hardware alike. In most cases, a vulnerability that results in a patch being released from the vendor pertains to a software product more often than to an actual piece of hardware. Regardless of whether the vulnerability affects software or hardware, the patch management process should proceed as designed for both instances. Therefore, *vulnerability* affects software or hardware. However, the vulnerabilities that affect organizations most often are in software and are the reason behind establishing the patch management process in the first place.

When a vulnerability has been identified with a vendor's software product, the vendor has the responsibility to make its customers aware of the vulnerability and to provide a patch for it. Doing this shows due diligence on the part of the vendor, because it protects the vendor's brand name and reputation. In the end, the vendor must show a strong effort toward helping its customers ensure that the vulnerable systems are patched appropriately. Ironically, vendors are not typically the source of a vulnerability announcement. Instead, they usually come from a third party that has reported the issue. Organizations such as CERT, BugTraq, and Symantec provide announcements to the general public, reporting the vulnerability and the patch availability to remediate the issue. The vendor's responsibility is established prior to the announcement being sent by the reporting organization to provide that a patch is associated with this vulnerability before it is publicly announced. When the vulnerability is released to the public, the chance of an exploit being released shortly thereafter increases. If a patch is not associated with the announced vulnerability, the vendor's reputation, customer base, and overall value are in question, especially if the exploit is in the wild before the vendor can get a patch prepared and announced. This is where the vendor's actions are critical. The vendor must provide guidance to its customers to mitigate against a potential exploit on a vulnerable system due to a vulnerability in its software. This is even more important if the vendor has yet to develop a patch for the threat. In these instances, instead of releasing a patch the vendor may provide a workaround that would need to be deployed.

Over the past years, Microsoft has received widespread publicity regarding the number of vulnerabilities being released for its software. Although Microsoft provides patches for all the vulnerabilities as they are released, it is the number of vulnerabilities that cause the negative publicity. Over a recent period of time, Microsoft has shown that it understands its customers by taking the appropriate steps to assist them in addressing the great number of patches released. For example, Microsoft has modified its patch release schedule so that one occurs on the second Tuesday of each month instead of releasing them as the vulnerabilities are identified. This limits the number of patches on a daily or weekly basis that customers need to address. Instead, customers receive a list of all patches for the entire month, which they can then use to plan for deployment on the vulnerable systems in their environment.

This has reversed the negative publicity effects Microsoft was seeing previously. Companies recognize that they are assuming the responsibility when it comes to vulnerabilities on their software products, and they are providing customers with a better way to address the release of patches. If a critical patch is identified during the course of the month, then Microsoft will break the monthly cycle and send its customers notice of the critical patch immediately. In these instances, the organization would need to have a critical vulnerability procedure, which is part of the patch management process. That ensures that the organization will deploy the critical patch onto the vulnerable systems in a shorter time frame.

Of course, Microsoft is not the only vendor with vulnerabilities identified in its software products. Other operating systems, such as Solaris and various flavors of Linux, must also be patched in the same manner. Therefore, the vendor of these software products must release the patch with the identification of the vulnerability. Neither of these vendors provides the monthly updates that Microsoft does. Instead, the patches are released as needed, so an organization must be prepared to start the patch management process at any time during the course of a month. The time it takes for a vulnerability to turn into an exploit is decreasing, as is the level of impact the exploit has on the organization. This makes the release of the patch when the vulnerability is identified a critical responsibility of the vendor that created and released the software product.

While vendors hold the ultimate responsibility to inform their customers and the general public when a vulnerability has been identified that impacts their software, there are others who are more than happy to do so. Of course, they do not always have the vendors' or their customers' best interests in mind. These other sources can be either white hat or black hat hackers. Hackers often inform the vendor directly when a vulnerability is identified in its software. If it comes from white-hat hackers, they are informing the vendor in an effort to ensure that a patch to remediate this issue is released in the near future. These individuals may also inform the other organizations, such as CERT, about this vulnerability so that CERT can further investigate and follow up with the vendors to obtain the information for remediation.

If black-hat hackers, who are malicious, inform the vendor of the vulnerability, the risk of immediate exploit is extremely high. These individuals may also release the vulnerability to the rest of the hacker community before it is publicly announced by CERT (or BugTraq). This poses an even greater risk for a zero-day exploit. These occurrences used to be a rare, but with all the discussions surrounding patch management over the past few years zero-day exploits are becoming more common.

A zero-day exploit occurs when an exploit for a vulnerability is released the same day a patch is provided to protect the organization's vulnerable systems. It is typically impossible for an organization to patch all of its systems in one day or upon immediate receipt of the patch. This is when an organization is most susceptible to an impact in business operations. If the organization cannot patch the systems immediately, the chance of the exploit making its way into the organization's network increases.

With each zero-day exploit, typically other remediation items can be executed to protect the organization. This might be a configuration change within the network. For example, it may be blocking certain ports on the external firewall to prohibit the entry of the exploit into the internal network. This would be considered a temporary fix, especially if these ports affect other business-required applications. This temporary fix would stay in place until the vulnerable systems in the environment are patched, and then the firewall rules would change to their original configuration. This is only one example of a temporary fix. These are usually provided by the vendor once the exploit is released into the wild and the vendor is assuming its responsibility in helping its customers protect their systems.

No vendor is more responsible than another when it comes to protecting its software and providing its customers with patches when vulnerabilities are identified. Most vendors of any software product today provide Web sites or mailing lists that provide information on vulnerabilities affecting their software. Vendors such as Microsoft and Linux have subscription-based mailing lists that e-mail the customer when a vulnerability is released. Other organizations such as CERT and BugTraq offer free subscription-based mailing lists that will alert the customer of a vulnerability and the availability of the corresponding patch to fix it.

2

VULNERABILITY TO
PATCH TO EXPLOIT

The purpose of this chapter is to discuss how a vulnerability is identified, when the patch is created, and who creates the exploit using the vulnerability.

There are countless numbers of people worldwide scouring source code to identify an exploitable vulnerability in a software product. Once the vulnerability is identified, it then comes down to determining how damaging the exploit can be. This includes the devastating impact the exploit can have against a business's operation, ultimately affecting its revenue. On the other hand, perhaps the exploit causes only an annoyance, such as a virus or worm that will not leave an environment. In addition, the difficulty in producing an exploit comes into play, because the more difficult the exploit, the less the chance malicious hackers have of completing it. Only hackers trying to accomplish extremely malicious activity will devote a lot of time and effort to exploiting a vulnerability. It is often the low-hanging fruit they go after.

Each organization may rate an exploit differently. Of course, this depends on how dramatic the impact is to its business operations. Overall, the security community does not rate a specific exploit unless it has had a dramatic consequence on the Internet. The effect of an exploit can be rated by the number of vulnerable systems within the organization, the speed of propagation, or the impact it has on business operations. If an organization has determined that the number of vulnerable systems is high or that a large percentage of its information technology (IT) infrastructure is vulnerable, the damage potential of an exploit can be exponential. If the vulnerable systems cannot be contained, or quarantined, the organization must put manpower in place to patch all the vulnerable systems before the exploit has migrated onto them. The speed of propagation can result in an exploit causing a lot of damage. If the exploit is through a worm traversing from one vulnerable system to the next, it will be very difficult for the organization to contain it until all the systems have been patched appropriately. However, if an organization is using an intrusion detection system (IDS) and intrusion prevention system (IPS) in an environment-wide deployment, the chances of detecting and quarantining the worm in a shorter time frame are higher than if it were not. If the impact to normal business operations results in a network outage or if business services are disrupted, the organization may lose revenue because of the exploit and the number of vulnerable systems within the environment. This is the worst outcome an organization can experience. A disruption to business operations can result in a loss of revenue because services, which the organization provides, may not be able to continue until the exploit is contained and the vulnerable systems patched.

The purpose of the following sections is to discuss who finds the vulnerabilities in the first place and how and when the product vendors are notified of such vulnerabilities. We will also discuss why malicious hackers spend time and energy trying to exploit them. Last, we will explore how a vulnerability goes to a patch and to an exploit, including which one comes first. Having an understanding of these items provides the meaning behind why patch management is critical to any organization today. Establishing the patch management process ensures that the organization is completing the right steps to protect itself from a vulnerability resulting in an exploit that is released.

Before starting down this path, it is important to briefly discuss hackers, including who they are and why they do what they do. There are two common types of hackers: white hat and black hat. There are books dedicated to hackers and how they think and act. A white hat hacker is the good guy, and, obviously, a black hat hacker is the bad guy. Either type can and will identify a vulnerability and will report it to CERT, a vendor, or other medium for notifying the appropriate people. Throughout this book, references to hackers are used to identify those who either report a vulnerability or develop the exploit pertaining to it.

Once the background behind the exploit creation is explained, the organization must arm itself with the proper mechanisms to track new vulnerabilities and patches as they are released. While monitoring for new patches can be a full-time position, the goal is for the organization to have a simplified procedure for identifying patches that have been released that affect any systems in its environment, or infrastructure.

Who Exploits When, Why, and How

It important for an organization not only to establish a patch management process but also to understand the background information regarding an exploit. There is the typical who, when, why, and how regarding a vulnerability turning into an exploit. In the security community, Web sites and organizations worldwide such as SANS, CERT, and OWASP provide information about malicious activity on the Internet. These sites can provide a lot of useful information, especially if the organization needs to understand more about an exploit and how it can be completed through the use of a vulnerability. While this section has nothing to do with the patch management process, it does explain the details of the behind-the-scenes activity that occurs with patches. Of course, not all vulnerabilities result in an exploit. Therefore, the information provided herein may pertain not to all identified vulnerabilities but instead to a limited number of vulnerabilities, which are then patched and potentially exploited.

It is important to understand who is behind the exploit and why they attempt to complete this malicious act. Ultimately, hackers are the ones who regularly create the exploits, depending on the severity of the vulnerability discovered, and what damage it can potentially cause. Their level and skill may be different, but they all have the same end result in mind.

Once the vendor is notified of a vulnerability, it has to make a determination on how quickly it will develop a patch to eliminate it. There is typically no inside information on whether this vulnerability will turn into an exploit; instead, the vendor should look at the severity of the vulnerability to determine the vulnerability's potential level of impact to its software and operating system. This can provide the organization with the understanding of when a vendor is made aware of a vulnerability that affects its software product. Once informed, the vendor must develop the patch prior to its public release. The exploit process is vastly different from that of informing the vendors, as not every vulnerability is exploited.

Hackers may choose to attempt to create an exploit or to cause malicious activity using the vulnerability simply because they can. If they are spending too much time creating an exploit, then they will move on to another vulnerability—one that is easier to manipulate. Hackers may choose to create an exploit for various reasons, including malicious intent, money, or reputation. Whichever the reason, the hackers realize the damage they are causing not only to a specific organization but also to individuals across the Internet.

How the vulnerability turns into an exploit that affects systems that have not been patched can be a very complex and technical question to answer. Examples will be provided to walk through a patch release, including sample advisories that are sent out from organizations. This should provide an organization with an understanding of the advisory and how the patch is related. It will also detail how an exploit is announced, including the patch that should be applied to the vulnerable system to protect the organization.

The Who

Hackers and developers are typically the two main groups that find vulnerabilities in source code or software products, although other groups such as OWASP assist applications vendors in attempting to find vulnerabilities in their source code in a nonmalicious manner, such as through secure coding techniques and recommendations. Hackers can go through publicly available source code and try to determine whether a vulnerability exists. If they identify a potential vulnerability, then they might make an attempt to exploit it. A hacker's motivations can be numerous. No matter what the motivations, it is the method in which the hacker informs the vendor of the vulnerability that has the most impact.

A nonmalicious user, such as a developer, programmer, or application tester, may review code on an ongoing basis in search of a vulnerability that has yet to be identified. Most vendors enforce secure coding when developing a new or updated software product and have employees within their organization ensure it is secure prior to releasing it to the market. Whether it is an operating system or an application, the vendor will employ resources to search for vulnerabilities in this code. Once the developer identifies a vulnerability, it would follow standard protocol to make certain that the vulnerability is mitigated prior to releasing the software to the general public. This is a common practice, and usually these vulnerabilities are identified before the software is released. If the vulnerability is identified afterward, then the patch would be issued in the normal fashion.

The security community has made it convenient for anyone to report a vulnerability that has been identified. CERT (www.cert. org), which is home to CERT Coordination Center and is located at Carnegie Mellon University's Software Engineering Institute, has a Vulnerability Reporting Form that can be completed by any individual who has identified a vulnerability. The form is completed and sent back to CERT via its Web-based format. While CERT will not look into all reports, it will consider each one and will then contact the vendor to discuss the vulnerability and to receive the related patch. CERT is considered one of the first places security-savvy individuals go to get accurate information regarding vulnerabilities in a timely manner.

Numerous other security sites are available on the Internet as well to provide a plethora of information regarding vulnerabilities, patches, and monitoring for malicious activity. It is recommended that for an organization to get up-to-date, unbiased information, they should ensure the organization they are trusting to keep them abreast of the latest security threats has the background and reputation to support said information.

The When

This can be considered in two ways: when the product vendors are notified; and when the exploit will be released. Product vendors' responsibilities are detailed in another section, although it is still worth mentioning that they must be notified in a timely manner about a vulnerability so they can issue the patch immediately. If the hacker, developer, or third-party organization does not inform the vendor about the vulnerability, the risk of it becoming a zero-day exploit greatly increases.

When this exploit becomes a reality is really what this section aims to discuss. Once hackers identify the vulnerability, they may attempt to develop an exploit that is built on the vulnerability itself. The creation of the exploit can be based on three main items: (1) the level of difficulty required to create the exploit; (2) the availability of systems to test the exploit; and (3) how much damage the hackers intend to cause with the exploit.

Depending on how complex the vulnerability is, the hackers may or may not be able to create the exploit. The level of difficulty and the hackers' skills can dictate whether the exploit can even be created. If the hackers are merely *script kiddies*—the users who try to do things for fun and seem to know just enough to be dangerous—and are trying to create an exploit based on tools downloaded from the Internet, this may not be good enough. It may take an experienced hacker who has actually created malicious tools to establish the requirements needed to exploit the vulnerability. While the level of difficulty is different for each vulnerability, typically a script kiddie will try to exploit an easy vulnerability or low-hanging fruit type of exploit. More experienced and knowledgeable types of hacker are the ones who will spend the additional time needed to create a more sophisticated exploit, which in the long run will cause more damage. Depending on how much time hackers want to dedicate to this task, if they cannot create an exploit after a certain period of time they will move on to something else.

Hackers must test the exploit prior to releasing it onto the Internet. If the vulnerability applies only to a small number of systems, the chances of a propagating exploit are slim. Instead, the vulnerability should affect a large number of systems that are widely used across the Internet. If this is the case, then hackers should test the exploit to ensure not only that it is working properly but also that it has a greater impact on the user community when the exploit is released into the wild. Just as with any other new software product or implementation, this too must be tested to establish that it will function as planned. Hackers will take the appropriate steps to confirm this as well.

Hackers' intent can also be a driver when attempting to create an exploit, such as whether it is being done for malicious intent, to prove worth to the hacker community, for monetary compensation, or for some other unknown reason. Depending on what the motivations are for the hackers, the exploit can have anywhere from just an annoyance effect to grave damage that costs organizations time and money. Hackers may be trying to exploit a vulnerability that is known in the organization from which they were recently fired. Hackers may be trying to get back at an ex-employer and, in this instance, may take the additional time to try to create the exploit versus giving up on it once they realize it will take a great deal of effort. Whichever the case may be, the intent of the exploit is dependent on the individual who created it in the first place.

The Why

The purpose of this section is to explain why hackers exploit a vulnerability and their possible intentions, including reputation, revenge, money or fraud, or simply for the fun of it. Hackers may not even attempt to create an exploit until after the vulnerability has been announced and the patch released. Hackers may not be going for the zero-day exploit but instead may be spending the time required to ensure that the exploit will cause severe damage.

Perhaps hackers have established themselves in the hacker community but need to make a name for themselves; this can be done by identifying and successfully executing a large exploit or, better yet, a zero-day exploit. Hackers do not use their real names on any of the underground Web sites, but there is still a community out there driven by reputation and malicious achievements. To gain this reputation and, therefore, respect within the hacker community, hackers must prove themselves in a fitting manner. One way to do this is by creating an exploit, which is the result of an unpatched system due to a known vulnerability.

While exacting revenge on an ex-employer may be the reasoning, hackers may also be trying to take revenge on a specific vendor. While this may seem a little far-fetched, it can be quite true. Microsoft is often used in this example. Hackers are still trying to prove a point with Microsoft, displaying that their software products are more vulnerable and easier to exploit than other operating systems or software products. If the same amount of time was spent trying to establish exploits against UNIX®-based operating systems such as Solaris and Linux, the same would hold true for them as well. In this instance, hackers may be trying to prove to a product vendor that the source code is not secure and is highly susceptible to malicious exploits. These hackers do this in the hope that the vendor will spend the extra time and effort in affirming that the code is secure prior to releasing it to the public.

While money and fraud are not typically the driving forces behind an exploit, they do need to be mentioned. Typically, money, fraud, and other more detrimental impacts are not completed in the form of an exploit but instead as a direct attack on the organization. An exploit can be used to obtain these things, but creating the exploit will not be at the top of the list for hackers trying to steal money from an organization.

To some hackers—usually script kiddies—there is fun or a challenge in creating an exploit based on a vulnerability. Maybe they are just becoming technically savvy users and are trying to learn new things. On the other hand, perhaps they are becoming security-conscious users and are trying to protect themselves by seeing what can actually be done.

The How

How does a vulnerability turn into an exploit that affects unpatched vulnerable systems? To explain this process in a clear summary, an example of the latest zero-day exploit is used.

As of this writing, the most recent zero-day exploit occurred in early January 2010. This hack affected Google, Adobe, and other organizations through an exploit of a vulnerability that impacted various versions of Microsoft Internet Explorer. According to the *Microsoft Security Bulletin MS10-002*, which was originally published on January 21, 2010 and last updated on February 10, 2010, this update has been rated as "Critical" and is titled "Cumulative Security Update for Internet Explorer (978207)." The security update resolves seven privately reporting vulnerabilities and one publicly disclosed vulnerability in Internet Explorer. The severest of these vulnerabilities can allow remote code execution if a user views a specially crafted Web page using Internet Explorer, and those with administrative rights on the system are more impacted than those with limited system access rights.

To take a step back to the information that was released approximately a week prior to the bulletin, the damage had already been done against a number of organizations' Web sites, including Google and Adobe. This is where the zero-day exploit comes into play. No patch was available when the vulnerability was discovered, and immediately afterward the exploit was created and deployed. Microsoft did provide recommendations on how users can mitigate the risk until the patch was created, but at that point the damage had already been done.

Google had announced that it was a target of a "highly sophisticated" and coordinated attack against its network. The hackers ended up stealing intellectual property and attempted to gain access to Gmail accounts of human rights activists. They were able to identify that the attacks originated in China.

Shortly thereafter, Adobe also announced that it too had been the target of the same, but neither would give much more detail on what specifically had occurred. Some of the companies that were breached, in addition to Google and Adobe, stated that it was through a malicious PDF e-mail attachment that exploited a zero-day vulnerability in Adobe's Reader and Acrobat applications. Through that vulnerability, the hackers then installed a Trojan Program called Trojan.Hydraq on users' systems to obtain credentials and other information, giving them another mechanism to breach said company.

The Adobe vulnerability is explained in detail in the *Technical Cyber Security Alert TA10-013A*, which is titled "Adobe Reader and Acrobat Vulnerabilities." The Adobe Security Bulletin is titled APSB10-02, and more information can be obtained from that security bulletin as well.

To summarize, the vulnerability in Adobe and the one found in Internet Explorer were combined to form a zero-day exploit that resulted in multiple organizations losing intellectual information. This is only a high-level summary of these two vulnerabilities and how they were used in conjunction to create an exploit. The bulletin numbers provided in the previous sections can be referenced for more details surrounding each vulnerability. Although there are now patches available for both, there were not any at the time of the exploit, thus making them more susceptible to this type of activity. The key to avoiding having an exploit affect the organization is to ensure that the systems are patched once the vulnerability is identified. Then again, if no patch is available, practicing other forms of security best practice—in this case limiting access rights of users to systems—can assist an organization in not being the target of this type of attack.

Tracking New Patch Releases

There are multiple ways to track the release of new patches. There must be a balance between obtaining the required information and not being overloaded with too much information to filter through. An organization must be able to focus on what needs to be identified and acted upon and what can be disregarded. The chapter describing the patch management process will provide information on how an organization can establish the procedures necessary in regard to monitoring for new patch releases, but the source of information should be decided upon early in the design process so that the proper mechanism can be established moving forward.

An organization can obtain information regarding new patch releases by two methods. The first is by going to various Web sites and becoming a member of various mailing lists to get information as it is released. While this can be a great method, it may also be information overload. It will not help an organization if it is being inundated with patch releases for operating systems and applications that are not in its environment. The organization must be able to determine which sites and mailing lists will provide the most benefit and focus on a minimum of two, with a maximum of four sites from which to obtain information regarding patches. From its perspective, Microsoft has made the notification of patches more efficient. Microsoft releases patches to its subscribers on the second Tuesday of each month. This way, organizations can plan accordingly for their Microsoft-based systems. Of course, an organization may have other operating systems and applications within the environment that would need to follow another means to obtain the information. Depending on how long an organization has been receiving these notifications, it may have a source of notification already in place; in other words, the organization has already determined which sites and mailing lists work best in its particular environment.

The second method for tracking new patches as they are released is through a third-party service or software tool. This excludes the use of mailing lists and applies instead to specific services, which an organization can pay for, that send patches or notifications of patches that only directly affect that organization. For example, an organization would subscribe to a service that would track patch releases that affect systems within its environment. For this to work properly, an inventory of the environment would need to be documented and accurately maintained. This inventory would then be provided to the third party, so that when a patch is released there would be a record on hand of what the organization has to clearly determine whether the patch affects it and to determine whether the notification needs to be sent to it. Depending on the method the organization chooses to use, the second option would need to be closely evaluated to determine which one is more feasible for the organization to put in place.

Resources for Information

There is a plethora of external resources where an organization can obtain information about a new vulnerability that has been publicly released. The following information is based on the most popular resources for this type of information. While an organization may need to go to only one source for the information it requires, multiple sources may provide additional information that could prove crucial.

The United States Computer Emergency Readiness Team (US-CERT) is the operational team within the National Cyber Security Division (NCSD) at the Department of Homeland Security (DHS). US-CERT is responsible for providing support and defense against cyber attacks for the Federal Civil Executive Branch. It also interacts with federal agencies, industry, the research community, state and local governments, and others to share cyber security information to the general public.

As part of US-CERT's dissemination of information, the National Cyber Alert System offers four different means in which to share such data (www.us-cert.gov):

1. *Technical Cyber Security Alerts.* Provide timely information about current security issues, vulnerabilities and exploits.
2. *Cyber Security Bulletins.* Provide weekly summaries of new vulnerabilities. Patch information is provided when available.
3. *Cyber Security Alerts.* Provide timely information about current security issues, vulnerabilities, and exploits. They outline the steps and actions that nontechnical home and corporate computer users can take to protect themselves from attack.

4. *Cyber Security Tips.* Provide advice about common security issues for the general public.

SANS delivers an e-mail every Thursday titled "@Risk: The Consensus Security Alert"; readers can sign up at www.sans.org/newsletters/#risk. @Risk explains in detail the first three to eight vulnerabilities for the week that impact organizations or users the most. It provides the reader with information on what to do and how damaging the vulnerabilities are and then summarizes how other organizations have reacted to those vulnerabilities. This provides the reader with a comparative analysis on how other organizations are reacting to vulnerabilities. The mailer then lists the vulnerabilities released in their entity for that week. The mailing list also will receive SANS Flash Alerts, which are released two or three times a year. It is a free subscription that is quite popular in the technical community. SANS is definitely the first place to go when looking for security-related information. It is also an excellent place to start for someone looking to learn more about security in general.

Table 2.1 provides examples of some other sources for vulnerabilities and patches.

Table 2.1

GENERAL SECURITY	MAILING LISTS	ADVISORIES
SecurityFocus.com: http://www.securityfocus.com	Bugtraq Archive: http://www.securityfocus.com/archive/1	Computer Emergency Response Team: http://www.cert.org/advisories
United States Computer Emergency Readiness Team http://www.us-cert.gov/	SANS http://www.sans.org/newsletters/	Common Vulnerabilities and Exposures: http://cve.mitre.org
Symantec Security Response: http://securityresponse.symantec.com/	United States Computer Emergency Readiness Team: http://www.us-cert.gov/	SANS http://isc.sans.org/

3

WHAT TO PATCH

This chapter discusses what an organization should include in the patch management process from a system and network device perspective. For the organization to determine what network devices and systems to include in the patch management process, an accurate and up-to-date inventory must exist. Asset management, also called inventory management, is discussed in detail in later chapters. Having this accurate and regularly updated inventory is critical to ensuring that the patch management process is successful. For the purpose of this chapter, the assumption is that the organization has a well-documented inventory of all network devices and systems within its infrastructure. If a documented inventory is not in place, this chapter will provide plenty of justification for the need for one to be created.

There are various types of systems and network devices within an organization's environment, and this list is ever changing and growing. The following sections provide a breakdown of what types of systems and network devices can and should be included in the patch management process.

Within desktops alone, various facets must be considered when designing the patch management process. During the planning phase of putting the process in place, the organization must perform an assessment against the desktops, determining what types of desktops are currently being used. Four factors should be included when adding desktops to the patch management process: (1) the use of standard builds; (2) providing user awareness and training; (3) using a tool to aid the organization in deploying the patches to all the desktops; and (4) regular checks via scanning tools to ensure all desktops are patched appropriately. Closely related to desktops, but treated differently when patching them, are remote users. Today there are a plethora of users who work remotely, in virtual environments, or out of the office, and they must be patched as well. This is to ensure that they have been patched with the latest releases prior to being permitted onto the organization's internal network or on the Internet in general. In most cases, remote users work by using a laptop versus the standard desktop that is used on site. Because laptops are mobile, they can be taken and plugged in anywhere. The organization must determine how these will be patched to make certain that they are protecting the organization's proprietary information as well as not endangering the network into which they are plugged. This holds true especially in the case of consultants, or virtual users who go from office to office, each connecting into another organization's network. Servers themselves add another layer of complexity to the patch management process. There are major factors to consider when determining which servers will be included in the patch management process and how the process will be designed to patch them appropriately. The different flavors of operating systems within the organization must be considered, deciding which ones can be supported in the patch management process. For example, the organization may start with including only Microsoft-based servers in the process with a plan to add the UNIX® servers into the process at a later date. Similarly, an organization may choose to patch its externally facing servers prior to patching its internal servers to mitigate the risk of the vulnerability. Compliance requirements may dictate which systems get patched first. For example, servers that fall under Payment Card Industry (PCI) compliance requirements may get patched first to guarantee that the quarterly scans come back clean, with no outstanding vulnerabilities due to a lack of installed patches.

Finally, there are the network appliances, including not only the routers and switches but also firewalls, virtual private network (VPN) concentrators, and intrusion detection appliances. These cannot be overlooked when it comes to patch management because they can have a dramatic effect on an organization if it is impacted by an exploit that is a result of a vulnerability not being patched properly.

Desktops

Desktops can be the most painful of all systems and devices that need to be updated within the organization's environment. Desktops require a different level of effort from that of servers. Typically, there are more desktops than servers within an organization. A method that will deploy the patch quickly while assuring that all servers have been patched appropriately is required. With servers, the decision is based more on the criticality of the applications residing on the server. The organization must be cautious and must apply due care prior to installing the patch on each vulnerable server. With desktops, patch deployment is related to and measured by time and effort. With servers, patch deployment is related to careful and accurate testing to establish that business operations are not negatively impacted. Any desktops that fall under PCI compliance most likely will be patched first to confirm that the quarterly scans, which organizations are required to perform as part of the PCI Data Security Standard (DSS), come back with no new vulnerabilities. Organizations must also perform annual penetration tests against the networks to ensure that systems under PCI compliance are patched in a timely manner. The issue of patching the desktops can be approached in three ways so that all desktops are accounted for and that the accounting is done accurately and efficiently.

One of the three ways to patch desktops is through the use of a standard build within the organization. The topic of standard builds being a requirement within the organization is referenced in multiple locations throughout the discussion on patch management. This is an important avenue for any organization to explore if it is not currently distributing desktops with standard builds on them. The second method in approaching patch management on the desktops is to ensure that desktop users are trained not only on the patch management process but also more specifically on what their responsibilities are. While an organization may try to avoid having any responsibility fall onto the users, typically this is not a realistic option. The organization needs to guarantee that users are clearly aware of their role and responsibilities regarding the patch management process. The third method of addressing patching desktops is through the use of a tool or, more specifically, a software-based application. An entire chapter is dedicated to the topic of tools and how an organization should use them for patch management. The use of the tool does provide the most benefit when an organization has a large number of desktops that need to be patched. It is not feasible in most organizations to manually go to each desktop and install a patch because of time constraints. A tool can deploy a patch to multiple desktops at one time, thereby reducing the amount of time and manpower required to make certain that all vulnerable desktops have been patched appropriately.

Standard Build

Having a standard build on the desktop to achieve patch management successfully is highly critical. Depending on the size, number of locations, and diversity of the organization (international), multiple standard builds may need to be deployed. A standard build can also be developed for specific departments or groups, based on their role or function. In these cases, the organization should implement a baseline, or minimum-build image, containing what every desktop is required to have installed. Once the baseline is developed, the organization can install the additional applications or software requirements depending on the user receiving the desktop.

The second question an organization should ask when designing patch management for the desktops is whether there are a multitude of operating systems, applications, utilities, installed across hundreds, or even thousands of desktops. If the answer to this question is yes, then the first thing the organization should do is plan to deploy a standard build on all the desktops included in the patch management process. This will make deployment and tracking of patch installs on the desktops a more simplified task, and this is explained in greater detail in a later chapter. For many organizations, it may not be possible to implement standard builds, perhaps because there is no budget for standard builds or because no resources are available to take on this task or, even worse, because the number and location of all the desktops are not known.

For the purpose of this writing and deployment of the patches onto the desktops, the recommendation is that the organization deploys standard builds. The topic of these standard builds is discussed further, and recommendations on how an organization can develop a road map for getting to that point are also provided. Many discussions on inventory management can assist an organization in achieving patch management without the use of standard builds in their environment.

User Awareness

Providing user security awareness and training to all employees is very important for any organization to integrate into its standard operating procedures. Regardless of the size of an organization, users must be trained not only on the organization's stance on security but also on their own responsibilities to protect the organization's assets. Once the patch management process has been designed and implemented, the members of the general user community must be made aware of this endeavor and its purpose and what their responsibilities are to ensure it is successful. Of course, the training can run in tandem with the actual implementation of the process into the organization. While they both need to be completed, the training can be done prior to, during, or after the process has been established. The best way to complete this is by conducting the training just prior to rolling out the process into full production. In this manner, the users are aware of the process and clearly understand what they need to do. If the process is rolled out first, then it can cause confusion on behalf of the end users because they will understand neither what patch management is supposed to accomplish nor what they need to do. Again, the size of the organization and the number of desktops are not relevant. The users must still be trained on this topic. In most cases, the organization will have a security awareness and training program. If this is true, the patch management process can be incorporated into this training and provided to all users moving forward. An additional module just on this subject can be added to provide a short training class or program instead of focusing only on new workforce members and updating everyone as the process is put in place.

Providing users with information regarding the patch management process is not enough to be considered sufficient. Instead, the organization must explicitly state what each user's role and responsibilities are. If a patch is deployed on users' desktops, they must know they have a role in getting it installed correctly. Putting a process in place that eliminates, or greatly reduces, the amount of work to be completed by the end user is strongly recommended. It is best to have the patches deployed on the desktops with little or no user intervention. The main way to achieve this is through the use of a tool to deploy the patch remotely to their systems. Tools are discussed in a separate chapter, in which we also include the best way to reduce user interaction. For the purpose of user awareness and training, once the patch management process is defined and documented, users must be trained on what they need to do to protect the organization from a potential exploit.

Use of Tool

An entire chapter is dedicated to the discussion of tools. It is important to note, however, that using a tool to deploy patches to the desktops will provide the organization with a great advantage. It can assist in ensuring that the desktops are being patched appropriately, with the tracking and reporting features included as well. When the organization is in the planning phase of the patch management process, the desktops that will be included are defined. Based on this, the organization must make certain that the tool it purchases will support the operating systems running on the desktops. If the standard build is in use, then ensuring compatibility will be an easier task. However, if multiple operating systems are running on the desktops, the organization must establish that the tool will support all of them.

The less user interaction required during the patch management process, the better. It should be as automated as possible for the desktop users, so that they do not have to do anything. In some cases, this will not work. This depends on various factors, such as the operating system in use and the type of patch. If the patch requires a reboot, which it often does, then is it fair for the operations or desktop group to reboot users' desktops without asking? If this is done, this can result in many unhappy users as well as the potential loss of productivity and important information. Users should have the right to determine when their desktops are rebooted—when it will be convenient for them. This does have a caveat: users cannot wait 2 weeks to reboot their system, but 24 hours may be acceptable, unless the organization is in a crisis. Having tools in place to assist the organization in deploying patches to the desktops can also prevent the organization from requiring user intervention when it comes to patching their desktops.

An organization should determine which method is best by conducting user awareness and training on this topic, should examine the current environment, and should develop a plan that agrees with the patch management process and one that will sit well with the user community. While the users should not have a strong opinion on this topic, putting a plan in place that they will be able to assist in supporting is important to the success of the process. The criticality of the patch can also drive the importance of setting a strict time frame for reboots or user interaction in deploying the patch. Because the patches are given different priority levels, the level given to the patch at hand will also affect the level of user intervention and automation available to the desktop user population.

Remote Users

Although desktop users and remote users can be the same group of individuals (i.e., within the same department), the patch management process can be deployed differently to these two groups of users. It is easy to centrally control the desktops in a specific location, but controlling the remote users—connecting to the Internet and the corporate network through an unknown connection—can be a daunting task. There is no one-size-fits-all method to do this effectively. Each organization must approach patching remote users' systems differently based on its requirements and architecture.

The most difficult question for organizations to answer when designing the patch management process will be how to handle remote users. Patches need to be deployed on their systems within a certain time frame and through an alternate means. The method of deploying the patch onto remote users' systems needs to be carefully thought out and defined to ensure that although a remote user is not in a static location the company's assets (e.g., laptop, PDA, proprietary data) are protected and patched appropriately. Various options, influenced by various options, are available to organizations to patch remote users effectively and efficiently. With remote users, there are three main concerns: (1) determining if the patch is required; (2) distributing the patch; and (3) ensuring that it has been properly implemented.

The first concern is determining whether the remote system requires a patch. While evaluating which tool to use to assist in the patch management process, the organization will need to decide if it will deploy agent- or agentless-based software. If the agent-based software product is chosen, the organization will have an accurate means of determining whether the patch applies to that system. Having an accurate inventory through asset management will also determine what systems need to be patched, regardless of whether they are a remote user. In some cases, the organization will require remote users to connect to the corporate network through the use of a VPN. Once remote users have established the VPN tunnel, they can be placed on a separate network segment where the system is scanned to determine whether it is missing any patches. This option is quite useful if the organization decides to use an agentless software product for patch management. Once remote users' systems have been scanned, the patches required will be deployed to the system automatically. Once this has been completed, users will then be able to access the corporate network.

Another concern is the actual distribution of the patch to the remote user's system. Again, the choice of agent or agentless software will influence the outcome of this concern. If agent-based software is used, the management console, located within the corporate network, will ensure that the patch is distributed to the client when connecting to the corporate network. Typically, remote users connect through a VPN session, and, once this has been achieved, the management console will be aware that a new system has connected and will deploy the patch. The scheduling of this must be defined, and users must connect to the corporate network on a regular basis to establish that they are not too far behind in patches. If the organization has developed an antivirus solution, the patches can be deployed when the new virus signatures are deployed to the system. If the organization decides to use an agentless solution, other tools such as Windows Update may be required to make sure that the system obtains the appropriate patch.

The third concern is then ensuring that the patch has been implemented on remote users' systems. The system has been identified as needing a patch; the patch has been distributed to it properly, and the organization must now report that the patch has been implemented. In an effort to avoid redundancy, the software product chosen to assist in patch management will influence how this reporting can be completed. Through the use of an agent-based tool, clients will report to the management console that the patch has been implemented and the system is not vulnerable anymore. The organization can also deploy the use of scanning tools to determine whether all systems have been patched appropriately. The scanning tool can be run only against VPN (remote user) connections, specific departments, or physical locations, but it should be run against all systems within the organization's network. The results of the scanning tool will show which systems are still susceptible and need to be patched and which ones have been completed.

Laptops

Laptops fall under the remote user category because they are typically the means by which users connect to their corporate networks while traveling, while working at a customer's site, or these days while working from anywhere in the world via either a wired or wireless connection. There are various means to ensure that the organization's laptops are updated properly, even if they are not patched on a consistent basis. Some organizations are deploying such options when users connect via broadband to a VPN session into the corporate network. They can be quarantined until they have installed patches available and provided by the organization. Antivirus updates can also be provided in this manner. If a laptop has not been patched and users are walking around connecting to various networks, there is a better chance they will get a virus or will be the target of an exploit. Laptop users must understand their responsibilities in addressing these patches in a timely manner.

Consulting companies, contractors, or third parties employed by an organization to perform work on site in most cases use a laptop to connect to the company's network. The means in which these individuals connect to the corporate network and what they will be doing should be considered in addition to the laptops they are using and whether they have been patched appropriately or whether they are spreading dangerous viruses, worms, or even Trojans on the network. Most companies are taking a stand on this topic and will deal with it in one of the following ways: (1) they do not permit the outsider to connect to the organization's network; (2) they allow them to connect from a specific location that will put them on a network segment separate from the corporate network, which may give them only Internet access; or (3) they can even have them sign an agreement at the start of their work, stating that their system has been patched appropriately and is protected from worms, viruses, and other malicious code. In some cases the system may be required to be scanned after the agreement is signed and before they can connect. Each of these methods is effective, and each has pros and cons. While this ties into patch management, it is a decision that should be considered prior to designing the patch management process.

Servers

Servers and desktops/laptops are typically owned, operated, and maintained by different groups. Servers are the core of the organization. Therefore, they will have more focused support and dedicated processes that are under centralized control. Other groups of systems, such as desktops, have dedicated support groups but have much more diversity and looser controls because they are replaceable. This is an interesting point when considering the vulnerabilities of the desktops, because they are typically the culprits. Servers are approached differently when it comes to patch management. The method in which they are patched is defined when the patch management process is designed. Compliance concerns must be considered when patching servers.

Servers cannot be updated in the same manner as desktops. Servers typically provide an important function for an organization. They may provide a business process or a business purpose; they can hold confidential information, such as credit cards, and they will hold sensitive organizational data. The testing of patches prior to installing on such critical servers must be closely regulated and monitored. The first time a server is patched and a negative impact results, executive management support will be lost, causing the patch management process to be banned or to be given lesser importance, to some extent. Testing a patch prior to installing it on a server is critical to the success of the process on these systems.

If an organization has a change management process in place, which it should, it will designate the maintenance window in which work can be conducted on the servers, especially the critical production servers. This time can then be used to patch and reboot systems if the patch warrants. Servers can also be grouped, with specific groups being patched, and then others being completed at a later time. It is easier to isolate an issue with the patch install if it has been implemented only on a specific number of servers.

Servers can also be patched based on whether they are externally facing servers, such as available via the Internet for either employee or business use, or if they are internal systems, such as supporting a back-end business function. In most cases, organizations will patch their external servers first. However, the order in which it is done can be based on criticality of the system, and of course proper testing of the patch on a development system should be completed first to ensure it does not have any negative impact. Internal systems tend to be patched much later, even after desktops. This is not always intentional; instead, in some cases support of the external systems takes priority and a majority of the support staff's time, so internal systems are overlooked until the proper time is available to support them as well.

Regular testing of servers through the use of various testing processes can also assist an organization to ensure vulnerabilities are not present. Organizations or a third party can perform a scan against the system to check for vulnerabilities. In addition, organizations may conduct an actual vulnerability assessment or penetration test against the servers to make certain that no patches are missing, that no vulnerabilities are present, and that they are secure from the numerous threats of the Internet. Many times, externally facing servers are tested throughout the year, whereas internal systems may be tested only once a year. This is mostly due to the higher risk of those externally facing servers being access via the Internet and all the threats that imposes.

Last, compliance requirements can be a major driver in patching systems and limiting the number of vulnerabilities associated on them. Regulations such as PCI, Sarbanes–Oxley (SOX), and Health Insurance Portability and Accountability Act (HIPAA) require organizations to continuously patch and test systems to ensure that from a patching requirement and from a vulnerability perspective they are current. The organization should work with their compliance teams to track systems that fall under compliance requirements and to guarantee that they have implemented the requirements of the regulation.

We discuss two main types of servers that reside within an organization's environment today, Windows and UNIX systems, as well as the differences and similarities between patching them. Although there are many UNIX systems, they are all grouped together for the purposes of this discussion.

Windows

Windows has begun to take a new approach to security. Microsoft has started to increase its focus on security as it relates to its server operating systems and applications. Microsoft has established an additional site that discusses the company's approach to security at great length. Microsoft has also developed a Trustworthy Computing solution that addresses security, privacy, reliability, and business integrity.

Microsoft has provided its users with a multitude of security information for the past few years now. They provide how-to guides, implementation manuals, and even free chat sessions for users when they have a virus problem. It has two patch management products that organizations can implement to aid them in the patch management process. Both WSUS and System Center Configuration Manager (ConfigMgr) can be used in an organization that has a large number of Microsoft systems. Depending on its size, an organization may choose to implement one product versus the other. However, the purpose of this section is to discuss not tools but instead how Windows servers should be integrated or included in the patch management process.

Microsoft servers really cover a large realm of systems within an organization's infrastructure. Depending on the size of the organization and its age, the number of servers can range from 1 to more than 1,000. If the organization has been in place for a number of years, it runs the risk of running legacy systems, which may be operating software that is no longer supported. Typically, Microsoft servers are updated and maintained more regularly than desktops. It is more common to find a few desktops running older versions of Windows versus a Windows server running a legacy operating system. Legacy systems usually include UNIX systems, such as mainframes. Microsoft servers can exist throughout the organization, running multiple applications, which all have to be taken into consideration when patching them. Obviously, a domain controller is patched in a different fashion and needs to be taken into careful consideration, versus a server that is running a noncritical application. Not only the operating system but also the applications and the purpose of the server itself must be considered.

An organization should have a detailed inventory of not only what operating systems are in its environment but also what application is running on each one. This will allow the organization to categorize and group the servers, so that the patch management process includes the various groups of Microsoft servers as they are patched. Building a server criticality matrix can also assist the organization in grouping these systems based on their business function. It is a recommended method to ensure that the most critical servers are patched in the appropriate time frame, after the patch has been tested. Any systems and applications with regulatory or compliance requirements should also be accurately documented to establish that they are patched accordingly.

Servers must be patched in a method different from desktops. First of all, testing the patch thoroughly prior to deploying it on any mission-critical system is a must, whether using a dedicated lab that can be used for testing or even a secondary or backup server. Testing can even be conducted on less critical systems within the organization prior to being rolled out to the mission-critical systems. Again, there is an entire chapter dedicated to testing, so granular details on this topic will be discussed at that point.

UNIX and Linux

In this section, the discussion includes all kinds of UNIX servers, which are referred to only as UNIX. Typically, organizations do not seem to be as concerned about patching UNIX servers as they are about Microsoft systems. This comes as a surprise because embedded in the UNIX operating systems are many packages that seem to be updated constantly. Some servers can have hundreds of packages installed on them, and determining which packages are on which systems can be a daunting task. This is typical unless of course the UNIX group has a very good inventory on the packages installed. In most cases, organizations will remove any packages that are not needed, but developers and programmers will need a surplus of them to complete their job tasks. Through the use of hardening requirements, the organization can dictate which applications, and therefore packages, can and will be installed on each server. This can be a base lining of the UNIX servers, with room for the group to add additional applications for the purpose of the server itself, based on proper configuration management processes.

The way organizations seem to update UNIX servers is through scripting and the frequent use of cron jobs. Update servers can be established that can rsync daily and then nightly with an official update server; the updates can get pushed out to the corresponding server on a daily basis. Administrators can be e-mailed the next day, so they know about the patch update and can reboot the server if necessary. Of course, factoring in whether the update actually needs to occur on the server and whether it will break anything needs to be analyzed when setting up a method such as this.

There are just as many vulnerabilities that affect UNIX servers as those that affect Windows servers. Moreover, to make matters worse, there is an overabundance of RootKits and exploits available to hackers to mount a malicious attack on an unpatched system, which can cause damage to an organization's vulnerable systems. These kits and exploits are also freely available on many of the underground Web sites that post this type of material. A basic search on the Internet produces a variety of Web sites containing information about and downloads for malicious tools that can be used to cause damage. However, if a comparison were to be done between a UNIX hacker and a Windows or Microsoft hacker, the former will be required to have more knowledge and technical skills than the latter.

Network Devices

Network devices are often overlooked in the patch management process. Organizations focus much of their attention and time on servers and even more on desktops, leaving the network devices to be patched when they get around to it. For clarification purposes, network devices are defined as routers, switches, firewall appliances, and others, including load balancers and VPN concentrators. The routers include not only internal routers throughout the infrastructure but also the choke routers, which sit on the edge of the network between the Internet and internal network. Firewalls should be updated with extreme caution because they protect the internal network from unauthorized access. A recommended practice with firewalls, whether software or appliance based, is to have two in place for redundancy. This allows the organization to update the secondary firewall, ensuring that there are no issues prior to updating the primary firewall. An organization can use failover capabilities to guarantee a smooth transition.

Cisco network devices are widely used within many organizations' network infrastructure and range from core router, to edge routers, switches, and even their PIX firewalls and VPN concentrators. Cisco does not release patches for its Cisco Internetworking Operating Systems (IOS) when a vulnerability is released. Instead, it requires an IOS upgrade. Cisco issues a different version of its IOS, which then needs to be applied to all affected network devices running that version of the IOS. If a network device is running a previous version (e.g., 11 vs. 12), then Cisco will provide information on whether those particular operating systems are susceptible. It also depends on what feature sets are being run on that network device. If an update comes out to address a VPN feature set and the organization is not running the VPN feature set on the core routers, then the core routers are not susceptible and do not need updating.

With Cisco's PIX, Catalyst, IOS Firewall feature set, and the VPN concentrators all require an IOS upgrade, just as their routers and switches. Cisco does not release any patches for its network devices. Therefore, they all require the same method for updating and upgrading them appropriately. Although an organization may choose to run the same IOS version on all its network devices, this is not always the best solution. Although having standard builds seems contradictory, it is advisable to have multiple versions of IOS running within the infrastructure. While these versions would all need to be documented and tracked, if a vulnerability is released that affects Cisco's IOS, not every device will need to be updated: only those running the vulnerable IOS version. It will be much easier for the networking group to upgrade 10 network devices versus thousands when a new IOS version is released due to a vulnerability in the previous version.

Of course, Cisco is not the only company that makes network devices. The purpose of this section is to discuss how vendors supply patches for network devices. While most follow the same method for updating as Cisco, it is important to mention a few other vendors.

For example, Nortel Networks supports Bay Networks, Synoptics, and WellFleet products, as a result of past mergers, and provides updates for them as a vulnerability is identified. However, once the product has been deemed end-of-life, Nortel ceases to support it from an updating perspective. This is similar with all products. Once they are deemed end-of-life, no updates or support services are provided.

Juniper runs an operating system on its E-Series, M-Series, and T-Series routers as well as on its NetScreen Firewall. Operating systems include JUNOS and JUNOSe for the E-Series edge routers and ScreenOS for the NetScreen Firewall. When a vulnerability is released that affects one of Juniper's network devices, workarounds are typically issued. Alternatively, additional security measures can be implemented on the affected system to eliminate the vulnerability on the device. Juniper also sends out an update to the operating system and recommends that the end user update the software to a version that is not susceptible to the vulnerability.

In summary, the same due diligence and care are needed when a vulnerability is released that affects a network device. The vendor, type of appliance, or IOS is irrelevant. What holds more relevance is the criticality of the device itself. Such questions as where is it located, what does it protect, and what is the level of risk the organization is willing to take if an exploit if formulated on that device need to be addressed. Whether the vulnerable system is a server, desktop, or some form of network device, each patch should follow the defined and documented patch management process to ensure accuracy, efficiency, and effectiveness.

4

NETWORK AND SYSTEMS MANAGEMENT

Information Technology Infrastructure Library

Patch management is very much an operational issue. The need for a patch may come from the security group or another engineering team, but patches are most often implemented using operations processes and operations personnel. The term that usually refers to the people, processes, and technologies used for managing information technology (IT) operations is *network and systems management* (NSM).

While it is possible to separate the duties of security management from those of NSM, the two are much closer in roles and responsibilities than an organization may realize. The operational aspects of security for the day-to-day activities are performed in much the same way as NSM. For example, if an e-mail application needs a patch to fix a feature, the operations organization should have a process in place to handle it. So, if the organization already knows how to deploy a patch for a feature issue, the difference in deploying a patch to fix a security vulnerability in the same e-mail application is not much different.

NSM and security management are alike in many respects, but it is important to understand how they differ so the organization can ensure that the appropriate attention is focused on implementing the specific security requirements that might not be achieved directly through an NSM approach. The principles of NSM are reviewed throughout this chapter to outline how they can be applied to the fundamentals of patch management. Primary consideration is given to processes. Chapter 5 then focuses specifically on the people, processes, and technology for supporting security management.

Network and Systems Management

The NSM industry is relatively mature because it has been struggling for decades with the issues of managing networked environments. More recently, security operations has been dealing with the same issues. By taking the basic principles of NSM and using the well-defined processes, procedures, and technologies that have been set out over the years and applying them to security management, organizations will be able to more rapidly implement robust security operations and to achieve the end goals quickly and cost-effectively.

NSM is a term that refers to the practices used to manage an IT infrastructure. As its name implies, NSM is what an organization does to manage its networks and its systems. However, it can be much more inclusive than just those two items. NSM may also include the management of applications, desktops, and practically anything considered part of the IT infrastructure, including security.

The history of NSM goes back to the early days of computing, where practitioners were managing some of the original computers. They were dealing with faults that happened on a much more frequent basis than what we are familiar with in today's computing environment. The practices of managing mainframes in the early days are how many of the fundamentals of systems management were developed. Managing networks started with the management of local area networks (LANs), progressed to the wide area networks (WANs) shortly thereafter, and then moved on to all other network-specific technologies over the years.

NSM historically has been implemented in a segmented fashion in different organizations, especially in large corporations. Systems management was usually performed by one group, whereas network management was performed by another. This may have also been further distributed by region or even subgroups, such as managing UNIX® servers versus Windows systems or LANs versus WANs. However, over the past few years, there has been a strong movement toward integrating the management of all technologies into a single operational group.

Product enhancements over the years have helped NSM mature and provide capabilities that are used to manage multiple technologies within a single organization. Although many tools still remain focused on managing specific technologies, numerous NSM applications are available to manage and monitor all types of systems and network devices.

Back in the original days of network operations or computer operations, there was a lack of industry-wide accepted standards. The main players, like IBM, have capabilities for managing their products, but these could not be applied to all networks and systems technology-wide. To develop NSM applications that could manage multiple technologies, a protocol such as Simple Network Management Protocol (SNMP) needed to be established to facilitate the basic gathering of telemetry information. SNMP then became the primary means for gathering device status and for delivering notifications when certain types of situations occurred.

As more and more devices became SNMP compatible and newer and more advanced software was developed, the amount of information that could be generated about the conditions in the network or systems was tremendous. In addition, much of the information may have been segmented by which vendors' devices were being managed or by the types of technology. Systems known as "manager of managers" were developed to take events and management information from various sources and to combine the information streams to a single console. Ticketing systems have also grown and developed into full-fledged workflow systems that are managing the delivery of information and individual workloads to all individuals in the operations organization. Furthermore, the workflow and manager of managers systems can now be connected via a two-way communication link and thereby both automatically notify the appropriate service personnel and log with the event management system that a critical event has taken place.

Therefore, over the years, NSM has grown from the practice of watching lights on devices to combining and managing telemetry data from tens of thousands of network and systems devices and turning it all into meaningful information. This is the primary achievement in NSM: turning data into usable information. All the data in the world will not help. Being able to gather enormous amounts of data, to process and analyze them, and to turn them into meaningful bits of information is a major accomplishment. Furthermore, because the operations teams and information are based on the entire IT infrastructure, this reduces the confusion over a problem's root cause. All too often in the past, there was finger pointing among systems, applications, and network folks, each blaming the others for a failure. Having all the information in a single location and managed by a single staff organization enables the smaller operations staff to accomplish greater management success.

This simplified summary of the history of NSM shows the tremendous progress this industry has experienced over the years. Although security has been on the minds of some folks in the industry, security standards and processes have never been well formalized into mainstream NSM practices. That is changing. A key driver of the convergence of security and NSM is that both experience the same fundamental problem: how to transform too much data, from too many sources, into useful and actionable information.

Over the past decade, the IT security industry has seen great improvements in its ability to monitor and manage network and system security with the introduction of devices such as new firewalls and intrusion detection systems (IDSs). Today, intrusion prevention systems (IPSs) are becoming more commonplace, yet all of these devices generate security data that must be processed. Although some companies separate security operations from network operations, the same fundamental principles of managing IT apply.

An organization with experience in operations will know that the processes, not the technology, are the foundation of managing an IT infrastructure. Technology provides certain capabilities and efficiencies, but without good processes no technology can help an organization. Throughout the history of NSM, a variety of formal standards have been developed. Most recently, the industry has realized that focusing on service management is the most important aspect of managing the IT infrastructure. Although knowing that a router, printer, or system has failed is important, understanding how a service to a customer is running is even more important. NSM has shifted from the silo management of the past to a more proactive and business-oriented approach to management by using what is called IT service management (ITSM). A *de facto* standard is quickly developing called the IT infrastructure library (ITIL). It defines a best-practices framework for service management.

Starting with Process

All too often, organizations look at process last when implementing operations capabilities. They are too quick to buy software to manage the infrastructure and to throw people into the mix to try to make it work. However, it is process that really defines an organization, and this should be the first thing investigated and developed when building or enhancing an operations organization.

IT operations have always been defined by process. The better operations organizations are those with well-defined processes and proper adherence to these processes; this makes the organization much more efficient and reliable. If processes are defined effectively and procedures are being adhered to, then the organization will operate consistently and probably more efficiently because everyone should know how to get his or her job done. This is extremely important during times of crisis. If a major outbreak of a virus or worm is occurring within the enterprise, it is important to have procedures for identifying the situation and reacting to it as quickly as possible. This is not a time to figure out who does what and how to get the job done.

An organization cannot claim that it has processes in place unless they are documented, adhered to, and enforced. Having informal, undocumented processes will not work. Individuals can interpret the processes and procedures in their own way, and, when things start to fall apart, employees can claim that this is the way they understood it. Without having the processes and procedures documented, employees will have no place to turn when they need to find out how they should act in a crisis. Employees should have a standard operating procedure (SOP) to follow and should be trained properly in their function. It is also important to identify interfaces between functional groups to understand exactly how work items are transferred from one group to the next. There should never be ambiguity about how to deliver something to the next group, only to find out that what was delivered is not in the right format or not the information they were expecting. This creates extra work and delays. In a crisis situation, this can create lost man-hours and can generate unnecessary costs.

Unfortunately, process is not something an organization can just go out and purchase a book on and implement verbatim. Process requires understanding how the organization operates, what the business drivers are, and the complexity of the environment. Typically, operational processes have been based loosely on concepts, such as International Standards Organization (ISO) and fault management, configuration management, accounting management, performance management, and security management (FCAPS). Today's best-practices approach to IT service management is ITIL. Because the IT operational process is so important to patch management, the following sections take a closer look at ITIL and then review an approach to implementing better IT operations.

ITIL

ITIL was initially developed in the late 1980s by the United Kingdom's Central Computer and Telecommunications Agency (CCTA). The CCTA has now been incorporated into the U.K. Government's Office of Government Commerce (OGC), which has continued to update ITIL, along with the British Standards Institute (BSI) and the IT Service Management Forum (ITSMF). The OGC has published numerous books on various aspects of ITIL, the foundation of which is IT service support and IT service delivery. ITIL has also defined a process for security management to lay out best-practice approaches to the broad topic of managing security in an organization. Many of these processes are based on the process areas of service support and service delivery.

The core of ITIL is defined by service support and service delivery. Between these two functional groupings, ITIL defines the majority of activities necessary to keep an IT infrastructure running properly. These processes cover most aspects of managing the IT infrastructure, including, but not specifically oriented around, security. However, ITIL also has books on other topics that augment these processes, including *ICT infrastructure management*, *ITIL security management*, and *ITIL application management*.

ITIL does not have a specific patch management process, but the process framework supports all aspects of patch management. When a review on how the patch management process is implemented, based on ITIL, the organization will be able to notice that it is primarily contained in the service support area. Therefore, before the process flow for patch management is discussed, the processes in the service

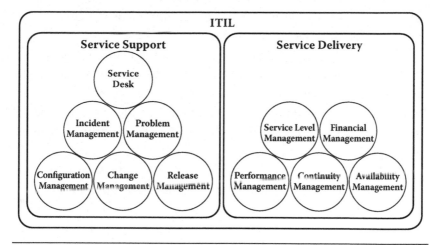

Figure 4.1 ITIL.

support area need to be described in detail. Figure 4.1 shows the two main aspects of ITIL—service support and service delivery—along with the components that make up these aspects.

Service Support

Service support is one of the two main areas defined within the ITIL process framework for service management and encompasses the grouping of services concerned with the day-to-day management of the IT infrastructure. It is composed of six highly integrated process areas. When implementing a patch management process, all six highly integrated process areas of service support are required:

- Service desk
- Incident management
- Problem management
- Configuration and asset management
- Change management
- Release management

Service Desk The service desk is actually not so much a process area as it is a function, yet it is extremely important because it is the entry point into the service management processes. The service desk drives many of the processes in service support, especially incident management and, in some cases, release management.

The service desk is the group that acts as the primary contact for end users and is usually responsible for monitoring the health of the environment. Also known as the help desk or call center, the service desk records all pertinent information from the caller and, if possible, provides a solution by researching whether a preexisting answer can be found in the knowledge base. If such a quick solution is not available, the service desk will forward the incident to back-line support, where further resolution activities continue. It is the responsibility of the service desk to keep the end users up to date on the status of the incident. Because of this customer-facing position, the service desk is the greatest participant in the next area, the incident management process.

A service desk does not have to be a single group that takes calls at a centralized location. Service desks can be organized in a variety of ways. Of course, there is nothing wrong with having a centralized group that receives all trouble calls for an organization or enterprise. This is probably one of the most common implementations. However, a service desk can also be composed of multiple groups distributed throughout an organization, joined by a common ticketing system. Each group can provide some sort of local presence or provide service in a particular language. Another implementation is the virtual service desk, where multiple regional groups provide the service desk service but the end users see it as one entity. The groups can be distributed around the globe and provide what is called "follow-the-sun" service, where, based on standard working hours, one group provides service until it hands it off to the next group in another region of the globe, usually to cover the next time zone. This is more common with large, global companies.

A service desk can also be provided using online technology. A majority of the service desk features can be developed within a Web-based application. In this case, users access the Web site when an issue arises and fill in information about themselves and the problem. The system may provide access to a knowledge base or frequently asked questions (FAQ) to provide immediate potential solutions. If a solution does not match the contents of the knowledge database, users can help categorize the problem and submit it to where it is automatically routed to the group most likely to be responsible. In some implementations, the call will be routed to a call center or help desk. Here, an associate will take ownership of the ticket and process it just like any phone call.

Regardless of the service desk implementation, the charter remains the same: to provide the single point of contact by which users can call for help. In some cases, the service desk may have additional duties, such as providing network management, security management, or computer operations. However, it is much more common to see the service desk interface with the network operations center (NOC) or security operations center (SOC) to share information and work on incident management together.

Incident Management   Incident management is responsible for restoring services back to their normal state as quickly as possible. Therefore, the incident management process helps identify the faults in the environment and records, classifies, investigates, diagnoses, and resolves the service issues. Incidents can be almost anything from a hardware failure to an application not functioning properly to a request for a password change.

The incident management process is usually worked by two groups: (1) the front-line support, most often service desk employees; and (2) back-line support, which may be a part of the service desk or part of various second-level engineering groups. Incident management will attempt to resolve the problem as quickly as possible or provide a workaround until a complete solution can be implemented. Incident records are closed only when the problem has been resolved and customers have confirmed that everything is back to normal.

Aside from notification provided by a vendor, computer incident response team (CIRT), or security firms, incident management is where most of the reactive needs for patches will be identified from within the organization. When users call with an issue or when issues are identified through the use of the management applications, the incident may require a patch to be applied before the issue can be resolved.

Problem Management   The overall responsibility of the problem management process is to reduce the adverse effects of incidents and problems on the organization. The problem management process has two aspects: reactive and proactive. The reactive process is tied directly to the incident management process, where unknown causes of incidents are passed to the problem management process to be identified and documented. The proactive process reviews historic data and looks to identify problems prior to an incident occurring and being escalated to problem management. In either case, whether reactive or proactive, a problem record is opened and worked. The problem management process identifies and classifies the problem, investigates and diagnoses it, and documents the resolution, possibly requesting a change to the infrastructure to fix the problem.

Problem management often causes confusion because people generally do not understand the difference between an incident and a problem. Something to keep in mind is that an incident never becomes a problem. An incident is just a specific instance of an error condition, and a problem is the documentation to resolve an error. Typically, a solution to a problem will resolve multiple incidents, so when implementing the incident management process and the problem management process it is imperative that the organization uses a workflow application that can link multiple incidents to a single problem.

In some implementations of the ITIL process, an enterprise will see the engineering organizations, such as the network engineering group or the tactical security group, participate in the proactive problem management process. These groups may look to be proactive, to evaluate potential problems, and to review trends of incidents to determine what a workaround and solution may be if this problem were to arise. These groups may also be called on by the reactive problem management process to help diagnose and determine a solution for a current problem.

Configuration and Asset Management   This process involves maintaining a list of the assets and configurations in the organization. To keep detailed information about what is deployed in the IT infrastructure, the configuration management process establishes a configuration management database (CMDB). In actuality, the CMDB ends up being a series of databases that depend on what applications are implemented to support configuration management. The CMDB is supposed to keep track of all the versions of assets deployed in the IT infrastructure and to maintain their current configuration. These records are known as configuration items (CIs). The configuration management process interfaces with all other process areas that require information about CIs and takes updates from those processes that make changes to the IT infrastructure.

Configuration management is one of the most important processes relative to patch management and general security management. To patch devices or software, as part of patch management, the organization must know what the scope of the needed patch is. Therefore, it is important that they can quickly identify what devices require a patch and where they are located. To do this, the organization must have an accurate inventory of all devices within the IT infrastructure, with specific hardware and software version information. Without this information, it is almost impossible to have a viable patch management capability. If the organization does not have a good CMDB, then it becomes almost impossible to implement a viable patch management process.

Another reason configuration and asset management is so important to security management is that the CMDB should have the capability to register each device's classification, whereby a level of importance relative to confidentiality, integrity, and availability is recorded. Therefore, in the CMDB, the database record for each device should have a rating of *high*, *medium*, or *low* indicated for each of the three security objectives.

As with many of the process areas in ITIL, configuration and asset management relies heavily on technology. Without the CMDB and other technologies to gather information to populate the CMDB, the configuration and asset management process would not exist. The CMDB may be implemented via many methods, where most rely just on a complement of vendors' element management systems (the software that usually comes with a vendors product to configure and record configurations for their devices). However, some asset management systems can be used to gather all asset information. Many of these may be associated with ticketing and workflow systems, yet the best method for gathering all asset information within the IT infrastructure into a single repository may be to develop it internally. If the organization has good database administrative resources, it may want to create a custom database application that pulls information from the various asset and inventory sources, such as the element management systems, and to build the appropriate CMDB, adding such fields as the security objectives ratings.

Once the organization has a CMDB, it is imperative that it be kept up to date. This is done in two ways. First, processes must be defined and adhered to for recording information properly throughout the configuration management process and all of the linkages to the other ITIL processes. Second, the configuration management process should have an audit capability that periodically compares the records in the database with what is actually deployed. This can be done with manual checks or with automated scans. These scans go out, poll devices for information, and compare the results with what is in the CMDB, flagging anything that is different, missing, or extra.

The importance of having a configuration and asset management process to suitably perform patch management cannot be stressed enough. This may be the area the organization focuses on first when improving or establishing a patch management process.

Change Management The change management process provides a mechanism to control changes made to the IT infrastructure to reduce the risks to the business and to ensure that changes are made in a predictable and orderly manner. It is run by the change manager, who processes incoming requests for change (RFCs). RFCs are initially evaluated and either accepted or rejected. The change manager then evaluates the priority of the change and processes the RFC in a manner that depends on specifics of the change. There may be various different change models to follow based on the scope of the change. If it is an emergency change, there should be a special process put in place to handle expedited changes. Otherwise, if the change is minor and is deemed to have little risk, the change may be immediately approved. However, most significant changes are brought to a Change Advisory Board (CAB), which is established to review the impact of changes and to gather the input from various groups that may be impacted. Depending on how the CAB is implemented for a particular organization, the CAB may have standing members of the board and other members who are called in based on the scope of the change. For example, someone from the systems group may be asked to attend the CAB meeting if a patch is being considered for application to servers. However, if the change is for a router, then the systems group probably has no need to attend.

The change management process is also tied very closely to the configuration management process, and in some cases the two processes can even be tied together as one. The change management process is responsible for approving changes to the CMDB and its configuration items. In most cases, change management is the only process that updates and makes changes to the CMDB.

Release Management   The release management process is responsible for the deployment of hardware and software in the IT infrastructure and the coordination of changes to these systems, such as a patch. The release management process works closely with the change and configuration management processes to perform what is known as a "release," which is the combination of all the RFCs for which it implements. The release management process is responsible for identifying when a release would be deployed and how it should be coupled with other changes to make the most effective release. Releases are usually categorized as major software releases and hardware upgrades, minor software releases and hardware upgrades, and emergency software and hardware fixes.

When a patch must be deployed, in most cases, the change management process will inform the release management process that a patch needs to be deployed. Depending on the severity of the change (i.e., whether it is determined if it is an emergency fix), the release management process will decide when the patch should be deployed and if it will be combined with other patches or software deployments.

Service Delivery

The service delivery of ITIL does not usually relate directly to the day-to-day activities of patch management or to the patch management process. However, it is best to understand the components of the service delivery area. An organization will develop the processes, procedures, organizational structure, and technology to support security management and patch management. When it does this, it is important to understand how everything interacts and what else the organization may need to develop to assemble the complete solution (service support and service delivery).

Service delivery has five process areas: (1) service-level management; (2) financial management for IT service; (3) performance and capacity management; (4) IT service continuity management; and (5) availability management. Many of these process areas have direct and important linkages to security.

Service-Level Management Service-level management focuses on properly measuring and reporting on the service levels of individual IT services and ensuring that the services committed to customers are achieved as best as possible. The service-level management process involves defining a service for a customer, establishing the tools and techniques needed to measure and develop reports on a service level, and reviewing with a customer the service that was provided and how it might be improved.

Service levels could be affected by security issues; therefore, they have a direct link to security management. Security risks place a risk on achieving service levels. Therefore, these service levels must be taken into consideration when defining the original service-level agreements (SLAs). Service-level management is a process that many organizations try to partially implement, thus doing it poorly. Service levels are typically defined around very specific metrics, such as network response times on a specific circuit or that a server's uptime should be a certain percentage of time, such as 99.99%. However, it is important that service levels be defined for an entire IT service, not just its individual components. When setting up an SLA the company should do the following:

- Work with the customers at the start of a service delivery process to understand their service requirements
- Implement methods to monitor the specific metrics that have been agreed upon
- Incorporate outside factors, such as other dependent service levels like network contracts, security threats, and scheduled downtime for maintenance
- Report the service levels to the customer appropriately and reliably

- Work with the customer to continue to modify service levels to be appropriate to what the service organization can commit to and meet what the customer really wants

A note of caution: beware of nonspecific service metrics. The agreed-to metrics must be clear and measurable. A service-level metric such as "must have good response time" does not mean anything. Pick a time, and define what the response time must be, such as, "When I click on the log-in button and after I type a valid user ID and password, the main screen of the application must appear in full in 2 seconds."

Financial Management for IT Services   This contains processes for many of the typical fiscal administrative activities, including budgeting for IT projects, accounting of how money is spent, developing charging mechanisms for IT services, and categorizing costs.

Performance and Capacity Management   An area that is not affected much by security is performance and capacity management. The performance and capacity management process is also known as the capacity management process. This is a proactive process that evaluates the current performance levels of IT infrastructure components and ensures that they are adequate enough to support the current IT services. Information is also taken from these processes, like change management or, from the business side, business plans and strategies, to guarantee that the IT infrastructure is correctly sized and costs are properly allocated to support these changes and plans.

Capacity planning interacts with most other service support and service delivery processes. Aside from the obvious tasks of the capacity management process, such as making sure that there is enough network bandwidth or that the servers are large enough, however, this process establishes that costs are managed properly, servers are sized accordingly, and bandwidth is allocated reasonably. The capacity management process should also help manage those all too frequent unrealistic expectations. It is easy to want amazing performance; however, the capacity management function needs to notify requestors what the costs are and to make certain that these costs are managed and charged back properly.

IT Service Continuity Management   IT service continuity management takes into consideration the need for individual IT services and the respective IT infrastructure to be restored in a certain amount of time in the event of a disaster. Many factors are taken into consideration, including budgets and importance of a service, on what the business continuity plan should include. Part of the IT service continuity management process is to determine what type of disasters to prepare for and try to prevent. As part of this planning, security management will provide information on what types of disasters may be related to security issues and how to best react to a disaster that is related to security issues. For example, if a data center is taken off line due to a denial-of-service (DoS) attack, how would an alternate data center provide redundancy, and what would the plan be to mitigate the DoS attack?

Availability Management   Availability management focuses on ensuring that IT services are up and running in accordance with the defined service levels. The role of this process is to manage IT service availability by evaluating service levels against other items, such as failures, maintenance windows, and additional negative effects on availability. Availability management has a strong linkage to security because security issues may present a significant risk to the availability of a service. Relative to patch management, the availability management process would make certain that there are plans in place to provide rapid deployment of patches should a software fault require the immediate need for a patch.

ICT Infrastructure Management

The service support and service delivery aspects of ITIL are based on the fact that the infrastructure foundation exists and is stable. The concepts of taking the technologies available in the marketplaces and engineering and implementing them are a part of the information and communications technology (ICT) infrastructure management practices. More important to the roles of NSM and patch management, ICT infrastructure management also includes best practices relative to operations.

In the OGC books on ITIL, ICT infrastructure management usually does not get as much attention as service support and service delivery. However, when the organization is setting up a new operations organization, it is ICT infrastructure management that covers the best practices in this area. Ironically, one of the key aspects of operations is a reference to ISO FCAPS.

ISO FCAPS has been a long-time reference for establishing the technical architectures for NSM, and there is a good chance that if the organization has an operations organization in place today it is related to the various parts of ISO FCAPS.

Security Management

Yes, ITIL addresses security management. However, security management is not so much a process unto itself but an overlay and focus for the processes defined in service support and service delivery. Much of this we will define within the next chapter.

The ITIL security management book does not give much detailed information on security practices. Actually, it refers to the *Code of Practice for Information Security Management* (BS 7799) for information on policies and activities. However, ITIL security management does describe how many of the practices are incorporated into the service support and service delivery processes.

Assessing and Implementing IT Operations

To implement a patch management capability, the organization must build it on top of a good operations capability. Depending on the current situation, the organization may be able to just add the patch management capability to the existing IT operations, or it might have to first establish a good foundation by building a solid operations organization. Whichever situation the organization is today, it is still appropriate to perform an assessment of the IT operations to determine what exactly needs to be enhanced, even if the improvement is small, before moving on. This may also be a good time to bring in an independent consulting firm to evaluate the current situation to help gain an unbiased view while also providing some vision and insight for the organization, based on experience with other firms.

Whether the organization performs the assessment in-house or with an external firm, it is important to take a look at how the organization would go about assessing what is in place and implementing it into IT operations.

Assessing the IT Operations Capabilities

As with any good project, success starts with good planning. The first part of planning is gathering data and performing a current state analysis and gap analysis. These activities are the primary components of performing an IT operations assessment. So before the organization can look at the people in the organization, the processes that are being used, or what tools are implemented, the organization must ensure that the appropriate time is spent gathering all the business requirements.

Gathering the business requirements helps set the charter for the entire program and may establish a good set of priorities from which to work. It will also be the foundation for establishing a vision, one of the most important results of the planning phase. The company must remember to investigate why the IT operations team exists: it is to enable the business to function, to be as productive as possible, and to positively affect the company's bottom line. Therefore, understanding exactly what the requirements are for the IT operations organization to enable the company to better achieve its goals is vitally important. Do not be afraid to get executive input. The organization may be surprised that executives are more than happy to share their thoughts on how IT can help the company. Also, if the company is large, gather requirements from various different sources, including end users. Getting these different perspectives will provide an objective solution overall. Sometimes, it is also quite advantageous to receive input from those who are known to have opposing views.

Some of the business requirements that would be gathered include the following:

- Determining what the budget is
- Identifying the stakeholders
- Identifying the scope of IT operations within the organization or company

- Understanding what constraints might exist, such as having to use union labor or consolidating everything into a single location
- Understanding what some of the current issues are with the IT operations organization
- Determining what the needs of the business are from IT operations, such as ensuring that SLAs are being met

One other thing to keep in mind is not to be judgmental about the requirements that are gathered. Listen, confirm, evaluate, and record the requirements, and then move on to the next task.

Once the business requirements have been gathered, the organization can begin gathering the technical requirements. In actuality, some of these may have already been collected because a few of the same people who provided the business requirements might also provide technical requirements. The technical requirements are not specific solution requirements, in the sense that the organization is looking for what products it should buy for the solution. This would be done as part of designing the solution. However, the organization needs to know what devices need to be managed, how things should be integrated, and what users or organizations will be involved in IT operations. The organization will also need to identify any constraints, such as the use of a specific tool that has been recently invested in. Furthermore, do not forget to ask about future plan, such as a newly rolled out technology that will need to be managed.

The next step in the assessment is to gather information on the current state. As part of this activity, the organization will need to gather all information on how the organization is structured, what all of the processes are, and what the tools architecture is.

Reviewing the organization includes the following:

- *Recording all of the groups that participate in IT operations.* Keep within the scope. If the scope is only NSM, then focus on the groups related to NSM; if the scope is systems, then keep the focus on that. However, because the organization will most likely be performing this assessment to implement a patch management process, it will look at the network, systems, and applications.
- *Looking at the skill sets of the folks who perform IT operations.* This may not mean interviewing everyone, but get a general

idea of what type of skill sets exist. Will the team have the skills to perform management of a new technology? Does the team know how to perform service-oriented management? How will the team handle change?

- *Reviewing how well the personnel work together.* Is the team collaborative? Does the team follow processes properly?
- *Gathering any information on roles and responsibilities.* Hopefully, the information will be documented; otherwise, just note who is acting in what capacity. See if a good organizational chart is available.

Reviewing the processes includes the following:

- Gathering all documentation related to current processes
- Observing how the organization operates

Investigate how the organization follows or performs actions that fall in the ITIL service support and service delivery areas. How are incidents handled? How is the root cause of a problem determined? How is a change made to a network, system, or application? How is a known problem shared with the operations team? How do end users or customers get help? How are service levels defined and tracked?

Investigating the current toolset includes the following:

- *Documenting all of the current software and hardware that is being used.* Record all information such as version numbers, licensing, and maintenance contracts.
- *Determining how all of the applications are integrated.* How is information shared between applications? Are connectors, probes, application programming interfaces (APIs), or other mechanisms used to connect applications?
- *Documenting the databases that are being used.* Do applications share common databases? Are the databases installed on the same machine as the NSM application or on a separate database server? What versions of the database are in use?
- *Documenting system redundancies.* Do the systems have any failover capabilities? Is there a redundant NOC?
- *Reviewing the features that are being used.* What features of the NSM applications are actually being used by the IT operations

staff? What major features are being ignored? Are two or more applications being used that have the exact same features?

Once all of the information regarding the organization, processes, and toolsets are gathered, the organization can start performing the gap analysis. The gap analysis is the process of comparing the requirements with what is actually implemented. The gap analysis can also compare industry standards and best practices with what the organization is currently doing.

To keep organized and to perform a thorough gap analysis, all requirements should be listed one by one; the requirements should be compared with what has been implemented. When this is done, once again review the current state of the processes against the ITIL best practices. Also, look closely at the NSM applications. Are they really meeting the needs? Have they been implemented well? Do any need to be replaced? Are there holes in the architecture that are not meeting the requirements of the organization? Can the toolset be optimized by integrations?

Once the gap analysis is in place, it is time to establish the plan. This is an important aspect of the assessment because this is where the organization sets the stage for success. The first step in the plan is to establish the vision. What is it you would really like to accomplish? What is the real goal you are trying to achieve? The plan need not be complex. It can be a simple message, but it should also be near-term focused. That is, do not make the vision the implementation of a tool. Make the vision something like, "Establish a world-class service desk using ITIL processes with an efficient and cost-effective toolset, operated by well-trained and organized personnel."

The vision helps set the stage, but now the organization needs an action plan and design requirements. This should be straightforward because the gap analysis has already been performed. Review the gap analysis, and create an action for each of the issues. Then take all the individual solutions, and ensure that they work together and create an overall plan. Do not worry about product selection or specific detail. This part will happen in the next phase, designing the IT operations solution. Once the organization has a series of recommendations that achieve a common goal, it can document the list of design requirements that the goal needs. For example, if one of the issues identified is that there is no central method for the distribution of software, then the requirement is that a software distribution solution needs to be implemented. Once the design requirements list has been completed, the organization can start the design phase of implementing an IT operations solution.

Designing an IT Operations Solution

Designing an IT operations solution is no easy task. It requires great knowledge of the tools and applications available on the market and how different products can integrate with one another to form a solid technical solution. This stage also requires in-depth knowledge of operational processes and procedures, such as those identified in the previous section on ITIL. Because the design aspect is complicated, this may be a good time to use the services of an independent consulting firm to design the solution or of an industry analyst for guidance.

The IT operations solution design phase requires developing solutions for the people, processes, and tools. The IT operations design, also known as the IT operations architecture, should include the following:

- How to organize the operations teams
- A solution for how all the tools and technology will be implemented, integrated, and used
- A process framework for performing all IT operations

To accomplish these design items, the organization should identify how to tie a high-level technology solution with a preliminary organizational structure and process framework. This sets the charter for the design and helps the individual teams go out and build a plan for each of the three areas.

Separate teams will be necessary. Individuals with good technical skills and knowledge of the NSM product sets to develop the technical architecture are a requirement. These skills are usually very different from those required to develop process or to assemble an operations organization with a well-trained staff. However, those with the skills to develop good operation processes may also have the skills to identify the operations organization and staff requirements. This may also be accomplished together by one team.

Once the teams have developed their detailed designs, the solutions should be mapped out to validate whether all of the processes, procedures, tools, and staff solutions will work together. For example, has all the training been identified for the tools, technologies, and techniques that staff will be required to use? Has the technology been developed for all of the process requirements?

After everything has been brought together and a solid IT operations architecture exists, it is time to figure out how to get it all implemented. A detailed implementation plan should be developed and approved. This is the foundation for the next phase.

One item to note is that cost will obviously be an overriding requirement for the entire process. It should be in the requirements definition, and it may be necessary to develop multiple preliminary solutions at first, each having different cost options, and then to present them to senior management prior to developing the detailed designs. When developing the implementation plan, all costs should be included, along with the resources necessary to implement and install everything.

Implementing an IT Operations Solution

Once again, implementation requires the proper skills. The organization will need to ensure that proper skills exist for the tools that will be implemented or enhanced. The organization will also need to have the skills to perform the training as well as to develop the detailed SOPs.

The implementation phase is basically laid out by the plan developed in the design phase. This plan should include implementing the technical architecture and the process framework and organizing or reorganizing the staff.

It should be noted that in many cases the detailed procedures that support each process or area are actually developed in the implementation phase. The high-level process and process interfaces should already be designed. However, because the design phase does not bring everything together until near the end of the design phase, based on timing and the specifics around how the tools are implemented, it may be difficult or impossible to develop the SOPs at the level required. Therefore, these procedures are usually developed at the same time the technical team is implementing all of its tools.

Once all of the IT operations solution is in place, everything can be moved into operation.

Putting the IT Operations Solution into Action

At this point, everything is in place and ready to become operational. The steps toward using the new tools and operational processes should probably be introduced slowly with a pilot. Instead of just picking a day and moving from one operational model to another, a subset of the team should try out the new tools and processes while the old model is still being used by the majority of the operations team. Once this pilot has been completed and everyone who used this new operational model is comfortable, the entire organization should start using the new IT operations solution. Those who participate in the pilot can champion the solution and can provide help to others.

The solution is now in place, and the assessment and implementation project is over. However, as with any good operations area, it should be continuously improved. Tools can always be made more efficient and better able to handle events. Processes can constantly be evaluated and improved. A program should always exist to identify areas that require improvement and implement enhancements.

Outsourcing to a Service Provider

Throughout the process of assessing and implementing the IT operations solution, the option of outsourcing or out-tasking has not been discussed. Both of these options allow the organization to put some of the control and responsibility for IT operations in the hands of an external service provider.

Outsourcing is the process of contracting a section of the operations to another firm. The magnitude of the responsibilities for contracting IT operations varies greatly, from managing routers in small locations, to entirely outsourcing the IT infrastructure and all operational responsibilities.

Out-tasking is the process of subcontracting specific tasks. In some cases, the organization may hire a consulting company or service provider to supply a resource on site to carry out performance and capacity management. Typically, out-tasking is used to enhance the operation with a capability or skill the company is unable to fulfill internally. Usually, this is either because of a lack of technical capabilities or because it cannot be justified, financially, to incur the expense when compared with that of an external contract.

Outsourcing and out-tasking should both be evaluated when planning and developing the IT operations solution. If contracts already exist, when performing the assessment, the organization should understand the impact and costs of the outsourcing solution and decide whether it has to be a part of the new design. When the design is complete and the implementation plan is developed, this may also be another good time to perform a build-versus-outsource analysis, especially if the implementation plan is a comprehensive build of a new IT operations capability.

There are many things to note about outsourcing the capabilities to a *managed service provider* (MSP). One major piece of advice is that an organization that decides to outsource must be committed to it. If a company outsources its IT operations and is uncommitted, the end result is building some capabilities to ensure that the outsourcing company is doing its job while still keeping some capabilities in place to allow them to maintain control. This is not plausible because the outsourcing is probably costing much more than was ever budgeted, as the organization is now paying for both an internal and external operations organization. The reason this happens is because of a lack of trust and control. Often, people do not entirely believe that the service provider is actually achieving what was committed to. Yet if the company does not have proof that it is getting what it paid for, it will create some operations to monitor the service provider. The other reason is control. Many companies have a difficult time fully committing to allowing someone else perform the IT operations function and want to maintain control. If the organization is unable to find a trustworthy service provider or cannot commit to fully moving away from performing IT operations internally, then it should stay away from outsourcing.

5

SECURITY MANAGEMENT

Although organizations have been establishing security postures within their environment since the 1970s, the term *security manage-ment* is still not a well-known term that is used in the same manner across various organizations. Security professionals may even refer to security management from a variety of different aspects or views. Security management can be used to define how the organization establishes and defines its security posture. It can also be used to perform the day-to-day security operations that occur. What security management is and why organizations are moving toward the establishment of this standard today will be answered in this chapter. Information on how to establish security operations to ensure that the requirements defined within security management are met will also be included.

Security management stems from the information technology infrastructure library (ITIL) processes. Because the patch management process is an output of the security management process, it is important to detail the larger picture. An organization may also opt to implement only a patch management process. However, it is important to show how this is just one part of a much bigger picture that organizations should strive to put in place.

One can view the term security management in two different ways. Security management can be any of the actions that take place within an organization to establish and maintain a certain level of security—that is, the desired overall security posture. By definition, security management is the policies, processes, procedures, and technologies instituted to protect the confidentiality, integrity, and availability of the IT infrastructure, which includes all of the organization's assets. Therefore, it actually includes both views, which can either be separated or combined.

Security management refers to the level of security the organization will establish and maintain. The day-to-day operations that maintain this are referred to as security operations and include the administration, maintenance, and operations of the security measures implemented to support the security management processes within the organization. Patch management fits into both of these aspects. Through their security management processes, an organization is defining what they believe their stance on patches is. Patch management also ties into the daily security operations because it is an ongoing task that is completed at various intervals (i.e., a patch being released).

A security operation, in turn, has its roots in two different areas. The first is that security operations are related to the general practices of security in security management. The second is that security operations' main source of information, or data, comes from the group that performs the network and systems management within the organization. This is also known as IT operations. The IT operations group is well versed in gathering data from various components of the IT infrastructure. An IT operation also analyzes and manipulates the data on a daily basis. It typically determines if everything is within the organization's normal operating parameters, which have been predefined. The practices of IT operations can be married with what the organization has defined in security management from a security operations perspective. It is at this point that the organization has the majority of the practices necessary to perform security operations. The intent of this chapter then is to focus on how security operations should be prepared for and established within the organization.

The purpose of this chapter is to concentrate on the aspects of security management and creation of a security operations group within the organization. This group of personnel will then assist in performing some of the aspects of the patch management process.

Overview

Security management is a broad and all-encompassing high-level process. It entails the security posture the organization chooses to define within itself. It can include the security measures the organization implements to protect the confidentiality, integrity, and availability of the organization's assets. Security management is divided into three functional areas: (1) strategic; (2) tactical; and (3) operational.

The *strategic* aspect of security management is where the corporate security policy is established. This defines the overall security posture that the organization will take and provides a high-level understanding of such. Security awareness and training programs are also driven by the strategic aspect. This ensures that all employees are educated on how the organization views security and what the employees' roles and responsibilities entail. Executive management commitment is also established here. This is where the chief information security officer (CISO), or equivalent, is identified and presides over the security group. Also within the strategic aspect, the documentation requirements are established. Because all the policies, processes, and procedures must be maintained in hard- and soft-copy format, a standard for maintaining and updating this documentation must be established. This is done at a high level, dictating how the organization requires documentation to be completed from the top down. The actual completion of the documentation would be the responsibility of a different group.

The *tactical* aspect of security management is where the security engineering tasks are performed. One of the tasks may include determining whether a security technology such as an intrusion detection system (IDS) or intrusion prevention system (IPS) should be implemented. The development of operating system hardening documents may also be created and implemented. Another task may also be to determine the antivirus solution to be implemented within the organization. The tactical aspect of security management will also be where potential vulnerabilities are reviewed and identified, and then security operations is made aware of this potential issue. Individuals assigned to the tactical aspect can be thought of as the "doers" who implement the required security measures to adhere to the strategic aspect of security management that has been defined.

The *operational* aspect is a vital part of security management. Once the infrastructure has been secured, the level of security degrades based on time, new threats, and constant changes in the environment. To constantly maintain an established level of security, it is important for the organization to closely monitor the IT infrastructure for new, emerging security threats. This is done by carrying out the day-to-day tasks of administering, maintaining, and operating the security measures to guarantee that the level of security defined in the strategic aspect and implemented in the tactical aspect is continuously adhered to.

Because the tasks are performed on a daily basis, this aspect is known as security operations. If the operational aspect is not taken seriously, the security posture of the organization is at risk. All the time and effort committed to establishing a safe and secure environment will become lost if security operations are not established. After time, and sometimes on a daily basis, new vulnerabilities and risks are introduced into the organization. Vulnerabilities applicable to the environment will provide new avenues for access and will create violations in policies that result in previously secure systems becoming insecure.

In contrast, the strategic and tactical aspects do not deal with the day-to-day operational tasks, which include monitoring the organization for security issues. This is one of the tasks for which security operations is responsible. Security operations are actually the act of performing the monitoring of the environment for malicious activity. It is also the act of performing the security-related management tasks of the security measures implemented within the organization. Some of the tasks within security operations can include reviewing logs and monitoring events from the antivirus solution and IDS events. Security operations can also include responding to end-user requests for secure ID tokens, password resets, and even firewall rule changes. Therefore, it includes the daily monitoring and management of the security measures implemented within the organization.

Security Operations

Patch management ties into the organization's security operations plan. It is within the security operations plan that many of the implementation aspects of the patch management process are performed. However, the actual planning and establishing of the patch management process fall under the tactical aspect of security management. And then, of course, the strategic aspect is where the requirement of patch management to be performed is determined. The high-level requirements of what must be met with the process are also dictated by the strategic group.

IT operations and security operations are similar in the way that data need to be collected from numerous devices. Security operations require data from many of the traditional network components that are also monitored by IT operations, such as routers and switches. Information from other network components, such as virtual private network (VPN) devices, IDSs, and firewalls, are also gathered by security operations. From the systems within the organization's infrastructure, data are gathered by security operations such as access logs, event logs, and application-related access. The method of collecting all this data is not much different from traditional IT operations methods.

What a security operation does with this information differs significantly from what an IT operation does with it. For example, IT operations are required to review event information in real time and to deduce that something is currently not working as it should. This could be caused by a circuit failing or a process on a server or application crashing and ceasing to run. It may also have something to do with a change that was made at a specific time that has caused a negative effect. In this case, the situation can be directly related to a specific change. For example, a change to the configuration on a router may have been done on Sunday evening and on Monday morning users start reporting that they are having issues with an application on a server due to slow network responses. After further investigation, the problem is identified that the router, which this server is connected to, is not routing traffic properly. The investigation also shows that this is due to the change that resulted in traffic using suboptimal routes. This then is causing the slow network response with the servers attached to it. Now that the solution has been identified, the router can be updated appropriately and validated to ensure that the issue is resolved.

The way IT operations and security operations review gathered data is different. Information from the environment is gathered regularly, but the continuous review of the information may show an issue over a period of time as opposed to a single, current event. For example, a trend showing a high level of traffic from one server going out to the Internet during various times of the day may be noticed. While a high level of traffic may be normal during regular business hours, this traffic now seems to increase after the end of the normal working day. After further investigation, including log reviews and network traffic monitoring, it may be identified that the system is compromised and hosting inappropriate content, which is then accessed over the Internet. Perhaps due to an already existing vulnerability on the server, a hacker has installed a file-sharing application enabling the transference of the content to be downloaded and uploaded to and from the Internet. If the data had not been gathered over a long period of time and correlated appropriately, the organization may not have identified what this server was actually doing. This is only one example of how data gathered over a period of time can be correlated to show a security breach. There is also the immediate identification of a security breach due to the data collected from security operations.

In most organizations, IT operations have already been established. The method used to establish IT operations could be carried over for the establishment of security operations. For example, the processes established for IT operations can be used as the starting point for the security operations processes, using even the same tools in some instances. While an organization does not need to implement security operations solely to perform patch management, it can be considered in cases where the organization wishes to improve the already established level of security management (or its security posture).

Preparing for Security Operations

It is only through the healthy combination of people, processes, and technology that security operations can exist and be successful within any organization. As with any new task, the proper steps up front must be accomplished. This entails gathering the appropriate requirements that the organization is striving toward in terms of security operations. The organization must also determine which tools or technology will be used for the day-to-day operational tasks. For example, the tool that will be used to correlate the events received from the various network devices must be decided in advance. This and other important decisions must be made by the organization prior to purchasing and implementing the tools.

Gather Requirements

As with the establishment of any new process, the organization must review the business and technical requirements that the process must address. The gathering of these requirements must be the first step because it drives what security operations must complete for it to be successful within the organization. The requirements can also drive the success of security operations and, in turn, be used to measure this success.

When the organization sets out to determine the requirements for security operations, it must review the requirements from a business and technical perspective. These two perspectives ensure that the business and technical needs of security operations are ultimately met. The following list of questions can be used as a starting point for the organization to ask and provide answers:

- Business requirements:
  - What regulations must the organization be compliant with?
  - Have previous security incidents occurred that caused a financial impact?
  - Has service ever been affected by a security issue?
  - Are there any specific security concerns today?
  - What type of budget exists for security operations?
- Technical requirements:
  - Has any particular security operations software been purchased or licensed?
  - Are there any contracts with security monitoring service providers?
- What type of reporting is necessary?

The business requirements tie into the business impact that security has on the organization. In many cases, laws and regulations can have a role in determining the level at which security operations must exist. The organization's compliance officer and even legal counsel can assist the security group during the requirements-gathering phase. This will guarantee that what the security group is looking to execute will meet the requirements dictated in the laws and regulations. If the organization has experienced one or multiple security incidents, the financial impact can determine that the security operations requirements are moving forward. If the financial impact was great, the organization may require a security operations solution that is complex and will reduce the level of risk in having a repeat incident cause additional financial impact. If business-critical applications have been impacted by a security issue, the organization may increase the requirements of security operations to protect these systems with additional security measures than those taken on less critical applications and servers in the environment. If past financial impacts have been minor, the organization may choose to start with a basic security operations plan, allowing for growth in the long run. Finally, probably the most important topic—which dictates what the organization can actually implement when it comes to security operations—is budget. The organization needs to determine how much money it can spend on security operations. This will be the overall driving force when it comes to what the organization can do in the way of security operations.

Technical requirements also must be defined during the initial stages of planning for security operations. The current security-related management tools should be documented and reviewed. In some cases, the organization can use these tools (or additional modules of these tools) in the new security operations plan. The organization may look into other third-party companies actually monitoring its environment. They may be a service provider used in a specific area within the organization. For example, a service provider may be used at a specific location or within a business unit (or department). If there is a security monitoring service provider in place, its role and tasks will be closely evaluated. If not, this may not apply. The reporting requirements are also evaluated to determine what types of reports need to be completed on a regular basis. While this does not hold a high level of requirement, it can have an impact on what the organization will put into effect at a minimum. Reporting can also tie into auditing capabilities, which again can go back to laws and regulations with which the organization must comply.

When an organization is collecting requirements, it must perform due diligence and ensure that all the requirements are gathered and documented appropriately. The organization, or more specifically the group establishing security operations, must understand what capability is being built within the environment. The organization must also clearly define, document, and agree upon the requirements before moving on to the next phase of establishing security operations. Once this task is completed, the design and implementation of security operations— including the tools required to complete the tasks appropriately—can commence.

Selecting the Tools

Within the realm of overall security management, it encompasses the three aspects of people, process, and technology. As with the decision to implement a technology to assist in accomplishing a specific task, the organization must carefully consider which technology will provide the result desired. In security operations, the same due diligence must be performed when determining which technology will be used to monitor and manage the security measures that have been executed within the network, systems, and applications. It is through the use of the technology or a tool that the security operations personnel within the organization can perform tasks in an effective and efficient manner.

Oftentimes an organization will purchase a tool for no other reason than to solve a specific problem. This holds true not only for patch management but also for security operations. This may work for the short term or from a high-level perspective. However, this may not work for the long-term goals of the organization and its view of security management. What typically happens is that multiple software and hardware technologies are purchased to solve individual problems. When this is done, the greater goal of using technology to assist the organization is neither evaluated nor taken into consideration, which results in a more expensive method to accomplish many tasks instead of looking for a method to group tasks together and use one tool to accomplish many things. In addition, this requires a more complicated method to accomplish these tasks, because personnel will need to be well versed in many areas instead of a more streamlined flow. After a period of time, frustration on the part of operational personnel will increase and can result in the technologies not being used at all. Many a network operations center (NOC) has systems that have been "shelved" by operational personnel, and they are noticeable due to the layers of dust on them.

The main goal in implementing a technology is to perform the appropriate monitoring and management of the environment. This applies to traditional IT operations as well as security operations. A holistic approach to security operations should be pursued, wherein all the requirements are reviewed and an architecture and vision are developed. It is only after gathering the requirements and performing an assessment of what tools are in use today within the organization that a plan for evaluating new tools can commence. Once the tools have been evaluated, the organization can make an educated decision on which ones to purchase and implement. Tools also come in the form of a suite, where additional modules can be purchased to accomplish multiple tasks. This can aid the organization in solving multiple requirements across different areas. For example, a tool can be used for monitoring system health and can also have security monitoring capabilities. Therefore, only a single tool needs to be purchased instead of two different ones. This requires the organization to investigate tools that provide both an IT and security operations function.

Once the requirements have been defined, the organization must assess its current environment and then must develop the vision and architecture for the security operations tools. This means investigating all the components of the environment that need security monitoring and management. The organization may ask what should be monitored and managed from a security perspective within the organization. The organization can then answer this question by working both forward and backward.

In working forward, the organization would list all the components within the environment that can be monitored and managed from a security perspective, such as the following:

- VPN concentrators
- Network intrusion detection devices
- Host intrusion detection devices
- Intrusion prevention devices
- Firewalls
- System log files
- Application log files
- Network devices (e.g., routers, switches)
- Remote access servers
- Traffic analyzers
- Enterprise virus console
- Web content filters

Now the organization can work backward, which is actually more important than working forward. This is because by working backward the organization is identifying exactly what it wants the function of security monitoring and management to do. The end goal is to identify and remediate abnormal conditions in the environment that may be related to a violation of a security policy. Therefore, the organization will want to focus on determining what events will require action. Once this is identified, the organization can determine which toolset will support the monitoring and management of these items.

Another item to consider when working backward is that if the organization monitors everything in the environment this will cause many alarms to occur on a regular basis. The security operations personnel will not be able to keep up with all of the alarms and will soon start to ignore everything until something severe happens, which is typically the result of operations being informed via telephone and not the tools suite. The personnel will need to be able to identify a severe incident that needs attention versus an annoying one. They will usually find out only after a few phone calls from panicked individuals instead of learning from the technology implemented to inform them directly. This results in the organization wasting time, money, and resources by implementing a complex infrastructure that is ultimately ignored and unused. When working backward, the organization will need to define what security situations or events it will react to, such as the following:

- Virus spreading through the organization
- Repeated "Access Denied" to a system or application (i.e., DoS)
- Unusual traffic activity
- Unusual device reboots
- Suspicious activity identified by an IDS or IPS
- Unauthorized configuration changes
- Unauthorized or unexpected changes in content

Once the organization has identified all the requirements based on the forward and backward analysis, it can then move on to identifying what is required from the tool and thus what type of tool is necessary and what it must do. For example, a common aspect in security monitoring and management tools is that the tool can be configured to forward events to a trap recipient or syslog server. This may not require any additional management application or an agent on the system or device itself. Where these events get forwarded to and how are important. For security operations, an application or device called security information management (SIM) performs data aggregation and correlation. The SIM will process events from the various sources and will identify specific types of situations that warrant a response. The SIM can be used as the main console for managing security, or events can be forwarded to any event management console being used by the security operations personnel. If this is a requirement of the tool, it must be included in the evaluation process. If the tool evaluated does not function in this manner, it should not be considered an option for the organization because it would not meet the defined requirements.

Tools purchased and used individually may not be as effective as tools combined and integrated together. To facilitate this properly, the organization needs to understand what the flow of events will be. The organization needs to take into consideration how an event or situation will be identified and processed via the toolset. The following example shows a security incident that takes place from start to finish. Individuals from the Internet are attempting to perform a denial-of-service attack. A machine on the Internet is rapidly delivering Internet Control Messaging Protocol (ICMP) echo packets to a server in the perimeter network. This attack is identified by the network-based IDS implemented in the perimeter network. A trap from the IDS device is sent to the SIM. The SIM processes the event, determines that this is a security event requiring attention, and forwards the event to the event management console, where the security operations personnel are notified of the situation. The personnel can then perform the appropriate actions to prevent the situation from causing harm to the infrastructure in addition to any other necessary tasks for this type of situation. This is a simple example; in many situations, information will come from various sources and be combined at the SIM. This illustrates that the SIM processes the information and identifies the security incidents and their root causes.

Establishing Security Operations

Various aspects must be considered when an organization decides to establish security operations, one of the most difficult of which is putting the right security operations personnel in the right place. Staffing security operations appropriately can be another hurdle for an organization to overcome when putting security operations in place. Each organization will establish security operations differently, based on a variety of reasons:

- The technologies implemented by the organization require specific skills
- The existing implementation of the IT operations group
- The size and complexity of the organization's infrastructure
- The organization's business need for security operations

Each organization is going to deploy different tools to appropriately accomplish the security monitoring and management required. Which tools the company purchases and how it uses them will affect what knowledge and skills are required by security operations personnel. Whether the technologies used are a VPN concentrator, a specific vendor's firewall, IDS, or a Web content filter, all will determine what skills will be needed by security operations personnel. A clear understanding of how IT operations are organized will help the organization in establishing security operations effectively and in leveraging the existing processes, procedures, and personnel from IT operations into security operations. However, how the roles are broken down and how the responsibilities are handed off from one individual to the next will affect how security operations can be integrated best. A side item to note is that lessons learned from establishing and maintaining IT operations can be used as a guide during the establishment of security operations. As it is best not to reinvent the wheel with the creation of every task, information from the implementation of the IT operations group can be used again in the establishment of the security operations group.

The size of the company and the company's requirements for certain types of security practices can also affect the security skill sets required and how they are organized. A large firm is going to call for a full staff of security individuals, whereas a small firm may be able to make do with a single skilled individual. A company that requires specific procedures to meet regulations, such as pharmaceutical companies complying with 21 CFR Part 11 regulations, may also need an organization dedicated to ensuring compliance. Also, organizations required to comply with Payment Card Industry (PCI) will have specific security monitoring requirements. The size and complexity of the organization may also aid it in determining whether security operations should be performed in house or outsourced to a third party.

Finally, the organization's business need for security operations must be considered when establishing security operations. The needs of the business drive security management and the establishment of security operations. It is executive management that also drives the success of both of these. Without the business need and the proper support, a successful security operations plan cannot be established. Gaining executive-level support in the early stages of creating security operations can aid in its smooth organization-wide establishment. This is also where the strategic group comes into play, because this group should receive the proper support from the business and executive management prior to determining it a requirement.

Methods of Implementation

Although security management is driven by the internal needs of an organization, there are methods of accomplishing security operations through external means. Some organizations think that they need to solve all of their own problems, but instead they may decide to look toward external entities to assist them. When establishing security operations, an organization can choose from four basic methods to establish this:

Method 1. The organization decides to implement a dedicated security group known as a security operations center (SOC), which contains both security operations and the supporting security engineering group, also known as the tactical group. The SOC is responsible for all security monitoring and management of the organization's assets and for incident response, including resolutions for all known security issues. An SOC is very similar to an NOC. The NOC provides the monitoring and management of the organization's infrastructure but does not perform any security-related tasks. SOCs are in common use within organizations today.

Method 2. The organization decides to implement a dedicated SOC, but this time with a separate security engineering group. The security monitoring is still performed by the SOC along with Level 1 support of security-related issues. All other security-related tasks are escalated to the separated security engineering group. The Level 2 and 3 supports of all items would be escalated to the separate group for resolution. With this method, the SOC may be in a different physical location. Different managers would also be allocated for the SOC and the security engineering group but would report to the same executive-level manager.

Method 3. The organization decides to implement an integrated security operations center (ISOC), which is where the NOC and SOC are combined to conduct all the monitoring and management from one central location. The network, system, and application monitoring and management, including those that are security related, are performed by one operations organization. A separate security engineering group is also established in this method, and any Level 2 or 3 support required is escalated to this external group. This method is becoming more commonplace today within organizations of various sizes. It can be a more cost-effective way, especially if the NOC and all the processes and procedures are already defined. The organization would need only to integrate the security functions into the current NOC processes. In this manner, both goals can be completed in one group, resulting in fewer resources being required. The time to implement this method can also be shorter, because all the steps need not to be completed but instead only modified. There would also be two groups of managers responsible for the ISOC: (1) a manager reporting up through IT; and (2) a manager reporting to security. This ensures that both goals of the groups are met, including maintaining the security posture required by the security management processes.

Method 4. The organization decides to completely outsource security monitoring and perhaps some security management.

This is where all monitoring for security incidents is performed by an external organization. The outsourcer would identify actual or potential security risks and would alert the security engineering group within the organization. The outsourcer would work with the security engineering group on any events identified that require additional information from the internal organization. The outsourcer typically does not perform the resolutions to the security problems, except in cases predefined between the two entities. In some cases, the external service provider can manage security-related devices. For example, a service provider might control changes to firewall rules for which it is responsible for monitoring. All requests for firewall changes would be approved by the organization, but the actual change would be completed by the service provider.

The end result of the aforementioned methods is that they all accomplish the same task. It is just a matter of how the organization decides to accomplish the task of performing security operations. It can be a matter of aligning the roles and responsibilities of the individuals involved to meet the needs and complexity of the organization. The organization must also determine which method can be established most cost-effectively. Depending on the budgeting and time constraints, one method might be better than the rest.

Roles and Responsibilities

When an organization is establishing security management, including security operations, the appropriate roles and responsibilities need to be defined, documented, and communicated to the appropriate personnel. When it comes to security operations, a few roles must be defined during its establishment. If the organization decides to implement an SOC, a separate group is established within the operations center to perform the day-to-day tasks required. The same roles and responsibilities can be carried over to the creation of security operations as they apply to both cases. In addition to management of the SOC, three levels of roles are defined within the SOC:

1. Security engineers
2. Security analyst
3. Senior-level security analyst

The security engineers are the individuals responsible for the ongoing monitoring of the environment and for identifying security incidents as they occur. These individuals also work closely with the NOC engineers to help identify incidents within the infrastructure, continuously monitor the tools implemented, and identify the incidents as they occur. The security engineers would also be the ones staffing the SOC around the clock if necessary. These individuals can be considered security professionals who have limited skill and knowledge. They must obviously have a security background, although the same level of knowledge would not be required for this group as with the others. One important item to note is that organizations can have different titles associated with the security engineers and should be incorporated properly when establishing security operations. These roles are provided as a guide, and the organization should tailor them to fit the needs and the organizational structure of the environment.

The security analysts are responsible for providing Level 2 support of the incidents as they occur. They look for security breaches that have occurred within the environment on a regular basis. The security analysts also receive notification of the events from the security engineers and provide Level 2 support for security operations (or the SOC). While these individuals are not on site all the time, they provide on-call services to the security engineers if required.

The senior-level security analysts provide the Level 3 support for the SOC. Depending on how well-skilled the Level 1 and 2 support personnel are, their involvement may come into play at different levels. The senior security analyst identifies the root causes of the incident or breach and implements the solution to remediate it. The security analysts contact the senior security analysts and obtain their involvement on issues that require their support. These individuals also ensure that resolution of the issue was implemented properly through receipt of the reporting information. Senior security analysts are skilled and experienced security professionals and are required to receive regular training to ensure their level of knowledge is maintained.

Additional roles can be established within the SOC, depending on the size and complexity of the organization, including the following:

- Security analysts specializing in different aspects of security within the IT infrastructure, such as a Linux/UNIX® specialist, Windows desktop and server specialist, or network specialist.
- A security operations manager who is responsible for overseeing the activities performed by the security analysts and approving any changes they make relative to resolving security issues. The security manager may also be the interface to the other security groups, including the security engineering group and the security policy group.
- A security incident response team that would include all the personnel who would be required to respond to a major security violation, such as a denial-of-service attack or a virus or worm infection within the organization. This team will most likely have various groups involved, including representation from those who manage the desktops and network devices and provide field support. The team will also have a designated leader who will coordinate identifying the resolution and getting it implemented.

While separate, stand-alone SOCs are somewhat rare and are typically established only within larger organizations, security operations are more rigidly implemented. Regardless of whether a formal SOC or a security operations group is established, it should report up through the security group within the organization. Although some of the tasks completed are closely related to IT operations, neither group should report to the director or equivalent of IT. This ensures not only a separation of duties but also that compliance with the organization's security management processes is being achieved.

Implementing Security Operations

Security operations are implemented in the same manner as IT operations. While this statement can be repetitive, the fact that it holds true must be conveyed. The policies, processes, and procedures to support security operations should be formally defined, documented, and communicated. The organizational structure should be established, including the proper training of the security operations personnel. Finally, the tools should be chosen and put into place as necessary and should go through thorough testing to ensure that it is meeting the requirements defined in the planning stages.

One thing to keep in mind, especially for security operations, is to understand what the interfaces are to the different security operations participants as well as to other IT operations groups. For example, when the incident response plan is established, the security operations personnel, along with the individuals they interface with, should clearly understand their roles and responsibilities. They should understand what their responsibilities are not only in identifying an incident but also in responding to it per the incident response plan.

The organization also must ensure the security operations group has a good interface with the tactical security group, which performs the audits and continuously identifies the vulnerabilities within the infrastructure. Having a clear channel of communication is vital for the groups to work together and to resolve any issues that may be highlighted as part of the functions that the tactical group performs. In addition, because the tactical group will drive the implementation of new processes and tools, it will need to work closely with the security operations personnel to make certain that these processes and tools are administered, maintained, and operated properly.

During the implementation of security operations, those who are performing the monitoring are educated properly, which will ensure the success of the security operations and the tool itself as well as that personnel are comfortable in their role within security operations. One method for an organization to do this is by teaming groups together to provide knowledge transfer. If there were a separate staff or group established to actually deploy the tool and to create the operational processes, this group would then provide the knowledge transfer to the personnel who are part of security operations. Another option is to provide third-party training directly to the personnel to guarantee they have a clear understanding of the tool and the day-to-day operational processes surrounding it. In some cases, depending on the complexity of the tool, the knowledge transfer process can take an extended period of time. Depending on the availability of the personnel who originally established the tool, they may not have the necessary time to provide the knowledge transfer appropriately. The security operations personnel will also need a clear understanding of how to recognize certain types of events within the tool itself.

Some events may require investigation and the use of other security operation tools and even IT operations tools. Performing all the actions with the new tools and following the documented processes may take some time to get used to and comfortable with. To make this transaction function smoothly, it is best to have the individuals on hand who developed the processes and actually designed the tool deployment. They should participate with the security operations personnel for several weeks to help guide them through the daily activities. This way, if something is not functioning properly or needs to be updated, the right personnel are on hand to identify and quickly resolve any issues.

Furthermore, if the personnel have a question, they can get the answer to it quickly and will not be apprehensive in trying different methods of using the tool. Typically, if operations associates are uncertain of how to perform something or react to an event, they may ignore the event rather than attempt to use the tool. Again, having the guides as part of the group for a few weeks will help everyone move forward more quickly and be a lot more knowledgeable about how to use the tools within the actual production environment.

The patch management process is a combination of security operations and IT operations tasks. Because security operations ties into the identification of the need for a patch (i.e., the release of the patch), it sets the priority and scope of the overall process. To establish the patch management process, an understanding of what security operations are supposed to be accomplishing must be defined and documented.

Incorporating Security into Operational Processes

Security operations follow the same processes and procedures as defined for IT operations. For example, if the organization is using ITIL as its process framework, an incident is an incident; it does not matter if it is a network outage or a security violation. The organization will still follow the same process but may need to engage different resources and expertise. Other processes may also be spawned from the incident management process, which further dictates what subprocesses and procedures need to occur.

The processes for security operations may vary slightly from the IT operations processes if the role of security monitoring has been separated into a different group such as an SOC or external security monitoring provider. However, the security processes would connect to the incidents identified through monitoring as the IT operations incidents are tied into the incident management process.

When an organization is planning for the existence of security operations, some key areas will need to be evaluated in detail. These include how the organization will identify a security issue, who will work on the security problems, and what type of incident response plan will be put in place. Although the same incident management process will cover security incidents the same as network incidents, how they are identified may be very different. Many of these can be identified using the security tools and technologies described in the previous section. Some will come directly from end users. In any case, the process should be clearly identified with what all the methods are for identifying a security incident or problem.

It is also important to understand who will work an issue. As security issues are very technical in nature and usually require specialized skills, these types of incidents are usually not resolved by Level 1 service desk employees. They are usually escalated quickly to a security analyst, part of the back-line support, either in the service desk or in a security engineer group, depending on how the organization is defined.

Similar to an IT continuity plan, whereby contingency plans are devised to deal with a disaster, an incident response plan should be developed for a major security violation. For example, if a rapidly spreading worm is loose within the IT environment, the procedure to rapidly deploy a team with the necessary level of knowledge to combat the problem needs to be clearly defined. If the organization has a global presence, appropriate representation throughout the globe that can assist must be in place. Numerous items need to be incorporated into the incident response plan. However, an organization should not wait until there is a major issue to develop one. Instead, it should have a formally defined and documented plan that is reviewed and revised regularly to ensure that it is adequate to combat new types of security problems that are being seen in the industry and as technology evolves.

Aside from the typical security operations, there may be some discussion on whether the role of auditing or performing vulnerability assessments is part of operations. Many see this as the responsibility of the tactical group. However, depending on the size of the organization and whether there is a separate SOC, many of these functions may actually reside in the IT operations group. If this is the case, then there needs to be a clear understanding and process developed on when these activities take place and how results are reported and responded to.

Process Example

The following example is provided to show how a configuration change is implemented on a system, based on a user contacting the service desk looking for assistance.

An employee of a company calls the help desk to complain about an issue. The service desk receives the call and opens an incident ticket. As part of opening the ticket, the service desk gathers the caller's information and basic information about the trouble. This is the beginning of the incident management process. Typically, the front-line service desk personnel continue to work the ticket, but this may be organized differently. Depending on how the skills sets and responsibilities are divided in the organization, it could immediately be handed to someone else to work the ticket. The trouble is investigated, and, most likely, the service desk person responsible will look through the knowledge base to see if this matches something that may already be known. At this point, the root cause of the incident may be determined to be unknown. Thus, a problem ticket is opened, and the incident record is mapped to the problem record. As stated earlier and worthy of repeating, an incident ticket does not become a problem ticket.

The problem management team then investigates the root cause of the incident. The team may try to reproduce the error in the lab and will continue to investigate the issue until it has identified the source of the problem. At this point, the problem is now referred to as a *known error*. This does not mean that a fix for the error is known but that a workaround may have been determined. If so, the incident management team is informed so that users who have incidents related to this problem can get back to work while the root cause of the known error is resolved. The problem management team will continue to work the problem until a solution for the known error is found to resolve the open problems or incidents. In many cases, the solution to a known error may be a system configuration change. The problem management team would then submit a request for change (RFC) to the change management team to have the configuration change implemented.

Regardless of the source, the change management team will review the RFC. In actuality, RFCs are submitted to the change manager, who will then review the RFC and perform any necessary filtering. The change manager will also help in classifying the RFC. Depending on the situation, the change manager might immediately approve the configuration change. In a more complex situation, the change might be brought to the Change Advisory Board (CAB). The board will be called, probably on its regular schedule, but it will also include only members who have an interest in the various changes being presented. Once an RFC has been approved for the configuration change on said system, the change management process informs the release management process that a configuration change to the said system needs implementation.

The release manager will receive the request and will initially determine how the release will be handled. Depending on the severity of the known error, the software package may be delayed and combined with several other patches or may wait to be combined together with a major release. Change management will also provide input on how many releases can be combined into one. Release management identifies releases in three categories: (1) a major release; (2) a minor software release; or (3) an emergency fix. A single configuration change for a high-severity security risk will almost always be deployed as an emergency fix. The release management process will identify what devices need the configuration change, using information from configuration management and details from the problem record. The release management process will also test the release in the development environment if necessary and the test environment prior to deployment in the production environment. The release management process should also identify a back-out plan if, for some reason, the configuration change causes an issue.

The release management process will also update the definitive software library (DSL) by providing the new version of the software. The DSL is where the defined authorized versions of configuration items (CIs) are stored and protected. DSL is controlled by change and release management and is a basis for these processes. The release management process will also inform change management to update the configuration management database (CMDB) by updating all the CIs related to the release. In actuality, some organizations choose to allow only change management to update the CMDB, whereas other implementations allow the release management process to update the CMDB directly.

The release management process will inform the change management process of the progress of the change, and the change management process will inform the problem management process on the status of the RFC. Once the changes have been implemented, the problem management process performs a postimplementation review (PIR). As part of the PIR, the problem management process validates that the change that has been deployed provided the anticipated effect on the security threat. The problem management process should inform the incident management process that the problem has been resolved and that all related incidents should now be fixed. The incident management process should confirm with the users who reported the incident that their problem has been resolved.

This example demonstrates how a configuration change to a system can be identified, worked through the process, and finally implemented. One item to note is that this example was based on a reactive situation. The following example shows how the process would be different for a proactive situation.

Several incidents might occur that would look like something else. For example, periodically, users throughout the organization cannot log in to their systems as usual. The users probably think that they mistyped their passwords too many times and just need them reset. The service desk, as part of the incident management process, follows the process for the password reset and closes the incident. However, the root cause of all these incidents, or maybe just some of the incidents, might be related to a security breach. It could be possible that user accounts are being compromised and that passwords are being reset as part of the unauthorized access by an external user. As part of the proactive nature of the problem management process, the problem management team might identify an unusual increase in password resets. After further investigation, they realize, working with the security team, that these password issues are related to a specific security compromise. If this is the case, the problem management team would open a problem ticket and identify the known error. The team would then follow the normal process for resolving the known error.

Next Steps

As previously discussed, security management, including security operations, plays an important role in driving the establishment of the patch management process. On the other hand, more specifically, establishing the appropriate security management processes, which include security operations, ensures that a successful patch management process can be established within the organization.

The strategic group established within the organization's security management process must develop the policy behind the patch management process. This policy dictates what the patch management process must have and what the business requires to be implemented to remediate this threat. The tactical group helps identify the need for the patches, the priorities, and, through the inventory management tool, which systems are vulnerable and need to be patched appropriately. The security operations group in conjunction with the rest of the IT operations group facilitates the patch management process and performs the actual deployment of the patch.

When an organization is establishing the patch management process, it is important to keep in mind all the aspects of IT operations and security operations that will participate in the execution of the process. Having the process properly contoured to the organization and making sure the roles and responsibilities are properly set will help guarantee the success of the patch management process.

6

VULNERABILITY MANAGEMENT

The previous chapter discussed security management and was intended to provide the organization with background on how to establish this process in the organization's current environment. To complete this discussion, it is important to cover vulnerability management and where it fits into an organization's security posture. The vulnerability management process itself is discussed, providing insight into the high-level steps an organization should include in the process. While each organization will tailor this process to meet its own needs and requirements, information regarding the process is provided to give the organization some background.

Vulnerability management, though vast in scope, will be discussed in this chapter for the purposes of patch management only. Vulnerability management is known as a management process that an organization employs to ensure that it is continuously protected from the threat of new and existing vulnerabilities to its environment or infrastructure. It is an ongoing process; one way it is similar to patch management is that it eliminates an existing vulnerability within an organization through remediation.

Prior to going into detail regarding the patch management process and how to put it in place, it is important for an organization to understand the difference between patch management and vulnerability management. Vulnerability management covers a broad spectrum of tasks and activities, whereas patch management deals with applying patches onto systems that are vulnerable. Patch management is only one piece of vulnerability management, as it pertains to the remediation of a vulnerability by applying a vendor-provided patch. Therefore, patch management is part of the remediation plan within the vulnerability management process.

Definition of Vulnerability Management

At its highest level, vulnerability management is the process by which organizations continuously monitor their environment for new or existing vulnerabilities. A vulnerability in this case is defined as a weakness in a process or technology that can be exploited to compromise organizational security. The vulnerability can occur when an employee in an organization is at fault for making the organization vulnerable at some level—for example, if an individual responsible for firewall administration has enabled access through a port from the Internet to the internal network. Without doing its due diligence, the organization may be vulnerable to an outside attack. If this is a well-known port that hackers focus on when attempting to compromise a machine, the organization has just increased its risk for an attack from an outsider. If, however, the firewall administrator has verified that this port is actually needed, this must be evaluated and validated to make sure no risks are incurred by the organization. The firewall administrator may determine that it is not a requirement or that another method can be used to accomplish the same task. In these cases, access through the port would not be permitted or the alternate method would be implemented. To take this one level deeper, if an application requires communication over this port across the Internet, the system administrator who is responsible for the application must ensure that the operating system and application have been secured appropriately. By adding this level of complexity, attackers must clear these various levels before they can compromise the server and successfully complete an attack.

A vulnerability can also be at the system level or the technology level. These are the most frequent types of vulnerabilities identified. In most cases, a system will have unnecessary ports or services enabled that are not required to be open on the system. These services are identified during the vulnerability scanning task within vulnerability management, which is discussed in detail in the next section. Issues with having services enabled on a system are twofold when it comes to vulnerability management. The services can be a focal point for hackers trying to compromise a system. This can be completed either externally or internally. For example, if a disgruntled employee was just laid off or will be in the next few days, he may have a medium level of technology skills, but if he is knowledgeable enough to know which server in the environment housed all the payroll information he might attempt to gain access to it. He may want to publish this information externally or just e-mail it to all of his coworkers to show them how much everyone in the company makes. Once the employee has identified which server houses the payroll information, he needs to gain access to it. The disgruntled employee can easily download a free scanning tool from the Internet that he can run against this system to determine which ports are open (i.e., which services are running). Once he has identified an open service or port, he needs to gain access to the system. Using a running service, perhaps Telnet or File Transfer Protocol (FTP), and if no access control is in place on the system or if the access is open to all employees, the disgruntled employee can obtain the information for which he is looking. Not only does this potentially make the payroll public knowledge, but also now the system has been compromised. A key point to note is that if Telnet or FTP is enabled on the system, appropriate access control must be established to make it more difficult for the disgruntled employee to gain access to the system in the first place. The second method in which an unnecessary service running on a system causes a vulnerability is when the service should be patched when a known vulnerability is released. As an example, the organization may have a Microsoft SQL Server that is responsible for housing a database containing customer information. Continuing this, if this server was put into production and Internet Information Server (IIS) was left enabled but was never configured properly, it would have just been left in default mode. If a vulnerability is released that affects IIS, then technically this system should be patched because the service is running. However, if the system is not patched and an exploit is released, this server is at high risk for being compromised because of the exploit. If all services that are not required are disabled or if all applications not in use are uninstalled, it provides an additional layer of protection for the systems in the organization's environment. It also assists the organization in ensuring that the appropriate applications are patched on all the systems in which they are running.

Now that we have a clear understanding of what a vulnerability can consist of in vulnerability management, where it fits into the organization's structure needs to be determined. Vulnerability management is closely linked to security management. Like patch management, although the security group may not be responsible for all of the tasks it should maintain ownership of the process. The security group would be responsible for ensuring that the steps within the vulnerability management process are completed and documented. While the security group owns vulnerability management, other groups play major roles in it and have specific responsibilities that must be completed. The operations group, along with the desktop, server, and network groups, is responsible for the actual mitigation of the vulnerabilities identified. The process involves a reporting structure that provides to executive management, including the chief information security officer (CISO) and chief information risk officer (CIRO), a status report on how the vulnerabilities identified have been mitigated to reduce the organization's risk.

Figure 6.1 shows a high-level depiction of vulnerability management and the various pieces included in and tying into patch management. The following section provides the phases within the vulnerability management process to detail what steps are included.

Vulnerability Management Process

Although multiple sources of information detail the vulnerability management process, this section is set up to provide an organization with a high-level overview of the five phases. The first phase of the vulnerability management process is to monitor for newly identified vulnerabilities. The second phase is gathering data on the organization's environment. This is typically in the form of inventory (or asset) management. If the

Figure 6.1 Vulnerability management.

organization does not have this information readily available, an additional step would be to document the inventory (systems and network devices) within the environment. This can be used for the remainder of the process. The third phase entails assessing the posture of the organization. This is where the use of a tool comes into play. For an organization to understand where it stands as far as vulnerabilities, a tool (or software program) is run both externally and internally on its environment. These tools will show the state of the organization's vulnerability posture. Once the organization's security position has been determined, the fourth phase involves making plans to remediate the vulnerabilities that were identified. This will include identifying any false positives that would not be included in the remediation plan. During the course of the vulnerability management process, the organization must perform various reporting tasks. This will include the results of the scans, a documented list of false positives, the remediation plan, and a final summary with the status of the remediation plan. The fifth phase is then repeating the process on a regular basis and every time a change occurs within the organization that introduces new or additional risk. The vulnerability management process should also go through a regular review and revision schedule to guarantee that it is still functioning as required.

Monitor

Each organization should establish its own means in which to observe various security services for vulnerabilities. A multitude of resources should be monitored to make certain that information received is accurate and up to date and that it matches the systems and applications within that organization's environment.

An organization should use multiple monitoring options. In some cases even a third party can be contracted to provide these services. At a minimum, resources that should be monitored on a regular basis include the following:

- Vulnerability scanners (e.g., Qualys, ISS)
- Third-party Web sites (SANS, vendor-specific Web sites)
- Mailing lists and newsgroups (e.g., CERT)
- Patch management tools

When monitoring for a patch that specifically applies to a vendor's application, that vendor is really the authoritative force in deciding to release a patch. Therefore, the vendor should be referenced when monitoring for vulnerabilities that impact its applications. That being said, a vendor will not make an announcement until it has a patch to actually release. Therefore, another means to monitor for the vulnerability can provide the organization with the forewarning it needs to put a remediation plan in place until a patch is released.

Gather Data

For an organization to identify what vulnerabilities exist, it must have an inventory of what is in the environment. The topic of inventory management has been discussed several times to stress the importance of having an accurate and up-to-date inventory on hand. Every organization should have a clear understanding of all the systems and devices within its environment. Having this knowledge will arm the organization with the knowledge it needs to perform all the processes established.

A subset of inventory management is to classify or group the organization's assets based on certain attributes. The classification of the systems and networks can be based on operating system, business function, criticality, or location either where physically located or where located in the organization network (i.e., internal, DMZ). Classification of assets is also recommended as part of the patch management process and can be used for patch management that has been established for vulnerability management.

Once the organization has gathered the inventory and classified the assets, a level of acceptable risk for each group must be determined. For example, some systems in the organization may not tolerate any level of risk. These may be the systems in the perimeter network or those that send application-based data over the Internet. All risks on these systems must be mitigated as soon as they are identified. For other systems, such as an internal Web server, a level of risk may be acceptable, as long as the risks are addressed within a defined time frame. While this system may be important to the organization, it will not be mitigated with the same level of priority as the externally facing systems. The level of acceptable risk may also be based on location. The data center systems may need to be locked down and more secure than the desktops at a remote location. Both systems house important data; however, a breach that occurs in the data center might have a detrimental effect on business operations, whereas a breach that occurs at the remote location may affect only the users on site. These situations need to be taken into consideration, not only when classifying the assets but also during remediation, to ensure that the vulnerabilities are mitigated in the time frame required to maintain a positive security posture within the organization.

Assess the Posture

Once the organization has a clear understanding of what systems and network devices are in the environment, the posture of these assets must be assessed. In most cases, a scanning tool is used to complete the assessment. It will identify where the vulnerabilities lie and will evaluate the vulnerabilities on servers (including the operating system and application), desktops, network devices, and the networks themselves.

For some organizations, the resources and manpower may not be available to complete this task internally. Organizations may opt to bring in a third party to assess their environment. This is typically called a penetration test or ethical hack. Books have been written on the topic of ethical hacks, so this is mentioned here only for the purpose of providing an alternate option. Through the use of a third party to complete the scans, a validation of the organization's inventory can be provided as well. In the final report, the list of all systems and network devices identified within the organization's infrastructure is provided. This list can be compared with the current inventory list to identify any discrepancies. An application-based test can also be completed. This is a more intensive version of a scan and is typically known as an application-based penetration test. Third-party consulting companies are available to complete these types of tests. If an organization decides to perform one, it should be completed prior to putting a new application into production. This type of test closely examines the applications on the system to make certain that the organization is not assuming any additional risk by using this specific application.

Table 6.1   Example Scanning Tools

COMPANY	SOFTWARE PRODUCT	FREE?
Tenable Network Security, www.nessus.org	Nessus Vulnerability Scanner	Yes, but professional feed for fee recommended
Insecure.org, www.insecure.org	Nmap (Network Mapper)	Yes
Qualys, www.qualys.com	Qualysguard	No
EEye Digital Security, www.eeye.com	Retina	No
NCircle, www.ncircle.com	Vulnerability Management System	No
NetIQ, www.netiq.com	Security Management	No
Symantec, www.symantec.com	Enterprise Security Manager	No
IBM ISS, www.iss.net	Internet Scanner	No

If the organization decides to run the scan itself, it would need to acquire the appropriate scanning tools to do so, and many are available (Table 6.1). If the organization decides to complete the scans internally, it will need to determine which tool to use. Some of these tools are free, others are part of another software suite, and others can be purchased as stand-alone systems. Prior to choosing a tool for use, the organization should identify whether an existing tool can be used to assess the posture of the organization. The organization will also need to ensure it has internal resources that can use the tools. The use of these tools by an inexperienced individual can result in dire effects as they can bring down an application, system, or even network unintentionally.

Once the scanning has been completed, the organization will have a plethora of raw data, which can be cumbersome to read through. The tool will most likely have a method to summarize all this raw data in an easy-to-read final report, which can usually be customized to provide the details only on specific systems, on networks, or even on the entire environment at once. Regardless of which tool is chosen, the organization must confirm that it provides an easy-to-read, understandable, and customizable final report.

This final report is then used to first eliminate any false positives that have been identified in the scans. For example, if a server has been scanned and a Web server is found to be running on it, the server may, in fact, be a Web server that requires the application to be running and established. However, the organization can dig deeper to ensure that the Web server has been configured properly to prohibit the introduction of any additional risks.

One way that an organization can identify repeatable false positives is through a baseline configuration that can be compared with the final report. If the organization is using a standard build for the desktops, this standard build or baseline can be used to validate which vulnerabilities identified on the desktops are considered to be false positives. The same can hold true for servers, although the servers may have additional applications or needs based on their business function. These may not yield the same false positives for all the servers in the environment. After the false positives have been eliminated from the final report, the organization should have a clear understanding of its current posture and can move on to the next phase.

Remediate

The output from the assessment posture phase is the final report containing the list of vulnerabilities that have been identified within the organization. The false positives must be removed from this report to ensure that plans to remediate a vulnerability are not taken if they are not required. The organization must now develop a plan to remediate these vulnerabilities. One step that can be completed first is to prioritize the identified vulnerabilities. Prioritizing which systems must be addressed first can be based on the classification, or group, in which the system has been placed. For example, a server in the perimeter network that has been identified as having vulnerabilities present might be addressed first. Other systems may be done secondary or tertiary, depending on the group to which they belong.

The operations group along with the server, desktop, and network groups should all be part of the planning phase when determining which systems to fix first. The organization's change and configuration management processes will also dictate when the vulnerabilities on a system can be addressed. Here, the organization may run into specific change management windows that guide when work can commence on a system. This is all based on the system's criticality and the nature of the vulnerability. All of this should be considered when the organization is deciding to remediate the vulnerabilities. This is also where the patch management process comes into play. If a vulnerability has been identified on a system because of a missing patch, then the patch management process would begin, with each phase followed through. There will be exceptions to this. For example, if the patch was released several months prior and all the other systems in the environment have been patched, the patch itself will not have to go through the testing process again. If the patch identified has already gone through the process when it was first released, the patch process will be accelerated.

The plan to remediate the vulnerabilities can take a long time to complete. The security group must determine the time frame in which all tasks should be completed, with input from the other groups. Because all groups will have a portion of the responsibility to mitigate the identified vulnerabilities, they must all work closely together to ensure that all systems have been addressed appropriately. Because vulnerability management is an ongoing process, the remediation cannot overlap with the next occurrence of the scanning. Otherwise, conflicting reports will exist.

A follow-up scan should be completed at this stage to guarantee that vulnerabilities identified as needing remediation have been done so accurately. The report then validates the fixed issues until the next scan occurs. The report goes to executive management, such as the CISO, to show not only the level of risk the organization is willing to accept but also what it has done to mitigate against the risk it is not willing to accept.

The final report is not a living document. When the process is completed, the report is archived for future reference. Each time this process is followed, the previous final document should be referenced to identify any differences. These reports can be compared to show the level of improvement. It is also good to show these reports to executive management, as this might even result in receiving additional budget, resources, or overall security support.

Rinse and Repeat

The steps in the vulnerability management process are not completed one time only. This process must be repeated on an ongoing basis. Typically, an organization should complete a scan of its entire environment once a year. However, a scan of a department or business unit can be done as often as once a quarter. Again, this can be based on the group or classification in which the systems or network has been placed.

In addition, the vulnerability management process should commence before a new system or application is put into production. The organization can conduct a scan to determine what vulnerabilities exist on the system to remediate any items before rolling it out into full production. The perimeter network can also be scanned more regularly than other network segments. Because the perimeter network contains externally facing systems, they must be protected at all times and the organization must ensure that there are no new or existing vulnerabilities. An organization may be implementing a new network segment altogether. Before this segment is placed in production or is linked into the production or internal network, the vulnerability scans need to be completed. Again, this is to remediate any vulnerability prior to allowing network traffic across the new segment. Any new customer or group added to the organization should be treated in the same manner. The scans are run against new customers prior to granting access to the organization's internal network.

Ongoing vulnerability management can also be completed by other methods, such as firewall log reviews. Though these can be resource intensive, one alternative is to hire a third party to monitor the logs to make certain the organization is protected from the threat of an attack. These third parties typically have an established SOC that provides continuous monitoring of firewall or IDS logs. IDSs can also be implemented by the organization to provide continuous monitoring of the network to detect malicious activity. Either host-based or network-based IDSs can be placed throughout the network to aid in protecting against a zero-day exploit or the threat of an attack.

Establishing Vulnerability Management

While vulnerability management is an entirely separate process from patch management, it takes commitment from the organization to determine whether it will be put in place and enforced. An organization may need to determine which process should be implemented first: patch management or vulnerability management. In some cases, the organization may decide to implement them both in tandem, but this will take a great deal of effort and manpower to complete.

If an organization is completing vulnerability management, this section is intended to provide some guidelines for putting it in place. An organization must first establish an understanding of how to deal with current vulnerabilities. A collaborative group of individuals that would play a role in the vulnerability management process needs to determine what the requirements are for moving forward. These requirements are defined and documented to measure the successes of the process once implemented and also to verify that the process is meeting the needs of the organization. The process itself must then be built as designed. The design is based on organizational requirements and industry best practices. While best practices can provide insight and guidance as to what an organization should be trying to establish, it must be designed to be achievable by the organization itself.

The use of tools to assist in vulnerability management should also be determined and acquired. In some cases, an existing tool may be leveraged to meet the needs. However, the organization may need to purchase an additional tool. Once the process is defined and the tools are ready for use, the process can be put in place and tested to ensure its effectiveness. If there is a flaw in any of the steps along the way, the process should be reviewed and revised as necessary. As previously discussed, the process itself should also be reviewed and revised on a regular basis or when a major change has occurred in the organization.

Assess

The steps for implementing a patch management process (discussed in Chapter 7) and a vulnerability management process follow the same plan, design, implementation, and operation criteria standard, but this section highlights the differences between the two.

The first step in establishing a plan for addressing vulnerability management is to understand how and if it is currently being done. While the organization may not be taking any formal, documented steps to manage vulnerabilities, some groups or departments may be doing it independently. While the overall process should be central-ized, an existing process used elsewhere in the organization may be modified to meet the organization's overall needs. If the existing process is not documented, part of the assessment would include formally documenting what is being completed today, as this will help when designing the process as it moves forward.

Of course, the organization will have a set of requirements when it comes to vulnerability management. This can include such items as the minimum necessary that must be implemented and the end result that organization is looking to accomplish. This can also include the list of "nice to haves." These might be items in the process that cannot be achieved in the short term but for which a road map for implementing them in the long term may be established. The security group alone cannot complete the determination of the requirements. Instead, the other groups that will play a role in the process must be involved when the requirements are documented.

Design

The design of the vulnerability management process is built on the organization's requirements and industry best practices. While best practices work well on paper, the organization should carefully consider them prior to including them in the process. The requirements should be the basis for the process, but industry best practices can provide guidance on how to achieve these requirements. Vulnerability management can either be a large, complex process that an organization is willing to dedicate a lot of resources and time to, or it can be simplified to achieve only a specific set of requirements. Part of the design phase is to make the determination on how complex the organization will make the process. This can also depend on the executive management support that has been given to drive the process out to the rest of the organization. If it is not treated as a critical element in the organization's security program, a simplified approach may be the best option.

One way to keep the process simple and highly achievable is to leverage the current process to some extent. This will apply only if the organization is currently performing some form of vulnerability management, and it must be functioning well to do so. If a process in place today is not working or is not spread across the organization, it will need to be redesigned or revamped to cover the organization's entire environment. The tools needed for vulnerability management must be evaluated, tested, and purchased prior to putting the process in place. Again, if possible, leveraging existing tools can be used to eliminate some of the costs associated with putting this process in place. The tool should be tested prior to documenting its use to ensure that it will scan the organization's network appropriately and will produce the desired results.

Implement

Once the new or modified process has been defined and documented, the organization should begin to communicate it to the individuals responsible for completing it. Because the user community is not involved in this process, it should be transparent to them. An official announcement that the organization has chosen to implement a vulnerability management process does not need to be provided to all employees within the organization. The security group must notify the appropriate individuals, such as the NOC or operations group prior to running the scans, but overall process information does not need to be dispersed to the entire user community. Because the respective groups would then remediate the vulnerabilities on their systems, these would be coordinated through the NOC in accordance with the organization's change and configuration management procedures.

During implementation of the process, the security group should schedule the first set of scans on a limited number of systems. There can be grave consequences when a scanning tool is run in any environment. The network may become slow or overloaded with the additional network traffic. This should be considered when scheduling the scans, which is why the appropriate groups must be notified before it can be completed. If there is a network slowdown because of the scanning, the NOC must inform the security group to stop scanning. In some organizations, the scan will be run at night or during off hours to guarantee that it does not affect business operations. This is why a small group of systems or small network segments should be scanned first, especially if this is the first time the organization is attempting it.

The first time the scan is run, the organization may get a large list of vulnerabilities that must be remediated. It may have a difficult time going through the list of items identified. As with any process, the frequency of the scan should reduce the number of vulnerabilities identified and the manpower required to remediate them. Once the process has been followed through the first time, the organization should go back to the design and make certain it has been documented accurately. If there are any discrepancies, the process documentation should be updated to include the differences.

Review

In accordance with the organization's overall security policy, the frequency of the process review and revision must be dictated. A vulnerability management policy should also be established to provide similar information as discussed in the patch management policy section. To avoid repetition, the policy in the future section can be referenced for details regarding policy structure and content.

The review and revision of a process and the supporting policy is a standard operating procedure within many organizations. The details behind this do not need to be provided. Instead, it must be noted that this is an important step in the process and one that must be completed on a regular basis.

Next Steps

Vulnerability management is a process that most organizations overlook. Instead, the incident response plan is put in place. While vulnerability management protects the organization from incidents on an ongoing basis or from the possibility of an incident, it is a much larger and intense process than an incident response plan or incident management from a security perspective. Organizations instead opt to implement an incident response plan so they will have detailed how they will deal with incidents that occur that could compromise the organization's confidentiality, integrity, and availability. A common misconception is that only incident response should be put in place; in truth, both should be. Organizations may feel that it is easier to put a plan in place that reacts to incidents instead of taking the proactive approach and managing the vulnerabilities that currently exist throughout the environment.

For vulnerability management to be successful within the organization, it must implement only what can be achieved. Of course, a third-party consulting company can assist in completing the defined process. Therefore, through a third party or internally the process must be completed as defined.

To avoid a tool management nightmare, consideration should be given in determining which tool to use. It is important for any organization to understand that a process is not driven through the use of the tool. Instead, it is the healthy combination of people, process, and technology that will make a task successful. It might seem easier for the organization to purchase a tool to satisfy the requirements in the vulnerability management process. However, this can lead to the issues surrounding support of the tool on an ongoing basis. If a tool that is in place today can be leveraged to accomplish this task, then the organization must consider that an option when determining which tool to use.

Now that all of these operational processes have been discussed, the organization must determine how it will approach these processes and which ones should be implemented and when. It would be a major undertaking to execute two or more of them at the same time. Therefore, prioritizing those that are most important and then building the road map to get them established is recommended. Depending on the size of the organization, it may take weeks or even months to get these processes established and functioning properly in the organization.

7
TOOLS

Up to this point, the focus has been on the patch management process itself. However, organizations are constantly looking for methods to streamline or expedite patch management. They are looking for a software-based tool—a tool that will solve all the issues occurring with deploying patches to all the vulnerable systems. While the use of a tool is not a requirement for a successful patch management process, it can help the organization in accomplishing this task. A tool can assist an organization in deploying the patches in a timelier manner. This will result in a requirement for fewer man-hours and will ultimately eliminate the vulnerability in a shorter time frame. Therefore, if an organization chooses to implement a tool to assist in the patch management process, it will reduce the risk of an exploit impacting business operations because the systems will already be patched. If a clearly defined patch management process is not in place, then use of the tool will be of little or no benefit. It is the combination of people, process, and technology that ensures success.

Before the use of a tool can be considered, the organization must do its own due diligence to guarantee it will provide the assistance it is looking for. In some instances, an organization will need to purchase a new tool, while in other cases an existing tool may be leveraged to accomplish the tasks required. The latter is the best choice: not only will it save the organization money but also staff will already be familiar with the software, thereby reducing the learning curve. Regardless of what software the organization is using today throughout the environment, three questions must be considered:

1. What is the desired end result of using the tool?
2. What tools are in place today that can be leveraged?
3. Who will have ownership of the tool?

The answers to these three questions will drive the tool evaluation process. It will make certain that the tool the organization decides to use or purchase will meet the requirements defined for a successful patch management process.

The end result of using the tool can be in the form of patch deployment, inventory management, or patch reporting. The following section goes into detail on the first two forms, with the third being more of a requirement for the patch management process itself. In the planning phase of the patch management deployment process chapter, the requirements of the tool will be established, answering this question in detail. The second question, regarding which tools are in place today that can be leveraged, can be a more difficult question to answer. Depending on the size of the organization and how information technology (IT) has been established, decentralized versus centralized, knowing which tools are in place can be a complex question. Of course, if the organization has a centralized IT staff, then a clear understanding of what tools are in use today should be clearly documented. There may not be a simple fit for patch deployment or inventory management, but in some cases the purchase of an additional module to complement an existing product suite can be leveraged. Having a clearly documented software inventory aids in answering this question with the most accuracy, further ensuring that once the tool has been chosen and implemented properly it will assist the organization with the patch management process. The third question—who will own the tool and provide the daily operations surrounding it—is probably the easiest of the three questions to answer. The solution will be based on the patch management process itself and on who will own various pieces of the process. In some cases, the security group will already be responsible for managing and maintaining security-related software. In other cases, the operations group will be responsible, especially if the tool is an additional module purchased to complement an existing software suite. Whichever the case, when the patch management process is defined, the persons or group responsible for the tasks pertaining to the tool will have ownership of that tool.

The following sections provide more detail surrounding patch-related tools, including a discussion of process versus tools, where to use them, how to determine which one is best, and a summary of tools that have been evaluated for the purpose of this book.

Process versus Tools

Most organizations are looking for that silver bullet, one-stop shopping, or instant gratification to fix all of their patch management problems. Typically, they look for this to be in the form of a tool—one that can protect them from the onslaught of viruses, worms, and various malicious exploits released into the wild on nearly a daily basis. Unfortunately, there is no miracle tool to solve all patch management headaches. This is one area that needs to be constantly reinforced. Any organization looking to solve its patch management problems must look at a healthy combination of people, processes, and technology to solve the problem in the appropriate manner. There is no doubt that a tool can assist the organization, as can a process and even people. It takes all three working together to solve the organization's patch management problems today and as patches are released in the future.

There are instances where the tool can drive the process and vice versa. For example, if an organization is looking to develop a patch management process around only its Microsoft systems (i.e., servers and desktops), then it might look at a tool that works best in a Microsoft environment. Once that tool is chosen, the process will be built around it, depending on how the tool works, how automated it can be made, and how the reporting structure is established. If the tool will monitor for missing patches and will deploy the patches, then those pieces of the process are built around the functionality of the tool. If the chosen tool or tool of preference automatically pushes patches to the affected servers and desktops, then the process must be tailored to push the patches during the appropriate time frame and scheduling. If the tool does not, then the process would need to include people to ensure that the patches are pushed to the systems appropriately. As explained earlier, in certain circumstances the process drives the tool and the tool drives the process. This is why organizations must be thorough in their evaluation prior to choosing which tool is right for them.

There may also be circumstances that do not require a tool to be used within the organization for patch management. This, of course, is relative to the size of the organization and the number of systems on which patches must be installed. For an organization that has hundreds of desktops, a method to push patches onto those many desktops will be needed. The number of resources and amount of time required to manually deploy patches on a large number of desktops would not be feasible for an organization to even consider. If an organization has, for example, a small number of UNIX® servers, it would be feasible to install the patches manually. In some cases, the patch management process will be different for each operating system and even for each of the desktops. Therefore, in this example, the organization may have UNIX system administrators who would be held accountable for installing the patches on those systems. They may be responsible only for those systems, which would not include the use of a tool to deploy the patch. Instead, a manual procedure would be followed to make certain the patch was tested, installed, and reported on appropriately. While the deployment of the patches on the UNIX systems would follow the overall patch management process, a subprocess would be established to address those systems specifically.

It is very important for all departments looking to establish a patch management process within their organization to understand that the tool will not solve the issues they are having with patching their systems in a timely manner. While there has been a lot of publicity surrounding patches, vulnerabilities, and exploits, these issues have only recently surfaced. Many organizations are now scrambling to put a process in place to protect themselves from the exploits that are being released. While it is a good practice to implement processes and procedures as needed, they should not be done in haste, nor should tools be thrown at the issues trying to solve a much larger problem. It is for this reason that this book focuses mainly on the patch management process and leaves one chapter dedicated to tools, including how to determine which one is best for each organization. This has been done to further stress the importance of people and processes when it comes to patch management, leaving the tools only to assist in the continuous inventory of what is in the organization's environment and deploying the patches in a set time frame.

Where to Use Them

It is important to note here that tools can assist organizations in two facets of patch management. It has been stressed repeatedly that it is critical to have an accurate inventory of the organization's environment. One way to gather this inventory—the most efficient and effective way—is through the use of a tool. Preferably, inventory or asset management software is used, although other tools are available to provide the same information. With the passing of time, more software products are being developed to specifically address the needs of patch management, including providing both inventory management and patch deployment to defined systems. Again, existing tools within the organization's infrastructure should be analyzed to determine whether they could meet this requirement.

Tools also provide effectiveness and efficiency during the deployment of the patch to the desktops or servers themselves. In an organization that has more than 10,000 desktops, it would take a great deal of manpower to physically patch each desktop. A tool that can automate this piece of the process, patching thousands of systems at one time, will reduce not only the manpower required but the cost associated with the process itself. An item to note is that an organization should not attempt to patch 10,000 desktops all at once. This task should be completed in phases with a thorough plan in place. More details surrounding this method are given in the explanation of putting the patch management process in place.

The following sections discuss tools that can be used for asset tracking, or inventory management, as well as tools used in the deployment of patches, along with how to integrate them into the organization's environment.

Asset Tracking

Successful patch management requires an accurate and current knowledge of what is in the organization's environment. This is essential for maintaining a smooth-running patch management process. For example, System Center Configuration Manager (ConfigMgr) hardware inventory retrieves specific hardware information by default. This includes information like computer drives, video card attributes, and random access memory (RAM) amounts, and it can be extended to obtain details of installed software patches and other information that will be required to support the end-to-end patch management process. A software inventory retrieves information about every file installed on the systems and needs to be analyzed to determine which applications or software have actually been installed on the systems. Software inventory should be configured to occur weekly, or at a minimum biweekly, for all systems within the organization's environment.

Software or inventory tracking, or management, is probably the most difficult piece in the patch management process for numerous reasons, including the rapidly changing environment that exists within an organization. It is important for an initial inventory to be not only gathered but then verified or validated on a regular basis. Any tool that is chosen for inventory management must have the ability to validate what is in the infrastructure versus what is in the inventory database and also should be able to provide discrepancies between the two. In addition, inventory management is a difficult task when multiple groups or business units within the organization have the ability to deploy new servers or applications without having to go through any formal review process. If the organization has a centrally located IT staff and a data center that houses all the networking equipment including all servers, then it is easier for the operations group to track what comes in and out of the network on a regular basis. If the organization is dispersed, then maintaining that inventory becomes more daunting.

The tools included in this book are for informational purposes only. Organizations can choose from multiple available tools, and this will continuously evolve over time. Therefore, an organization is advised to evaluate tools prior to purchasing or implementing any of them. During inventory, tools can be used to determine what is in the organization's network. The following tools are examples of what an organization can use to develop and maintain asset tracking. While other, larger software suites provide asset management, these tools are listed as inventory management tools to assist specifically in the patch management process.

GFI LANGuard Network Security Scanner (NSS) checks the network for possible security holes. It scans the entire network and provides information such as a machine's service pack level, missing security patches, open shares, and open ports. GFI LANGuard NSS also offers complete patch management. Missing patches and service packs, both at the operating system and application levels, can be automatically deployed to all devices within the infrastructure. Both freeware and commercial versions of the tool are available.

Lumeta may be the best choice for an organization that is not sure of its infrastructure. Lumeta can provide a leak detection, and network, and server discovery. This capability identifies what systems and devices are within an organization's network and need to be added to its inventory. This tool will actually go out into the network and identify what is there. It will then report on the systems and network devices that have been identified, which are then put into an inventory tracking database.

Qualys is recommended when the organization can provide some information about its environment. If the organization has an accurate range of Internet Protocol (IP) addresses and systems, the Qualys tool can perform an in-depth analysis of the devices and systems within the infrastructure. The Qualys tool will scan for not only system vulnerabilities, such as unnecessary services running, but also what patches are missing from the system itself.

Other tools can scan an organization's network to determine which systems are missing patches and provide the option to deploy the patches to the tools. *HFNetChk*, created by Shavlik, is a command-line tool organizations can use to assess a system or selected group of systems for missing security patches. Organizations can use HFNetChk to assess patch status for multiple types of operating systems and applications such as Exchange or Internet Explorer.

The *Microsoft Baseline Security Analyzer (MBSA)* is a free tool provided by Microsoft that can scan the security base level of each system on the network. It includes a graphical and command-line interface that can perform local or remote scans of Windows systems. MBSA can scan one machine by domain name system (DNS) or an entire range of IP addresses. The output of the scan is Web based, and the reports can also be saved to be reviewed at a later time.

ConfigMgr, formerly known as Microsoft System Management Server (SMS), is a server-based systems management application that gives administrators the ability to track hardware and software and provides application distribution. Additionally, it can provide site metering, remote desktops support, and reporting without installing additional servers.

Patch Deployment

Once the organization's inventory has been accurately identified and documented, the same tool or another can be used to deploy the patches onto the servers and desktops, as required. For some organizations, gathering an accurate inventory of the environment is more difficult than actually deploying the patches. Over the past years, many new products have been designed to assist organizations in deploying patches on a network that is either simplified (one main operating system) or diverse (many different flavors of operating systems). Although these tools have seen many successes, it is important for an organization to carefully analyze its options prior to purchasing a new piece of software. Not only must the primary function of the software be analyzed, but also the management of that software must be taken into consideration.

An entire section in this chapter discusses tools that have been evaluated for the purpose of this book. It is recommended that any organization interested in purchasing or using a tool for patch deployment should do its due diligence and conduct the proper testing prior to purchasing the tool. Purchasing a tool to successfully deploy patches throughout an organization can be either a great asset or a major hindrance. Organizations should think about how adding a piece of software into an already understaffed or software-dense security group or operations group can negatively impact an organization. Depending on the complexity of the software chosen, management of that system itself can be a full-time job for at least one staff member.

The following are a couple of tools that have been evaluated for the purpose of deploying patches to multiple systems. In some cases, there is overlap with the previous section because many tools provide both inventory management and patch deployment for the purpose of patch management itself. Again, although other software suites can provide these two features, these are only as they relate to patch management and Microsoft. In a later section, other vendor-independent tools are evaluated that provide the same information.

Windows Server Update Services (WSUS) replaced *Microsoft Software Update Services (SUS)* in 2007. WSUS enables information technology administrators to deploy the latest Microsoft product updates to systems that are running a Windows operating system.

ConfigMgr, formerly *SMS*, is a systems management software product that is intended to manage large groups of Windows-based computer systems. Configuration Manager provides remote control, patch management, software distribution, operating systems deployment, network access protection, and hardware and software inventory.

How to Determine Which One Is Best

Now that an organization has determined that using a tool in the patch management process is a requirement, it must decide which one to use. The organization will also need to determine which criteria will be used to make the tool decision. During the design phase of putting the patch management process in place, the requirements for the tool would be established and documented. During this time, the organization must decide on which criteria to base the tool, with the supporting documentation provided to measure the success of the tool based on the requirements defined. It is then within the planning phase that the organization moves forward with planning how the tool will be integrated into the organization's environment. During the implementation phase, the tool is first implemented and then piloted on a predefined group of systems, including both servers and desktops. It is important to note here that proper planning must be incorporated to ensure that the tool functions successfully during the inventory management or patch deployment piece of the patch management process.

While implementing the tool can be extremely time-consuming and resource intensive, it is important for the organization to take the proper steps when determining which tool it should use. If the wrong tool is chosen and this is not determined until the process is in place and in operation mode, the organization may have to go back to the drawing board and reevaluate the tool chosen and perhaps even purchase and implement a different tool. This can result in the loss of money because most tools must be purchased, in the loss of manpower and resources used to initially set up the tool, and in an impact to the time frame required to put the process in place and have it functioning accurately. As an organization tries to implement a patch management process rather quickly to protect itself from the vulnerabilities and exploits that associate themselves with the patches, it is important for it to do its own due diligence and carefully choose the tool that is best for it.

This section provides a detailed discussion of the criteria for determining which tool would be the best for the organization. The following is a list of possible criteria the organization might define prior to evaluating products that could be integrated into the organization to assist with the patch management process:

- Price
- Leveraging existing software
- Supported operating systems
- Agents-based versus agentless software products

Price

Within every organization, pricing and budget are cautiously divided out and spent on areas where there is the highest need. This also holds true for the purchase of a tool to assist in the patch management process. While patch management tools are not necessarily high-priced commodities, they still will impact the organization's budget, including the manpower resources required to implement and operate the tool on an ongoing basis. Regardless of what a software product is used for, it comes down to pricing and feasibility of spending the budget on that product without knowing for certain whether it will meet the organization's requirements.

In some cases, a vendor will provide a customer with a trial version of software at no charge so that the organization can do the proper testing in its own environment prior to purchasing it. This recommended practice is discussed in the evaluation section of the tools. The organization must weigh the costs versus benefits prior to purchasing the tool to ensure that it is not wasting money on a product that will not fit its needs. The organization may need to present a return on investment (ROI) to executive management to justify the purchase of a tool. Can the organization measure the budgetary figures that were spent addressing patch management in a reactive state, such as the amount of overtime or off hours work by the staff? Can the organization show how much revenue was lost because of a vulnerability being exploited within its environment that used an unpatched system? If so, then the cost of implementing the process including the cost of the tool should be less than what it has cost the organization to function in a reactive state. Of course, having only one incident within the organization over the course of 6 months does not warrant an accurate ROI. However, multiplying that by four incidents throughout the course of the year may give a more accurate estimate of the costs today versus the costs once the patch management process is in place.

The standard basic cost model is as follows:

Cost = Employee labor hours × Hourly rate × Number of systems

This formula can be used as a start for an organization to determine how much cost it associates each year, or even down to the month, when addressing patch management today. This cost model can then be used when the process is in place to show how the cost has decreased due to the patch management process and, more specifically, through the use of a tool to assist in the process.

If purchasing a new tool, or piece of software, can reduce the manpower resources required to manually deploy the patches on servers or desktops, the savings should be reflected in the business plan to show the ROI. The cost of the tool should be taken into consideration when evaluating which one is best for the organization. It is also important to ensure that the tool purchased will scale with the organization over time. There is no reason for an organization to use a free tool if it will outgrow that tool in the year to come. This will only incur additional costs, as the process will need to be completely reevaluated once the new tool is purchased and planned to be integrated into the organization's environment.

Leveraging Existing Software

Another criterion is leveraging an existing piece of software. If this can be done, then this is the recommended choice of action. While a piece of software can be found to solve almost any problem an organization is facing, it is not always the best choice. When a new piece of software is purchased, several other factors drive its success. The organization absorbs not only the cost of the software but also its installation and its day-to-day operations and management. This comes down to resources and knowledge. Training must be provided to the persons responsible for implementing, operating, and maintaining the software. Dedicated resources may also need to be hired to fulfill these tasks. Once this has all been taken into consideration, the cons of the tool will outweigh the pros, especially if the organization already has a product suite in place that can be leveraged to accomplish the same tasks.

Depending on the size of the organization, many software products may already be integrated into its environment, providing day-to-day network and systems management. In many cases, the larger network and system management suites offer additional modules that can be purchased to assist in deploying patches. This is another option for the organization to carefully investigate. Not only will it reduce the price and manpower to install a new product suite, but the network operations center (NOC) and operations group will already be familiar with this product so there will be less of a training curve. Typically, the infrastructure is already in place as well to support this module, thereby reducing the costs associated with purchasing the additional hardware to run the tool itself. This all depends on the size of the organization, because a small to medium-sized organization may not even have an NOC or a large systems management suite to assist in managing the infrastructure.

During the planning phase, the security committee must have a clear understanding of what software tools are currently in place within the organization. This will allow them to accurately determine, with the assistance of the NOC and operations group, which products have the potential to be leveraged to accomplish patch deployment and inventory management (if this is not being done already). The security committee, also known as the group responsible for overseeing the process (not owning it), is established in another chapter. They are used in the remainder of this chapter because they will have a voice in which tool will be used to assist in the patch management process.

Supported Operating Systems

As part of the planning phase, the security committee must also determine which systems will be included in the patch management process. This can be addressed in a phased approach, with the process-only patching desktops and then at a later time servers and even possibly UNIX servers. Once the security committee makes the decision of which systems will be included in the patch management process, a requirement from the tool is that they support these systems.

When systems are mentioned, it means the operating systems that will be part of the patch management process. If the organization currently maintains various flavors of Microsoft and all of these systems are included in the patch management process, then the tool must be able to support all of them. If the organization has desktops that are running current or even older versions of Windows, then it must decide whether all these systems will be included in the patch management process or if the older ones will be upgraded to the organization's standard build prior to including them in the process.

This also holds true for UNIX systems within the environment. While many tools are available for patch management, only a few support multiple versions of UNIX systems. Linux, Solaris, and Novell seem to be the most widely supported; however, if the organization has AIX servers, it will need to determine how these servers will be patched if the tool does not support it. In some instances, UNIX systems are patched on a manual basis; this is a decision that the security committee must make because it can affect the efficiency of the process and the time required to protect the organization against the vulnerability.

The decision to purchase the tool, depending on which operating systems it supports, is based on the requirements defined in the planning phase. It is within these requirements that the required operating systems and systems in general are listed to ensure that those required are patched appropriately, regardless of whether it is through the use of a tool. Once the systems have been identified, then the choice of which tool to use based on the operating systems it supports is determined, again, by the security committee.

Agent-Based versus Agentless Software Products

Another key criterion to consider when determining which tool to use for patch management is whether an agent is required to be installed on the client system. While this does not impact the patch management process itself, it can make for a longer implementation phase when the organization is ready to put the process in place throughout the environment. During tool evaluation, products that require agents to be installed and those that do not should be evaluated to determine which one integrates better into the environment. The decision of whether to install an agent on each system that will be included in the patch management process is solely up to the organization. It can also be based on cost because, typically, patch management tools that require an agent are more expensive than those that do not. In addition, the supporting infrastructure for the tool may incur more costs because management consoles need to be dispersed throughout the infrastructure if the clients all have agents running on them.

There are pros and cons for each side of these situations. It is a more controlled environment when every system including desktops requires the installation of an agent. If an agent is installed, it does provide assistance with inventory management because a record of each system with an agent installed on it is maintained in that tool's database. The agent also aids in the monitoring of new systems as they are placed within the environment. If every system must have an agent installed on it prior to placing it into production, a formal review process can occur at this point to ensure that all security policies are being followed prior to putting the system live. If the tool that requires an agent is chosen, the standard agent configuration can also be established within the organization's standard build, guaranteeing that all systems have been configured in an identical manner as they are put into production.

There are also downsides to having an agent installed on each client system. With an agent-based tool, the patch is deployed from the management system to clients in encrypted format. If an agent is not installed on the client, the patch is not encrypted when it is sent to the client system. This leaves the system and the patch itself susceptible to malicious activity prior to being installed. If a tool is chosen that does not require installation of an agent, the setup and configuration of the patch management tool is generally less time-consuming because each system does not need to be touched, thus ensuring the agent is installed. This can result in a patch management process being integrated into the organization's environment in a shorter period of time. This is another piece of software that must be managed on a daily basis, and it can have the most negative effect on the desktops. If there are issues with the agent or with the communication between the agent and the server, NOC personnel must be trained on the software to remediate any issues without affecting business operations. The organization's help desk must be prepared to address any troubleshooting or configuration issues with the agent on the desktops because the users will be contacting them as soon as any problems arise.

While this criterion should not play a major role in determining which software tool to use, it should be taken into consideration, especially in environments where there are a large number of desktops and users in multiple locations. There are pros and cons to this decision, and each must be weighed and the final decision agreed upon by the security committee prior to purchasing the tool.

Tools Evaluated

Detecting what systems need to be patched and which systems are vulnerable to an exploit is part of vulnerability management. However, the security group should not rely on only one product to do all security testing. Each product has its own pros and cons. The tools chosen for use within the environment should be used only for that which they were designed for. While some vendors will provide updates to their software to meet the needs of a customer, it is recommended that the organization go with a vendor that already has the features the organization is looking for rather than relying on the vendor to update its software to fit those needs.

With this being said, the tool chosen to assist the organization must be thoroughly evaluated prior to being purchased and implemented within the environment. There is no need to hastily choose a tool to use to deploy patches just because the "latest and greatest" has been released. With the publicity surrounding patch management growing over the past years, so has the number of software vendors providing the silver-bullet fix to an organization's patch management problems. There is no one silver-bullet tool that fixes every organization's patch management problems. Instead, each organization should examine its own needs and requirements prior to choosing which one to implement.

Table 7.1 provides a summary of several patch management tools. A limited amount of information is provided because there is such an influx of patch management tools being released on a regular basis. This is used only as an example of the various types of patch management tools available today along with a brief description.

Table 7.1 Examples of Tools

NAME	DESCRIPTION	FEATURES	AGENT NEEDED
BigFix, www.bigfix.com (now part of IBM)	BigFix Patch Management is a comprehensive solution for delivering Microsoft, UNIX, Linux, and Mac patches, as well as third-party application patches, through a single console. A single server supports more than 250,000 endpoints—regardless of their location or connection type or status. With policy-based and dynamic bandwidth controls. Integration with the BigFix asset discovery, configuration management, endpoint protection, and systems management.	Scalability: manage more than 250,000 endpoints from a single server No loss of functionality over low-bandwidth or globally distributed networks Ability to manage computers on or off the network Increase in first-pass success rates from 60–75% to 95–99+% Coverage for a variety of software vendors, such as Adobe, Mozilla, RealNetworks, Apple, and Java Real-time reporting that provides information on which patches were deployed, when they were deployed, who deployed them, and to which endpoints	Agent based
Ecora, www.ecora.com	Ecora's Patch Manager provides patch management capabilities. Patch Manager automates system discovery, patch assessment and patch installation on workstations and servers.	Intuitive UI Installs in minutes, auto-discovers servers and workstations Patch ANY Windows application Microsoft supports Patch other companies' Windows-based patches Patch for home grown applications Automated patch roll-back on one or more machines Logically groups systems for ease of management Scheduled patch deployment	Agent or Agentless
HP, www.HP.com	HP Client Automation (HPCA) Enterprise software	Single console for physical and virtual clients with a common toolset and process It supports traditional desktop and notebook PCs as well as thin clients, server-based computing and virtual desktop infrastructures Integrates security and compliance management. It scans client devices across the environment for PC security vulnerabilities, regulatory and corporate compliance, and security tool status	Agent based

Company	Description	Features	Agent
Lumension, www.lumension.com	The Lumension Vulnerability Management solution delivers automated vulnerability assessment and patch management through an integrated solution that enables businesses to automatically detect risks, deploy patches, and defend their business information across a complex, highly distributed environment with greater efficiency and minimal impact to productivity.	Results are summarized in simple dashboards and reports that allow you to identify and focus on the highest priority areas. By consolidating vulnerability data with centralized policy enforcement and compliance reporting, the Lumension Vulnerability Management solution enables you to effectively manage the entire vulnerability life cycle and transition from a reactive security model to a proactive risk management approach	Agent based
Shavlik Technologies, www.shavlik.com	Shavlik NetChk Protect finds and deploys missing patches for third-party applications and Microsoft operating system and applications.	Third-party application patching. Single console to manage both physical and virtual machines. Agentless or agent-based implementation. Trusted, proven patch assessment technology—first to market with patch data. Most flexible, precise reboot options in the industry	Agent based or Agentless
VMware, www.vmware.com	VMware vCenter Configuration Manager (formerly EMC Ionix Server Configuration Manager) ensures enterprise-wide system compliance by collecting, storing, fixing, provisioning and managing configurations for servers and workstations across physical and virtual environments. With this critical data, Configuration Manager increases IT efficiency and lowers costs by eliminating the hassle and expense associated with using multiple tools for managing changes, provisioning, patches, configurations, remediation and compliance.	Automated collection, analysis, remediation, and patch lower IT audit costs by significantly reducing the time and labor associated with time-consuming manual processes. Consolidate tools to increase IT efficiency, removing the hassles, headaches and time associated with using multiple, separate systems for managing server changes, patches, configurations and remediations. Improve visibility through one, centralized view into configuration, security and operational compliance	Agent based

Conducting Comparisons

Open up any magazine over the past few years, and chances are an article on patch management is included. Several magazines and Web sites provide "bake-offs" or product comparisons with a certain number of patch management tools. These articles and sources of knowledge provide great insight into and high-level comparisons of the various tools available today. These can also be used as a great starting point for patch management tools an organization may wish to consider implementing in its environment. However, the results of these bake-offs alone should not be used by the organization to determine which product to purchase for its environment.

Vendors can be very helpful when it comes to clients wanting to evaluate their tools for purchase. They will offer free trial versions of software and sometimes will come in to provide a live demonstration. Depending on the level of detailed evaluation the organization wants to dig into, it should evaluate a minimum of three and a maximum of five tools to be used to deploy patches. If a comparison is done with too many tools, the results can be confusing, and the evaluation itself can become very time-consuming, slowing down the rest of the process. If too few are evaluated, the organization is not open to other tools to see what they can achieve for it.

The first step in evaluating tools is determining the criteria by which the tools will be evaluated. They can be ranked from 1 to 10 or can be graded, or a specific checklist can be completed that states how well they comply with the requirements. The latter is preferred, with a summary of grades, because it provides a detailed measuring mechanism and can evaluate each tool based on the same criteria. The checklist can include criteria such as pricing, supporting operating system, and agent based or agentless. This is similar to the one detailed earlier in this chapter. Once the checklist that will be used during the evaluation has been established, the organization will need to set up an environment that can be used to put the tools through the evaluation process. Depending on the size of the organization, a lab environment may be used to evaluate the tools. The number of systems available to the evaluators, whether within a lab environment, or not, can dictate how many evaluations can occur at once. It is recommended that all the evaluations occur at the same time to compare products immediately, but if this is not feasible then the evaluations can occur one at a time. Again, in some cases vendors will even bring in their software and will assist the organization in walking through the evaluation process to ensure that the organization understands all aspects of the tool prior to making a decision. It is recommended that organizations take advantage of this benefit from the vendors. It is more difficult to learn a tool and evaluate it accurately unless there is an individual available who can explain all the aspects to the organization during the evaluation process.

As the tools are being evaluated, the results must be documented separately so that they can be compared at the end of the evaluation. The personnel responsible for conducting the evaluation may be members of the security committee or operations group. However, the security committee would oversee the evaluation of the tools and receive an update from the personnel assigned to monitor the evaluation environment, along with the documented test results. Once the evaluations have been completed for all the tools, the results are then compiled into one report, grading each tool perhaps from an A to D level. The security committee would make the determination on how each tool ranks and what grading score it should receive. Once the tools have been graded, the tool with the highest grade would be chosen as the tool the organization will purchase and implement.

It is true that this is easier said than done. Completing a tool evaluation can take a tremendous amount of time and effort with the input from everyone in the security committee. This is a task that should be completed only once in the planning phase. An organization should not have to go through this exercise again. This is why it is important for the organization to take great care when choosing which tool to use for patch management, so that this level of effort does not have to be repeated. Just as the organization took due care when the first firewall was implemented in the environment or even when the first e-mail tool was chosen, the same care should be taken for the patch management tool. Regardless of the task the software or tool is supposed to achieve, organizations should evaluate all their options prior to purchasing one and integrating it into the environment.

Once the tool has been chosen, the organization can move forward through the purchasing of the tool and the integration of it into the organization's infrastructure. These steps are detailed in the implementation phase, which is explained in a future chapter.

8
TESTING

Effective testing of patches before deployment to a production environment cannot be stressed enough. If the business environment is disrupted because of nontested patches applied to production systems, then what is the difference between a worm attack or security breach that disrupts my operation and self-inflicted downtime from deliberate patching, both of which have the same end result?

Historically, many organizations tended to place too much trust on the vendors that release patches or on the source from which they downloaded those patches. Due to a high number of patches that were not tested by a vendor prior to public release and patch download sites from nonvendors posting altered patches, most eventually learned their lesson not to trust these sources to produce an error-free patch the first time.

The vendors eventually got better about testing patches before releasing them to the public, and many download sites began to offer MD5 hashes that one could compare with the hash value of the downloaded file to ensure that the file's integrity was intact. However, these improvements alone are not reason enough to forego proper testing of patches before deploying them into the production environment. It is not feasible to expect a patch vendor to be able to test the millions of different configuration and deployment scenarios that exist for a single product. What might work fine in one environment might totally devastate another because of the environmental conditions.

In addition, most vendors have not shared their testing methodology with the user community to show that complete testing was performed prior to release. If a patch is meant to fix one thing but inadvertently opens a hole elsewhere due to forgotten system file dependencies, the organization does not know if the vendor tested anything other than the vulnerability it was trying to fix.

Although most businesses are aware at some level that they should be testing patches before deploying them, they do not. The reasons for this vary. Some of these are explored in this chapter, along with some recommendations that may allow them to address these concerns.

Common Issues with Testing

One of the reasons some organizations fail to properly test is that they believe there is not enough time to test a patch prior to deploying it. Given the shortened patch management life cycle from when a vulnerability is discovered to when a patch is released to the time an exploit is running rampant over the Internet, this almost becomes a valid argument. However, most of these organizations made this claim when there were several months between the release of a patch and an actual exploit.

The organizations asserting this are usually considered to be stuck in reactive mode as opposed to being proactive when it comes to patching their systems. They wait until an exploit has actually affected them before they begin to react. This method of addressing patches is chaotic to say the least but becomes more chaotic when systems react negatively to a bad patch or misconfiguration that could have been caught with an effective testing process. Many hours of needless remediation then follow in determining what caused the problems when applying the patch to systems, fixing systems that were affected by early production release of the patch, and trying to keep the remaining operational but unpatched systems from being exploited. An effective patch testing process can shorten the time to production release of patches while minimizing the chances that a patch will have an adverse impact on operations and allowing the organization to become more proactive in managing its exposure.

Another common problem, even for those who have a documented testing process in place, is failing to rate patches properly. Knowing that the organization may be more exposed to certain vulnerabilities over others can help it determine which patch needs to be tested and deployed first. Rating the criticality of vulnerabilities to operations, being aware of mitigating controls that may be in place that reduce the organization's exposure, and staying aware of changes to the exploit landscape can become overwhelming. Developing a simple yet effective patch rating system with target deadlines for production deployment can aid in sorting through myriad patches being released today.

Along with lacking a patch rating system, organizations often fail to prioritize which systems should be tested first in their testing process. This can leave companies scrambling when an exploit hits as they test and deploy patches to production systems that had less of an exposure level. Guidelines should be created that serve a business in making sure that systems with higher exposure levels are addressed in proper sequence. Doing so can save valuable resource time and hopefully decrease downtime of nonpatched systems that are needlessly suffering from an exploit.

Others tend to excuse themselves from effective testing because they think they need an elaborate and expensive testing facility. Depending on the size and complexity of the environment, this may or may not be the case. Typically, if an organization is not just trying to make excuses, it can create an effective testing facility consisting of a few pieces of additional hardware set up in an area that will not have its coworkers tripping over Ethernet cables. In addition, the money that proactive testing of patches will save in lost production system recovery time can be used to work toward a more elaborate environment at some time in the future, not to mention possibly saving jobs within information technology (IT).

Virtual machine software can also alleviate a portion of the traditional costs associated with loading test systems. Given ample random access memory (RAM), disk space, and processor capacity, virtual machine software can eliminate the need for large quantities of hardware that take up expensive office space, increase environmental costs for cooling, and lead to other drawbacks that are normally part of hosting a dedicated facility. Moreover, because of virtual machine capabilities, the expensive resource time necessary for setting up replicas of production systems and reconfiguration of systems can be greatly reduced.

This chapter explores these issues as well as provides more detail on how to effectively address each of these common problems.

The Testing Process

The patch testing process should be as well defined as possible to allow for maximum efficiency and consistency. Such a testing process minimizes not only time and resources required to thoroughly test a patch but also the potential chaotic fallout if required functionality is not accounted for during the testing process, leaving critical production systems that may not operate properly after a patch is deployed. Following a proper test procedure can reduce costly resource time during testing and deployment. It will also save the revenue that may have been lost due to an ineffective testing procedure. Figure 8.1 is an example of a high-level patch management test process, explored in the following sections.

Preinstall Activities

Preinstallation activities can consist of a number of variations, depending on the requirements of the patch, known requirements of the target applications or operating systems, and the creation or modification of scripts and deployment software for the distribution of patches. During testing, the same methodology should be used during both deployment of a patch to production systems and the test process to ensure error-free deployment. During this stage, release notes for a patch should be referred to for helpful information on dependencies or incompatibilities, and then they should be incorporated into the overall deployment strategy.

Some patches also have a corresponding hash file, most commonly created using the MD5 hashing algorithm, which allows an organization to verify that the patch has not been modified since its release from the vendor. Even if a patch is downloaded directly from a vendor or one of its approved mirror sites, if a hash file is available it is in the best interest of an organization to check this file for integrity by running a hash against the patch file and comparing the value with that provided by the vendor. If the hash run against the patch does not identically match the hash value provided on the vendor's Web site, do not install the patch. Reasons for nonmatching hash files can include alteration of a patch, Trojan horse programs, or other malicious code that can have an undesirable impact on an application or system. In this instance, the organization should look for an alternative download site and run the hash against the alternate patch file until an unmodified version can be located.

Many times, scripts will be written and modified throughout the test process as installation issues are discovered that will need to be

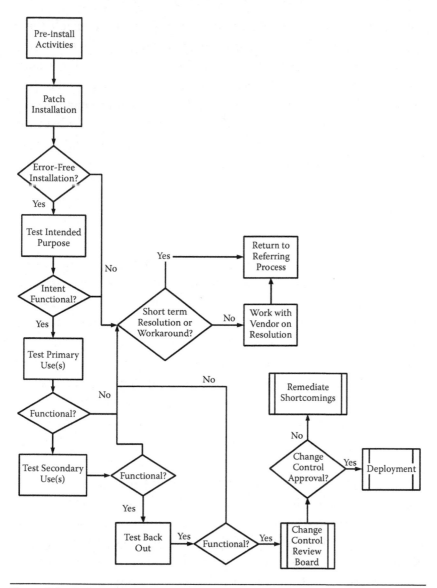

Figure 8.1 Test process.

retested prior to production deployment. Typically, scripts will be used for disabling and enabling services on the target system during installation or to automate other pre- or postinstallation tasks that make deployment less of a manual task. For example, it may be necessary to develop a script that disables a host intrusion detection system (HIDS) agent, antivirus software, or a service such as sqlservr.exe prior to running the patch executable and then to have it enable these services in proper sequence, logging errors throughout the process.

Part of the testing activities during this phase should also include monitoring bandwidth and system resource loads to gauge what impact the chosen deployment methodology will have on the production environment. If the projection shows that this methodology may have too great an impact on the production environment, the testers may need to find and test an alternative solution that will ease the level of impact.

Patch Installation

Once the preinstall activities have taken place, the patch can then be installed on a target test machine. During installation, it will be imperative to monitor log files for errors, for network use for any postinstallation increase, or for a severe decrease in traffic that could indicate a serious patch malfunction and system resources, such as processor load and memory usage. Any errors or anomalies should be analyzed to determine the source of contention. It is worth noting that any errors indicated in a log file should be verified to not have existed prior to installation of the patch to rule out any preexisting conditions.

It is also suggested that a reboot occur prior to installation of a patch on both test and production systems, especially those that have not been through a reboot process for some time. On more than one occasion, a patch has been blamed for a system not coming back online after installation, only to find out that the system had not been rebooted for some time prior to this installation and that the issue may or may not be caused by this patch. To rule out preexisting conditions and the time spent troubleshooting these types of issues, a reboot prior to installation can save valuable resource time and unnecessary "finger-pointing."

In troubleshooting noted errors and anomalies, it will often be necessary to trace back through the preinstallation activities to verify that any installation scripts were written correctly. To rule out a misconfigured script, it may be in the best interest of the testing team to run the script without actually installing the patch and to include task logging verifying that each step has been performed with an output log that tracks success and failure for each task.

Another troubleshooting task will be to verify that the patch was not corrupted during delivery to the target system. This can be done by running a hash function against the patch file on the test system to verify that the hash matches the hash value of the patch file on the delivery system. If the hashes match or if a hash is not available, attempt to deliver the patch file via an alternative means to the target system. Once the initial patch file has been backed out and the installation has been run with the newly transferred file, successful installation will help rule out whether the delivery mechanism is at fault.

If a resolution or workaround is discovered, the testers should modify their preinstallation checklists and restart the entire process to accurately track the steps required for a successful installation. If these methods do not help resolve the issue or help in discovering a workaround, it may be necessary to involve the patch vendor for resolution. During the past several years, vendors have gotten better about testing patches prior to release, but it is impossible to account for the millions of variations that exist in client environments. However, if vendors are aware of the particular settings and applications of the system the organization is having trouble with, they will be better able to determine if something within their patch may be responsible for any anomalies, as they may be aware of file modifications that are taking place behind the scenes.

Test Intended Purpose

Once errors and anomalies have either been ruled out or a workaround found, the next step in the process is to test to ensure that the intended purpose of the patch is actually successful. Oftentimes, this is verified by the vendor prior to release; however, it may not be successful for the organization's environment for several reasons. Sometimes the vendor's testing process was not complete and the patch was released prior to thorough testing. In addition, the environment may contain a variable that was not able to be accounted for during the vendor's limited testing. Whatever the case, it should not be assumed that because a vendor releases a patch it will always work appropriately.

Sometimes it will be difficult to test the intended functionality of a patch. Lately, soon after a patch is released the vendor releasing the patch or other interested parties will release a tool that can help an organization test a target system to ensure that a patch was successful in fixing the intended vulnerability. If these test programs are not available for a specific patch, and sometimes even when they are available, it will be desirable to run targeted tests against the target host. If it is found that the patch does not appropriately fix the desired deficiency, it will be necessary to first backtrack through the test installation activities to determine that all required steps were performed and that these did not result in an error. Once this has been completed, the organization may wish to begin discussions with the vendor for further assistance in determining why the patch did not fix the intended shortfall.

Test Primary Uses

Many systems will have certain primary functions that are required by the user of that system. Primary functions are those that are critical to system end users for them to fulfill their job requirements. Once the intended purpose of a patch has been verified to have been fixed, the tester will want to ensure that none of the primary functions of a system have been negatively affected. For example, a patch was installed to address a buffer overflow vulnerability on a Web server whose primary function is to deliver Web pages for the company intranet. After confirming that the buffer overflow vulnerability no longer exists, the Web server should be checked to make sure it is still able to load the desired Web pages and that uniform resource locators (URLs) are not mysteriously broken. Some other things to verify include the following:

- Does basic network and Web service functionality still work as desired?
- Does the Web server service start and stop without error?
- Have all Web pages and links been verified for integrity?
- Are other systems still able to access all previously available content?

These are but a few of the items that one will want to verify, and they will vary greatly based on the intended function of a system as well as other environment variables.

If all of the steps up to this point have been followed and there is still an issue with a primary function, it may be necessary to work with the vendor of whatever functionality is not working properly. The vendor may or may not be the same vendor that released the patch. At times, it may even be necessary to involve multiple vendors in the resolution. The reasons for involving all parties vary; however, typically each vendor will not be familiar enough with the other's product, and finger-pointing will prevail as to why a desired function no longer works correctly. If all parties are involved, some of the "blame game" can be eliminated, and everyone can work together with the organization to find the cause and resolve the issue at hand.

If a resolution cannot be found to restore whatever primary functionality is not working correctly, it may be necessary to find an alternative solution to fixing the initially targeted vulnerability. Sometimes the involved vendors can and will help in finding the resolution, but at times it will require that the organization rely only on other mitigating factors to lessen the likelihood of a successful exploit. Whether this will be acceptable to the organization will largely depend on the circumstances of the situation and whether an alternate solution is forecast in the foreseeable future. In any case, this decision should be left to a formal change control board to decide what further action should be taken.

Test Secondary Uses

Once the primary uses of a system or application have been tested for functionality and accepted, secondary use functionality will need to be verified. Secondary use can be defined as a desired function that is not critical to ongoing use of the system but that provides complementary services to users or owners of a system. Referring to the intranet Web server example, a secondary use of that system may be collecting usage metrics for particular pages. While this may be deemed a desired function for whatever reason, the immediate availability of this particular function will not adversely affect the ability of users to continue accessing necessary internal information.

As in the previous phase, if all steps were followed up to this point, it may be necessary to involve the vendor that released the patch as well as the vendor of the now nonfunctioning application to find an acceptable resolution. However, as this is a secondary function, it may not be as essential to have this functionality prior to deployment of a patch to production systems. If it is decided by the security committee that this secondary function is less important than patching a system, an organization may decide to deploy a patch before a resolution has been identified. This will allow for continued use of the intended system's primary functions as well as patching the intended vulnerability. Once a resolution has been identified, the testing team can retest and deploy the changes necessary to restore any secondary functionality.

Testing Patch Back Out

After a patch has been tested as thoroughly as possible, the testing team needs to ensure that the patch can be backed out without any complications. Testing the back-out procedure is important, especially for critical devices. If any issues arise at a later time that were missed during the testing process and no other remediation can be found, the organization will at least have the last resort of a back out available. As patches will often modify system files, it is realistic that the originals may not restore correctly.

Again, it will be important to refer to the release notes that come with the patch to determine if there are any special instructions for the back-out procedure. Many times, specific steps must be followed in sequence for the back out to work correctly.

Similar to other steps throughout the testing process, if the back-out procedure does not appear to work as expected, testers will need to retrace their actions. After verifying that all actions were executed correctly, they will want to determine if they are able to find a resolution by examining the log files and error messages for an indication of what the problem might be. If there are still issues that cannot be resolved in a timely manner, it will probably be necessary, as in the other steps of the process, to work with the patch vendor to find a resolution to the problem. If a resolution cannot be found, the change control board will need to know this information to determine if the risk of a system not being patched outweighs the inability to back out the patch should a problem occur during deployment to a production system.

Approving Deployment

At this point, a patch has been through the testing process, and the testing team will have the results of the tests that have been run against a patch. Prior to going to production deployment, testing results and noted anomalies, shortcomings, and recommendations should be approved by the security committee. The recommendations should indicate the desired and tested method of deployment, the desired prioritized targets for deployment, tested and approved back-out strategies, and information regarding projected downtimes, network and system impacts, and any unresolved issues that were discovered.

The security committee at that point can either approve of the patch deployment or can choose to turn the request back for either continued testing or resolution. The organization should have a Change Control Review Board or the security committee review and validate the findings from testing prior to deployment. This will provide the organization with much of the desirable information that is really not found prior to actually testing, and it will allow the board or security committee to make an informed decision regarding the patch.

Patch Ratings and How They Affect Testing

Patches are being released for operating systems and applications at an ever increasing rate. To keep up with the increase in release frequency and the decrease in time before exploits are available, it is necessary for an organization to establish a prioritization process for evaluating acceptable timeframes for testing and deploying patches. Table 8.1 provides a high-level example of a release schedule based on security priority.

Table 8.1 Release Schedule Based on Security Priority

PRIORITY	RECOMMENDED TIME FRAME	MAXIMUM RECOMMENDED TIME FRAME
1: Critical	Within 48 hours	Within 2 weeks
2: Urgent	Within 2 weeks	Within 4 weeks
3: Low	Depending on availability, deploy a new service pack or update rollup that includes a fix for this vulnerability within 1 month	Deploy the software update within 2 months
4: Maintenance	Depending on availability, deploy a new service pack or update rollup that includes a fix for this vulnerability within 3 months	Deploy the software update within 5 months, or choose not to deploy at all

The release schedule is broken down into four main categories:

1. Critical priority: Patches should be tested and deployed in a maximum of 2 weeks
2. Urgent priority: Patches should be tested and deployed within 2 but no longer than 4 weeks
3. Low priority: Patches should be deployed between 1 and 2 months.
4. Maintenance: Patches should be tested and deployed on a regularly scheduled basis. This is done normally on a quarterly basis or when a service pack or rollup package becomes available.

The determined release schedule and type of patch to be deployed will impact the testing process used. If an organization has determined that it has only 48 hours to test a patch before it needs to be deployed, the amount of testing that can be performed will be much less than that for a patch that has 1 or 2 months before it needs to be deployed. The testing process and time frame available will also be affected by the ease of exploitation, even for critical patches. For example, if a vulnerability is discovered that is determined to be critical in nature but for which no known exploit currently exists, it may be decided by the organization that additional testing may be performed and that patches need to be deployed within 2 weeks instead of 48 hours. However, if 2 days later an exploit is published and begins rapid circulation, the testing process will probably need to be accelerated to accommodate for this change in risk.

To minimize multiple changes that may occur affecting the criticality and thus the amount of time before deployment, some organizations have chosen to simplify their testing and deployment processes into two primary categories: emergency and maintenance. Emergency patches include the critical, urgent, and some of the low-security priority definitions from Table 8.1, whereas maintenance priority includes all other categories (Table 8.2). This is done to facilitate the decision-making process and to minimize changes that can become disruptive to testing.

To apply this to the discussion of a consistent testing process covered in the preceding section, little would change from the general methodology. The organization will still want to perform the

Table 8.2   Expanded Patch Priority List

CRITICAL PRIORITY

Vulnerabilities for applications or operating systems of Internet-facing hosts (e.g., Web servers, routers, firewalls, switches)

Vulnerabilities that will allow self-propagation without user interaction (e.g., worms)

Vulnerabilities that may allow for internal or external compromise of critical hosts

Vulnerability that may allow for widespread impact with an available exploit in the wild

URGENT PRIORITY

Vulnerabilities that may allow for exploiting weaknesses in commonly used and necessary network services but that are normally blocked by a firewall (or can be) without adversely affecting end users

Widespread application or operating system vulnerability that requires user interaction to initiate

Vulnerability that may allow for widespread impact but for which no exploit currently exists

LOW PRIORITY

Vulnerability that may affect a minority of hosts or applications, and exploit success is low or does not currently exist

Impact of vulnerability is low to medium, due to other mitigating factors that decrease the likelihood of exploitation

MAINTENANCE

Required to fix an uncommonly used service

Impact of vulnerability would have minimum effect on host or application functionality

Upgrades to application or operating system functionality that are not essential to usability

---

preinstallation activities as before to determine necessary steps for a successful installation. Once the installation is complete on the target test device, it will also still be necessary to ensure that the installation is error free, that the intended vulnerability the patch is meant to address has been remedied, and that at the very least the primary functions of the target system are operational.

For emergency patches, however, an organization may decide at this point to forego testing of secondary functions until a later date to ensure a speedier deployment of the patch. Many times, the lack of these secondary functions are outweighed by the potential impact of not having the patch deployed and the high risk of an exploit causing havoc on the organization's network. It will probably be necessary to readdress the secondary capabilities at a later date, depending on their nature and continued importance to the organization.

Another aspect of the testing process that may be affected by a heightened security priority of a patch will actually be the approval process from the change review board. Typically, the change review board may be more accepting of certain shortcomings that were discovered during the testing process that normally can delay a patch deployment. If the board determines that the cost of delaying a patch might outweigh the consequences of proceeding, the board will generally accept some minor deficiencies and will allow the deployment to production systems to proceed.

When major discrepancies are discovered, the review board should not let media sensationalism about a vulnerability impact its decision making when weighing the consequences of patching versus not patching. A detailed understanding of the vulnerability, what functionality will be lost by deploying before a resolution is discovered, the organization's risk exposure, and whether any other controls may help mitigate the exposure should all be taken into consideration.

Prioritizing the Test Process

Although the security priority ratings and how they affect the testing process have already been discussed, this does not really explain the order in which systems should be tested for a particular patch. Since many variations of system settings, applications, uses, and other factors may need to be accounted for, there may be as many variations in the number of tests that must be run. Especially when preparing to test a critical patch, it will be essential to prioritize the order in which systems will be tested to ensure that systems with the greatest exposure to a vulnerability or that would suffer the greatest loss if exploited are patched first.

Although the testing methodology will primarily remain the same throughout the testing of various systems, the services and applications that are tested for continued functionality may differ based on the role or primary use of a particular system. For example, it is expected that a vulnerability that can affect all Linux operating systems will require that different tests be conducted for a Linux server running an Apache Web server than for the system administrator's desktop that is also running Linux but in a desktop role. For the server running Apache, it will be critical to test the continued functionality of the Web server, after the patch is installed, as that is this particular device's primary function. For example, an administrator's desktop may have primary functions of word processing, a secure shell program for secure remote management of devices, and several auxiliary management programs, each of which must be tested for continued functionality.

These varying devices, because of their different uses and applications, will each be required to go through a separate instance of the testing process to guarantee complete testing of the continued functionality after the patch is applied. Many times, one will find that a patching error will create issues. For example, the Web server may have no effect on the functionality of the management programs for the administrator's desktops.

In the previous example, let us assume for a moment that, by default, the server will receive higher priority, as this is a typical default prioritization scheme for systems in many organizations. However, consider that the example patch addresses a vulnerability that can be exploited only via direct access to an open transmission control protocol (TCP) port on a device from an infected machine, allows only a security socket layer (SSL) through the firewall from inside to the Web server, and cannot be accessed from the outside (i.e., Internet). Now consider that the other Linux host is a laptop the administrator is using for remote management of certain network devices from her broadband connection at home. In addition, to make things worse, this administrator relies on the functionality of her desktop as the only device with an allowed media access control (MAC) address that can traverse access control lists to manage critical network devices. To connect to these devices, the administrator has also had to disable all filtering on her firewall so that the management software will function correctly. If the administrator's laptop is infected by the example exploit, millions of dollars may be lost if she loses connectivity to those devices. In this instance, the administrator's laptop will probably receive a higher priority over the Web server for testing the functionality of the emergency patch.

Although this example might seem unlikely, more complex scenarios certainly exist that will have an impact on priority of testing. It will be difficult in most circumstances for those responsible for determining the patching priority of systems to be aware of all or even a majority of situations such as the one just described. A method of prioritizing which systems will be tested first will more than likely follow a more static matrix that can be broadly applied on a consistent basis. The following list is a common hierarchy used for prioritizing the testing and deployment of patches:

- Externally facing hosts
- Mission-critical hosts or those hosting sensitive data
- Critical users (finance, executives, directors)
- Mobile devices and remote users
- Client systems of critical hosts
- Standard user systems
- Internal network devices

Externally Facing Hosts

In almost every organization, externally facing hosts will and should receive first priority for testing and deploying patches. "Externally facing" could mean a Web server that resides in a perimeter network that serves as the organization's Internet Web presence, a virtual private network (VPN) concentrator used for remote access into the network, a perimeter firewall, a border router sitting outside the perimeter firewall, or a business-to-business (B2B) server that is used for data sharing with a business partner. These systems allow connections from outside the network as a normal course of operation, so they are at much greater risk of exposure to a vulnerability. Although the organization may employ mitigating techniques to limit this exposure, such as a perimeter firewall protecting hosts residing in the perimeter network, they are still normally considered as having a higher exposure.

Notice that we do not specify just Internet-facing systems in the top level of this prioritization hierarchy. Organizations that need to share data with other companies for B2B transactions tend to implicitly trust the capabilities of their business partners and do not secure these systems as well as they should. While some companies downplay the significance of the exposure of B2B systems, these systems may be more prone to certain exploits than others due to ineffective access control mechanisms, such as firewall rule sets that, if set up appropriately, could limit the exposure of these systems.

Mission-Critical Hosts

Typically second in a prioritization hierarchy are mission-critical hosts or those hosting sensitive data. While some of the aforementioned devices might fall into this category as well, also included are systems such as the active directory root servers, database systems, and application or middle-tier devices that connect directly to database systems; file servers that host sensitive files such as human resources data; or any other system a business relies on for day-to-day activities. These systems have stricter access controls and additional exposure-limiting capabilities in place, but extended and unexpected downtime of these systems due to an exploited vulnerability could have a devastating impact on the organization. It is also likely that these systems will provide services to a large number of internal clients, thus increasing their exposure to certain vulnerabilities. Depending on the vulnerability discovered, methods and likelihood of exploitation, and what additional mitigating controls are in place, these systems may at times receive higher priority for testing of a patch than externally facing hosts.

Critical Users

Critical users are client systems whose downtime can also have a large or devastating impact on an organization. Desktops in the finance department that are used to process payroll, organizational executives, director-level systems, and the like all fall into this category. It is in the best interest of administrators to ensure that they can feel safe in knowing their paycheck will be processed on time. Executive- and director-level workstations tend to be important; depending on the type of processing and time sensitivity of activities, these client systems may be responsible for producing critical data and must be able to do so with no chance of downtime. Sometimes, for internal political reasons alone, it will also be important to ensure that executive management and their entire chain of command are not subjected to downtime from an exploited vulnerability.

Other systems may fall into this category, depending on when a vulnerability is discovered. For example, public companies are required by the Securities and Exchange Commission (SEC) to file quarterly financial reports. If these reports cannot be processed for some reason and the company is late in filing, the company can be subject to substantial financial penalties. In this case, it becomes critical that these systems do not suffer downtime from an exploit and will command a higher priority in testing and deployment of a critical patch. A majority of enterprises may choose to always categorize these systems with a higher priority, regardless of timing, as a means of eliminating the guesswork that might be associated with it being a critical time period or not.

Mobile Devices and Remote Users

Mobile devices such as PDAs and laptops as well as remote users who may have a standard desktop but work in a virtual office from their homes are generally considered to have a higher risk exposure to certain vulnerabilities than other client systems located on the company network. These systems may have adequate protection mechanisms in place to aid in defending themselves against a network-based exploit.

Remote users, such as those working from home, may not have an effective firewall protecting their system from the Internet. On the other hand, they may be exposed because they share a broadband connection with their personal computers that may not be effectively protected against network-borne exploits.

Mobile devices are difficult to protect from network-borne exploits as well. Due to their nature, these devices usually will be exposed in a number of environments, such as wireless Internet access in a user's favorite coffee shop, a complacent business customer or partner network, or their own homes. Not only can these devices be exploited, but also as soon as they plug back into the corporate network they may reintroduce a threat that was thought to have been eradicated. It will be essential for an organization to account for these often forgotten systems and to address their exposures accordingly for the testing and deployment of patches that may affect these systems.

Clients of Critical Hosts

Critical hosts not only are exposed to vulnerability exploits but also tend to provide client systems services that introduce an additional level of exposure. If one of these client systems is compromised because of an unpatched vulnerability, an organization will also be exposing its critical hosts. In this instance, a human resources server hosting the personally identifiable information (PII) of its employees may relinquish information that is subject to federal regulation. Alternatively, an application server with direct access to a critical database could be compromised, thus threatening the integrity of data hosted on that system. For these reasons and many more, an organization will want to minimize this exposure by patching these systems before moving on to the general client system population.

Standard User Systems

By this time, most of the critical systems that would pose the largest adverse impact on an organization will have been addressed. However, standard user systems tend to have the highest population count. Although these systems are further down in the patching priority, they cannot be forgotten. A compromise of one of these systems, due to a missing patch, could still expose critical systems. General systems tend to also have the highest exposure to certain vulnerabilities that take advantage of widely deployed client software, such as Web browsers, e-mail clients, and office productivity software (e.g., word processing or spreadsheet software).

Depending on the type of vulnerability and method of exploit, these systems may actually receive a higher priority than other systems, such as if the vulnerability at hand is one whose primary means of exploitation relies on a user opening an e-mail attachment. Systems that do not have e-mail clients installed but are still subject to the vulnerability will likely receive a lower priority for receiving a patch. In some cases, this group may also include systems from some of the previous categories, depending on their configuration and primary uses.

For testing purposes, these systems will generally be the easiest to test and deploy patches to. As they will likely make up a majority of systems on the network and commonly have a standard build, the testing process can be done in a short amount of time. Once the testing process has been completed for standard user systems, a large number of devices can be deployed in rapid succession. Caution should be taken for how patches are deployed to these systems in the event that a problem was overlooked during testing of a patch. This can easily be remedied, however, by logically dividing which systems receive a patch so that errors might be detected before the patch is deployed to the entire user population.

Internal Network Devices

Finally, internal network devices will need to be addressed. These systems include those that are not directly exposed to the Internet or other external network devices, such as switches, routers, hubs, noncritical network management devices, print servers, and other hosts. Internal network devices tend to have a lower risk of exposure as vulnerabilities typically can be exploited only from inside the corporate network. This does not mean these devices can be forgotten and in certain cases may receive a higher priority rating, depending on the nature of a vulnerability.

Dynamic Prioritization

While the prioritization list just discussed can be used as a general guideline in deciding which systems to test and in which order, in reality, this list largely depends on the vulnerability in question, mitigating controls in place and where, methods of exploit, and other factors. Therefore, patching priority becomes dynamic in nature as a vulnerability is dissected and understood by an organization.

On rare occasions, devices that fall into each of the previously mentioned categories may all be affected by the same vulnerability. However, many may remember the Simple Network Management Protocol (SNMP) vulnerability from years ago that essentially affected all network systems. Using the aforementioned static prioritization scheme as a guideline, internal network devices may have received the lowest priority for applying this patch. However, if most of the other devices by default had SNMP disabled and thus were less likely to be exposed to this vulnerability, dynamic prioritization would allow an organization to address internal network devices first and to effectively patch systems with the greatest level of exposure.

Depending on the type of patch that is released, certain categories from this guideline can probably be eliminated. Approaching the guideline in a systematic fashion, one would work down the list sequentially to determine whether a vulnerability affects each type of device by vendor and what exploit exists for each device and then to factor in known mitigating controls that make an exploit of that device unlikely. If an exploit is determined to be unlikely, the organization can ignore the patch, wait for a rollup patch, or at least move the device down in order of precedence for testing and deployment.

The Test Lab

Test labs exist for a variety of reasons. One is to ensure that nonproduction systems are not inadvertently affected during testing, because of either patches or nonpatch-related configuration changes. For example, testers have at times rushed to simulate a scenario they are currently testing and have mistakenly removed a cable from the production firewall, in turn affecting all external communications. Or, even more common, test configuration changes are applied to a production system with an Internet Protocol (IP) address of 10.10.10.10 that were meant to be applied on a test system whose IP address was 10.10.10.100.

To eliminate the possibility of incorrectly applying physical or logical changes that are meant for test devices from being applied to production systems by mistake, some organizations have developed dedicated test labs. These labs can vary in size and complexity, but their primary purpose is to make certain that production systems are not unduly affected by user error during configuration testing and that the physical elements (e.g., cables, on–off switches) of a test device are not mistaken for those of a production device.

If a maintenance-level patch does something similar to fixing the unreadable fonts of the operating system's calendar program, it is probably acceptable not to use a nonproduction-dedicated lab to test this patch. It is always a good idea to first try even these types of patches on a system that has a recent backup or on a noncritical device. However, the chances of having a widespread impact on the organization in this case will be very small.

In most other patching scenarios, however, a lab will be desirable. Oftentimes, loading a patch will affect only the host operating system or application that it is applied to. However, it is not out of the question for an untested patch to be capable of affecting other systems on the same network segment or even an entire network as the host to which a patch has been applied. And, for servers, it will be necessary not only to test the functionality of those particular hosts after applying a patch but also to test client functionality by simulating client connections across the network. This simulated network traffic can have an undesirable impact on network performance or can cause unexpected and erratic behavior. For these reasons, an environment that is logically, if not physically, separated from other network segments is the preferred testing environment.

Ideally, a lab will have multiple devices where a miniature replica of the production environment can be reproduced for fully testing deployment and postpatch functionality of a majority of the various systems on the network. Such a lab may have a mirror image of whatever patch deployment mechanism will be used in the production network, enough network and security devices to enable full simulation of network traversal, and one or two target systems on which the patch can be tested. For large organizations, this could mean a fairly large lab that even has its own heating, ventilating, and air conditioning (HVAC) system for controlling environmental conditions.

At the very least, a lab should consist of a single target system whose network connectivity is limited from the rest of the production network through a combination of access control lists and a separate virtual local area network (VLAN). In this example, a separate room would not be required for the "lab" to perform limited testing of application or operating system functionality after a patch is applied. This initial target system may or may not be a production host, but if it is production it is highly recommended that a noncritical device be used before applying the patch to any other production systems. Testing on production devices is not recommended by any means for most patches, but if there is no other choice due to budgetary constraints or for some other reason it may be better to take chances on the least important host first. If physical resources are not immediately available, the organization may also want to consider the use of virtual machine software for this purpose, as described in more detail later in this chapter.

In addition, a minimal lab configuration should also include a nonproduction instance of the production firewalls or any other host whose loss, attributed to a faulty patch, misconfiguration, or otherwise, would have a large impact on the organization. In addition to testing patches on these hosts, it is usually in the organization's best interest to test major rule sets on firewalls, or any other configuration changes to these types of hosts, before those changes are introduced into the production environment.

The lab may also need to simulate network traversal paths of the production environment. This could be to test the patch delivery method, client connectivity functionality, or a network issue being addressed by a patch. Testing network traversal typically will not require identical hardware as the production environment and can usually be simulated with smaller-scale devices, assuming that no extraneous bandwidth needs or services such as quality-of-service (QoS) or load-balancing functionality need to be tested and for which smaller devices may not be able to support.

At times, it may also be desirable to run pre- and postpatch installation vulnerability scans against the target test systems. Depending on the type of patch being tested, changes made to operating system files, application configuration files, or other system files may inadvertently expose a target system. Vulnerability scanners such as Nessus with an updated vulnerability signature file may detect the presence of a weakness on the target system that was introduced by the applied patch. A network service scanner such as nmap can aid in ensuring that no network service ports are inadvertently started. In addition, other typical "hacker" tools, such as those that scan for known and unknown vulnerabilities on Web servers, will allow an organization to test a patched system preproduction for holes that may have been introduced. Critical and Internet-facing systems should receive the highest consideration on whether to perform these tests before "going live" with a patch, as these hosts typically have the highest exposure to vulnerabilities that may be inadvertently introduced by a patch.

Virtual Machines

The maturation of virtual machine software over the past years has had a profound impact on the patch testing and deployment process.

Software such as Microsoft's Virtual PC and EMC's VMware line of products enable an organization to install multiple guest operating systems with varying configurations on a single host. The numbers of guest operating systems that can be loaded on a single device are normally limited to those that support Intel-based hardware and to the amount of physical RAM, disk space, and processor capacity of the host device. However, the use of virtual software can help eliminate some of the costs of redundant hardware for a separate testing environment, the physical footprint of a lab, and the lengthy resource time typically required for device configuration or reconfiguration and testing of postpatch installation functionality of the various host types found within the organization's production environment.

As shown in Figure 8.2, an organization can load and be operating several instances simultaneously on a single host using virtual machine software. The figure shows that this particular user has separate virtual machines created for Windows Server, Red Hat Linux 9, and Windows. During setup of these virtual machines, the user is able to determine what amount of RAM and disk space each guest operating system should be limited to. Users also have the ability to determine whether all operating systems should receive equal processor priority or should use other options for improving or limiting the performance of either guest or host operating systems. They can

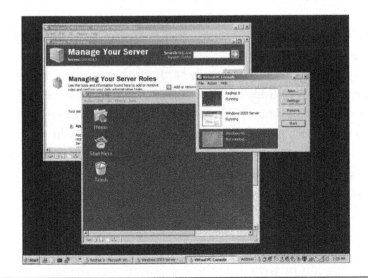

Figure 8.2   Virtual machine screenshot.

additionally determine whether each guest system should employ a virtual network adapter, which will allow the guest system to obtain a separate IP address, or whether the guest system should share the same IP address as the host system via built-in network address translation (NAT) functionality so that only one IP address is advertised external to the physical system.

Now take a look at how an organization can take advantage of some of the capabilities of virtual machines in a patch test lab in an effort to save resource time as well as reduce hardware costs. For this example, let us assume that a new vulnerability has been discovered that affects different types of applications running on different operating systems, similar to the ASN.1 vulnerability discovered in 2004. Because of the critical nature of this new example of vulnerability, the widespread use of the affected applications, and the various operating systems that the vulnerable applications are run on, it will be necessary for this example organization to test multiple patches for the same vulnerability. In addition, some operating systems will have different configurations that may react differently when applying the appropriate patch, requiring yet another separate testing scenario for each role type.

To simulate the operating systems in our production environment, we load an instance of Windows Enterprise Server, an instance of Red Hat Linux, and an instance of Windows XP on our host system running virtual machine software. After creating the initial virtual images with baseline configurations for each type of system, we create a copy for each of these baseline images, which serves two purposes. First, any configuration changes necessary to simulate another application on the same operating system; time can be saved by using this baseline image. Second, any adverse effects from loading the target patch file may make the selected virtual system inoperable. Thus, having a baseline image will save the tester time in having to reload the operating system software and making any necessary configuration changes to get back to the desired starting point. All that will be required is to eliminate the now corrupted test image and to point our virtual machine console back to the baseline image.

Now that we have our baseline images with all appropriate configuration changes and applications loaded, we can work our way through the testing methodology described earlier for each desired target virtual system. Each of these target systems either can be loaded sequentially in order of testing priority or can be run simultaneously assuming ample resources exist on our host system. As we have decided to load all target systems on a single host, our sample organization is able to both reduce footprint size to this single host as well as significantly reduce hardware costs that would normally be associated with testing multiple host types simultaneously.

Assuming that the target patch was loaded sequentially on each of our target virtual systems without error and that the intended vulnerability has been tested to have been patched, we can move to the next phase of the testing methodology: testing primary functionality. Our client virtual system running Windows XP was configured to use DHCP to obtain an IP address, with our host operating system serving as the DHCP server. Our Windows Server, which will be simulating a production intranet server, and a Red Hat Linux instance with Apache Web server simulating our production Internet Web server are each configured with static IP addresses. Our host operating system has two physical network interface cards (NICs), and we will configure our virtual Red Hat server as the only system using this second NIC. The diagram in Figure 8.3 illustrates this virtual lab environment.

After appropriately configuring our lab firewall, we can begin simulating our production environment to test client–server functionality. All of these tests can be run simultaneously from a single host. If a production host with a different functional role needs to be tested, the baseline configurations created can be modified to accommodate this need in a streamlined manner. One would simply copy the baseline to a separate image, make the appropriate configuration changes or load the appropriate software, and then continue testing additional devices.

With more time, one could also establish multiple VLAN segments on our lab switch and could configure access control lists to simulate production VLANs and to provide greater traffic separation between the hosts, as described earlier in this chapter. On the other hand, multiple test routers or a Layer 3/4 Ethernet switch, which can route between VLANs, can be introduced to test multiple network hops for testing production deployment scenarios.

Taking further advantage of virtual machine capabilities, one could also have production systems loaded as virtual machines.

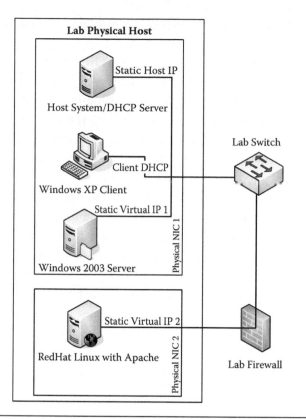

Figure 8.3 Example lab using virtual machine software.

On each production device, we could have a host operating system with limited additional functionality configured so as to reduce the impact on physical resources. Then the production operating system could be loaded with virtual machine software, which is configured for the greatest possible performance from physical resources of the host system.

The first benefit an organization would receive by doing this is the ability to copy the production virtual image and to port it directly to our virtual machine lab environment. This would even further reduce the amount of time needed to perform operating system loads and configuration changes that would be necessary to support simulation of a production system. Errors occurring in the lab environment, when attempting to deploy a patch to production, or as a result of a forgotten system configuration could be avoided by using this setup. Testers would also not be required to have all of the latest system configuration changes documented or available to ensure a mirror image of a production device.

In addition, other issues may prevent us from fully testing all possible functions of a particular production system. In the event that a patch causes an unforeseen problem unaccounted for during testing, the production system can be restored from the baseline image that was captured prior to deploying the patch, saving costly downtime to the production system in addition to the resource time that would be required in getting the system operational.

Of course, there may also be some limited drawbacks to using virtual machine software in testing patches, the biggest of which is for any maintenance-type patches or otherwise where a patch is intended to address an issue with a particular piece of hardware. The ability to test this in the lab with virtual machine software may not be possible unless the host system in the lab has the same hardware configuration as that of the production system. Other issues may also arise involving incompatibilities with the virtual machine software itself. Factors such as these should be weighed against the many advantages that can be gained by using virtual machine software to reduce some of the costs associated with a dedicated lab environment.

Wrapping It Up

Even with thorough testing of patches, it is still a good idea to incorporate an effective disaster recovery plan. The operations group can test and retest, but problems with a patch may not surface until a patch is actually in production, potentially causing downtime of a critical device or loss of data. Often, the team responsible for testing patches, much like a vendor, will not be able to conceive of every possible gyration a user may impose on a system. At times, it is likely that these actions by the user of a system or even from a behind-the-scenes system process can trigger an event that clashes with changes introduced by a patch and may cause a system to fail.

Having a good disaster recovery plan can also affect the resource time allowed for testing of certain patches. If an operation is able to test at least primary functions and the patch deployment methods, having a recent backup of a critical system may allow the security committee to approve emergency patches to be released, knowing that a critical system can still be restored should a problem arise due to a patch that is not fully tested. This may allow faster turnaround for critical systems that have a high level of exposure to an exploit.

We are not suggesting that a good disaster recovery plan can completely eliminate the need for proper testing. Patches still need to undergo certain tests before deployment to at least ensure critical functionality and operation. And backups can and will fail. The two processes should go hand in hand to hedge against costly downtime, system availability, and resource requirements that can occur from a botched patch deployment while still allowing an organization to protect its systems from increasing vulnerabilities and exploits.

The existence of an adequate inventory management program, as discussed at multiple intervals throughout the various chapters in this book, can have a profound impact on successful testing. The more production processes used on a system that the testing team is unaware of, the greater chance of them not addressing the functionality of those processes during testing, which may cause unnecessary delays or service availability problems once a patch is deployed to the production systems. Thus, the inventory management program should strive to address not only systems and data but also critical processes and services to best serve the testing team.

This chapter may not be inclusive of the issues companies face in today's challenging world; however, the issues that have been discussed are those that seem to be the most prevalent in the industry. Using the recommendations given herein as a guideline, the organization should be able to show the business the benefits of proactively testing patches before deployment and how effective testing processes can end up saving the organization money in the long run. This will also reduce the chaotic nature of keeping up with all the vulnerabilities that threaten the livelihood of operations.

9
PROCESS LIFE CYCLE

A patch management process is a best practice that should be employed in any organization, regardless of size, to govern how to respond to security-related vulnerabilities. Even if not given the necessary attention, updating patches on a system is the most common method to protect a company's assets from a threat. This process is initiated whenever the organization becomes aware of a potential security vulnerability, which is followed up with a vendor release, or hot fix, to address the issue. Figure 9.1 shows a high-level walkthrough of the patch management process, which is discussed in further detail in the following sections.

The process covers the following key activities:

- Monitor for security vulnerabilities from security intelligence sources.
- Complete an impact assessment on new security vulnerabilities.
- Develop and test the technical remediation strategy in alignment with the organization's change management policy.
- Implement the technical remediation strategy on all affected hosts.
- Document the life cycle of each vulnerability, including reporting and tracking of remediation measures implemented by each department.
- Integrate the patch or configuration changes into the related application or system baseline and standard build.

All these activities are subject to status reporting requirements.

While developing the patch management process, various milestones should be considered. The process should be centrally managed. In a smaller organization, this can be a simple task, as the security department may consist of only a few individuals. In larger organizations, information technology (IT) and the security group may be

Figure 9.1   High-level patch management flow diagram.

decentralized, making it more difficult to ensure that all groups are following the patch management process similarly. Even if the IT department is decentralized, a centralized committee should always oversee the security posture, including the patch management process, of the entire organization.

One of the primary reasons the patch management process fails is the absence of a supportive culture. Whether the security group consists of 1 person or 10, collaboration between the security group and other individuals who have tasks within the process is required and is built into the process. This raises the level of communication among various groups, which may not exist until a procedure such as this is put into place. Security vulnerabilities affect many different systems and applications; all entities must be willing to work together to ensure the risk is mitigated. Frequent meetings also take place during the process, which again promote interaction among the various groups. Formal processes are tied into the patch management process, including IT operations, vulnerability, change and configuration management, intelligence gathering, retention of quality records, communication, network, systems, and application management reporting, progress reports, testing, and deploying security-related patches. Having these processes defined in a formal manner guarantees consistency and the success of the patch management process, as one relies on the other.

Another crucial step in implementing patch management is taking an inventory of the entire network infrastructure. An infrastructure inventory will provide an organization with the systems that make up the environment, such as network devices, operating systems and applications, including versions, what patches have been applied, and ownership and contact information for each system and device and potentially what network range, location, or segment said system resides.

A patch management process requires not only centralization, collaboration, and formalization but also accountability in the process for employees. It requires prioritizing not only for the security group but also for the system and application owners. In some organizations, these roles can be tied to the same entity or to multiple employees spread over various departments. Placing a priority on a security vulnerability ensures that the organization is protected against both significant vulnerabilities and critical security-related patches. A waiver process is also established in case there is a significant reason to prohibit the organization from implementing a security-related patch when it is released. Formalized procedures are necessary to handle disputes as they arise, especially related to business-critical systems.

Figure 9.2 shows the detailed patch management process flow, which is broken down and explained in the following sections.

Roles and Responsibilities

The patch management process should define the roles and responsibilities of groups and individuals who will be involved in the remediation of a known vulnerability. This should align closely with the vulnerability management process when it comes to remediation regarding installing patches on systems, the same as remediating findings during the vulnerability management process. A description of these groups and individuals follows.

These are just an example of roles and responsibilities that should be defined within an organization. Although within different organizations this varies, it needs to be carefully determined and defined prior to putting the patch management process in place. This is completed during the planning and design phases of implementing the patch management process.

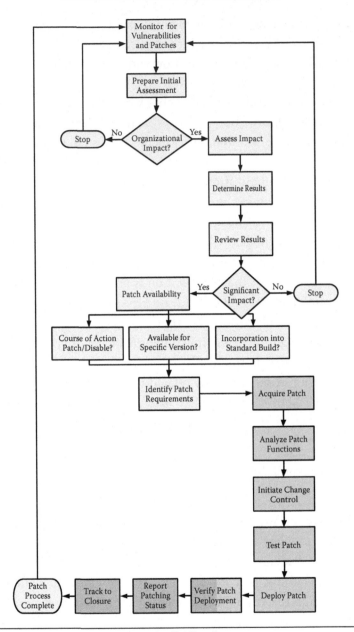

Figure 9.2   Security patch management detailed flow diagram.

Four main groups of roles are defined within this section: (1) the overarching committee for the process; (2) the security group; (3) operations group; and (4) the system and application owners. The overarching committee, or security committee, for the process should be defined within the organization that is installing a patch management process. This group is responsible for overseeing the process, and, regardless of the size of the organization, it should be established. Each organization should have a security group or a team of individuals that is responsible for overall security of the organization. If this group has been defined, then this role will fit well within the organization. It is within the operations group that organizations will vary the most. In some cases, operations consist of the group responsible for the servers, desktops, and network infrastructure. While in some cases there may be a separate group for each, in other cases this may be one team of people responsible for all operations within the organization. This is where each organization will need to map the roles and responsibilities defined in this section to its own organizational structure to determine which groups will be responsible for which piece. Certain responsibilities also fall under the network operations center (NOC) or, for the purposes of this book, the systems and application owners, in the event the organization implementing the process does not have an NOC. As some of the duties of the patch management process require working after hours or during the change management window, the system and application owners are involved to ensure it is completed accurately. As stated, these defined roles and responsibilities are provided as a guide for an organization and should be formally defined during the design phase of putting the patch management process in place.

Security Committee

Since patch management overlaps across the entire organization and various groups are already defined in the organization, one group needs to be defined that is responsible for overseeing the process, making changes, revising as necessary, and ensuring individuals are held accountable for their actions as defined. This group is called the security committee for the purposes of this book; however, it can also be called the governance committee or patch management group. The title of the group is not relevant; the responsibilities of the group are the most important aspect.

It is during the planning phase of putting the patch management process in place that the security committee would begin to be formulated. Until the patch management process is fully implemented, the security committee can change, or be modified as necessary, to accommodate the needs of the organization. At a minimum, the security committee should include one individual from the security group, one from the operations group, and system and application owners. Depending on the size of the organization and the number of individuals in the mentioned groups, the size of the security committee should be relevant to this number. In a medium-sized organization, the security committee should consist of two individuals from the security group, one of whom is the security manager, and one individual each from the operations, desktop, server, application, and network infrastructure groups. All group members should have a backup individual assigned in case of their absence. In the case of a large organization, in addition to the previously mentioned members, the group should extend to business unit managers or department heads—individuals who may not be responsible for IT but who are impacted or whose systems are impacted by the implementation of the patch management process within the organization. Although these individuals are not centrally managed under IT, they must adhere to corporate IT policies and procedures, including the patch management process.

Table 9.1 shows a breakdown of the minimum requirements for the security committee. In areas where one member is identified as part of the committee, a backup member should be identified if the primary is unavailable. The recommendations are also based on the establishment of specified groups within the organization. If the groups have not been identified, a satisfactory equivalent can be used.

Through the creation of the security committee in the organization, a formalized security policy must be created that drives the patch management process. This group will take stewardship of the process to ensure that it adjusts to the realities of changing business requirements. The security committee will establish minimum baseline requirements for analysis, communication, testing, deployment, verification, and reporting. The baseline requirements would also define the output requirements of the patch management toolsets employed by the operational units. The security committee will be responsible for the following activities:

Table 9.1 Security Committee Member Recommendations

SIZE OF ORGANIZATION	SECURITY GROUP	OPERATIONS GROUP	SERVER GROUP	DESKTOP GROUP	NETWORK INFRASTRUCTURE GROUP	NOC	EXECUTIVE MANAGEMENT (E.G., CIRO, CSO)
SMALL 1–1,000 employees	1	1	N/A	N/A	N/A	2	1
MEDIUM 1,001–5,000 employees	2	2	1	1	1	2	1
LARGE 5,001–10,000 employees	3	2	2	2	2	3	2
EXTRA LARGE 10,001+ employees	3	3	2	2	2	3	2

- Own and maintain the overall process. A strong process will maintain its rigid core elements while flexing to accommodate new technologies, business processes, and corporate challenges. The security committee should hold annual review sessions with operations stakeholders to ensure that the process continues to maintain its effectiveness. This feedback is necessary to assess the performance and effectiveness of asset management, testing, deployment, verification, and reporting processes.
- Enforce compliance through the regular audit of status reporting information. The organization relies on the various departments or business units, depending on how the organization is structured, to maintain the corporate infrastructure or the systems within its business unit. The security committee defines base requirements for patch management and relies on the business units to implement the process. The patch management process defines reporting requirements for closeout of each patching cycle, although it must engage in regular audits to ensure compliance. The regular cycle of a patch release and its corresponding attacks will provide plenty of performance metrics for the audit process. With the support of upper management, business units are held accountable for their inaction or divergence from this policy.
- Drive organization-wide education of the patch management process. To be successful, the security committee must regularly reach out to the organization, including the business units and various departments, to provide familiarization sessions and collaterals to ensure that stakeholders are familiar with their responsibilities.
- Define baseline standards for asset management, testing, deployment, verification, and reporting. The security committee must rely on the cooperation of the groups defined in the patch management process to maintain the corporate infrastructure. This group will define base requirements for patch management and will depend on the predefined groups to implement the process. For each phase of the process, the process defines minimum requirements for the patch management process itself.

- Notify the user population in support of critical patching operations. Critical patching operations have uncomfortable side effects on the user population and require users to abide by reboots and other interventions. A message from the security committee should encourage the user population to cooperate.

Security Group

Typically, organizations feel that the patch management process falls under the responsibility of the security group that is defined within the organization. In some instances, the organization may not have a security group. In these scenarios, individuals with the appropriate backup should be assigned to the security group and would then take on this role for only the patch management process. The security group within an organization can consist of one individual or as many as necessary to accomplish these responsibilities in a meaningful time frame. This depends upon the size of the organization, the number of business-critical applications, and the number of employees within the company that can be dedicated to this full-time responsibility. It also depends on how management views security and how it wishes to mold its security posture. In today's age, almost every organization has a security group defined and is taking strides to improve its overall security posture. It is for this reason that the security group should have a set of roles and responsibilities within the patch management process; however, the entire process should not fall on this group's shoulders. This, along with separation of duties, is the driving reason the security committee should be established. The security committee will also alleviate some of the strain of ensuring that the entire organization is adhering to the patch management process and that the organization is reducing its risks to not having systems patched.

During the planning phase of implementing the patch management process, which is explained in great detail in a later chapter, the responsibilities of the security group should be clearly defined. It is then during the design phase that the security group's responsibilities are put into action and documented clearly to be accurately understood. The security group's responsibilities should include the following:

- Select and monitor security intelligence sources for new security vulnerabilities.
- Respond within 24 hours to any request from any employee to investigate a potential security vulnerability.
- Generate internal advisories based on threats enumerated by monitored intelligence sources. Advisories should be published using the organization's internal advisory template.
- Analyze source information for general applicability to the organization. Applicability is determined through knowledge of the types of systems deployed within the organization.
- Coordinate the development of action plans with timetables for addressing vulnerabilities.
- Collect and maintain tracking status information from operations groups.

All major vendors, government institutions such as the Department of Homeland Security and United States Computer Emergency Readiness Team (US-CERT), and private- and open-source security groups have advisory systems in place to notify users that their software has a problem. Microsoft also issues its patches on the second Tuesday of each month unless a critical patch is identified, and then it is released to the public immediately. The security group is tasked with monitoring these intelligence sources. In some instances, an employee within the organization, whether IT staff or a member of the general user population, will identify a vulnerability that exists within the environment. A process for how these are reported to the security group must be put in place, and then the security group must respond to each of these instances, determining whether there is in fact a risk to the environment.

The security group manages the analysis and management of security vulnerabilities. It is responsible, along with the security committee, for determining the action plans and the time frame for which the patches must be applied to all the affected systems within the organization's infrastructure. The security group also sends out internal security advisories, alerting the responsible individuals of the vulnerability, the patch, the action plan, and the time frame for completion. There is more discussion regarding the contents of the security advisory, but is it ultimately the security group's responsibility to issue the advisory. Finally, the security group is responsible for collecting status information at the end of the patching cycle that will be rolled into reports for the security committee.

Operations Group

It is within the roles and responsibilities defined for the operations group where the most differences will occur on an organization-by-organization basis. These should be molded to fit the needs of each organization based on its organizational structure and various group definitions. For the purposes of this chapter, the responsibilities of the operations group are also broken down into the server group, desktop group, network infrastructure group, and system and application owners. Because these individuals are responsible for various systems, individuals from each must be part of the security committee and closely tied into the patch management process. For the purpose of this section, the operations group refers to the entire IT department within the organization. If the said groups do exist, then members of those groups are responsible for the same tasks. The only difference between the separated groups and the operations group is responsibility. If a server group has been established within the organization, it is typically responsible for all the servers under IT control. This could include Microsoft, Linux, UNIX®, or Novell servers; the type of operating systems running on them is not relevant. The server group would also report from an organizational standpoint, up into IT, or operations, typically under the chief information officer (CIO) within the said organization. Therefore, where the operations group is referenced, this can be either one group or three or more, if applicable. The desktop group is typically responsible for all the desktops throughout the organization's environment. Again, depending on the size of the organization, a dedicated group of individuals responsible for all the desktops may be established. In some instances, the server and desktop groups are combined. Finally, the network infrastructure group's responsibilities lie within the network of the infrastructure itself. This would include the routers, switches, and perhaps even the firewalls and virtual private network (VPN) concentrators. Because patches do not apply in the same manner to network devices as they do to servers and desktops, their involvement in the patch management process will not be as intense; however, they must still be part of the security committee and will clearly understand the process and their responsibilities surrounding it. Therefore, where the operations group is referenced, it includes the server, desktop, and network infrastructure groups.

The operations group within the organization is usually responsible for the actual deployment of the patch on the vulnerable systems. They are important members of the patch management process because they must coordinate the patch implementation efforts with the security committee and security groups. The operations group's responsibilities can be numerous, for example, assisting the security group in developing the action plans and time frame for completion and monitoring progress and providing insight during the development and testing phase. The operations group can respond to requests from the security group to assist in the analysis of security vulnerabilities and development of a suitable response to be communicated to all parties involved. Last, the operations group can recommend approaches to remediation, especially when a vendor patch is not available and until it becomes available, or for deployment of the patch to the affected systems and therefore removal of the vulnerability.

These responsibilities can be changed or tailored according to the needs of the organization and are to be used only as a guideline for a recommended successful patch management process. The first task is working with the security group to develop an accurate action plan that can be well executed. The operations group will also assist the security committee and security group to determine a reasonable time frame to deploy that patch to all the vulnerable systems. This is where having an accurate and up-to-date inventory is so important. Once the operations group is made aware of the vulnerability, it must know not only what systems are affected but also where they all reside.

As discussed in a previous chapter, the operations group is involved in the testing of the patch to guarantee that the action plan is built accordingly and that there are no ill effects from the installation of the patch on the vulnerable systems. The operations group is responsible for deploying the patch and then for reporting the status of the patch install to the security group, which then gets presented to the security committee to track the effectiveness of the patch management process and elimination of the vulnerability.

Network Operations Center

Though not all organizations have an NOC or security operations center (SOC)—perhaps they outsource this to a third party—it is important to discuss their responsibilities when it comes to the patch management process. While it may be assumed they would have no role, they do in fact have several. There are also cases where an organization has an SOC in place. While this has become more common recently, it is not a general practice for small and medium-sized organizations. In some cases, the SOC is outsourced to a third-party company that would be responsible for monitoring the firewalls and intrusion detection systems from an external perspective. These situations are not included in the patch management process. Instead, for the purpose of patch management, the SOC would need to be an internal function that monitors not only the system logs but also any firewalls, IDSs, and audit logs and continuously performs incident monitoring and response. By staying aware of the deployment of patches, the SOC is involved in the patch management process but not in the day-to-day operations. Instead, the NOC is ultimately responsible for making certain that all systems are operating properly.

NOC responsibilities pertaining to the patch management process include the following:

- Maintain the change management process.
- Maintain the configuration management process.
- Maintain the inventory, or asset management process.
- Coordinate not only all activities that affect these processes but also the systems they are responsible for monitoring.

When the patch is released and it is going through the patch management process, the NOC can play an important role in ensuring that the patch goes through the standard operating procedures the organization has in place. These include change, configuration, and asset and release management. While every organization will not have all of these processes clearly established, the ones that are in place should be followed appropriately.

The change management process will dictate when the systems can be updated. A change management process can have limitations regarding a time frame that controls when any changes can be made and can also state which systems can be updated at which times. For example, production or Internet-facing systems may be able to have changes deployed only once per month, but other internal back-end systems may be permitted to have changes occur weekly. The change management process will also establish the staging requirements on how many systems can be updated at one time so as not to affect the overall performance of the organization's network.

The configuration management process will track what changes have been made to what systems. For example, a Web server will be tracked in the configuration management tracking database as running a specific operating system, versions of applications, and any additional information regarding that system. Once a patch has been installed on the system, the configuration management database is updated to reflect this new patch or version number of the corresponding operating system or application. The configuration management database is closely tied into the asset management database, as they both store information about systems, but configuration management deals more with how the system is actually configured, excluding any hardware-related information. The system or application owner can also track this type of information, depending on how the groups are organized.

The hardware information is included within the asset management database. Asset management is important for a successful patch management process to establish that all the vulnerable systems have been patched appropriately. The NOC is responsible for ensuring that both the configuration management and asset management processes are adhered to and updated properly once the patch has been deployed onto the vulnerable system. The NOC itself may be responsible for completing these tasks. However, this might depend on how the organization's operational processes have been set up and defined.

The NOC is also responsible for coordinating all activities surrounding the patch management process. It is typically the "eyes and ears" of the organization. It has a view into the infrastructure and can accurately pinpoint any issue or situation that needs to be examined. For this reason, prior to making any changes to the production environment, the appropriate groups must coordinate all activities through the NOC following its standard operating procedures in this regard.

Analysis Phase of Patch Management

Now that the roles and responsibilities have been defined, it is time to move into the various phases of the patch management process. As stated in the previous section, this information should be used as a guide for implementing a patch management process. Each organization is different; therefore, the process should be tailored to meet not only its needs and requirements but also its make-up. During the design phase of implementing the patch management process, the requirements defined will set the stage for which of the following sections will be included and who will obtain the roles and responsibilities required. Figure 9.3 shows the analysis phase of the patch management process, which have been taken from the detailed patch management process flow diagram.

The following sections discuss the *analysis phase* of the patch management process. The monitoring and discovery phase includes how security vulnerabilities or new patches are discovered and taken through the process. The initial assessment is then completed once the patch is released, determining at a high level whether the organization has systems susceptible to the vulnerability or is in need of the patch. Once the initial assessment is completed, an impact assessment is the next step. This looks at the vulnerability in more detail, determining whether it is feasible for the organization to go through the patch management process for this vulnerability and how much risk the organization will have to accept if it chooses not to install the patch. The final phase in the monitoring and discovery phase is the creation and distribution of the security advisory. While an advisory or some type of general communication was sent out when patch management first came into play, this means of communication is recommended but is not a requirement. However, it is an important step in the process, and through the use of a template it can be completed in a consistent and well-communicated manner.

Monitoring and Discovery

Once established within an organization, the security group is responsible for daily monitoring of all appropriate security intelligence sources for exposures that might impact platforms or applications

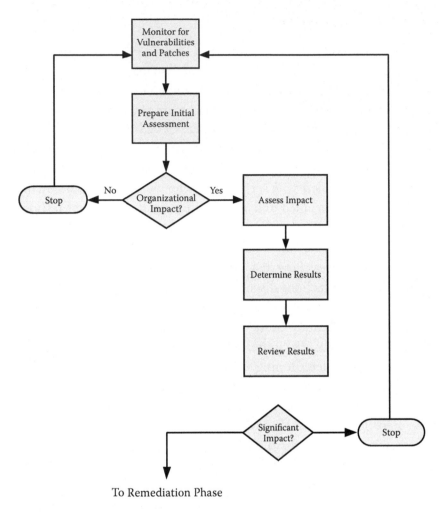

Figure 9.3 Analysis phase.

used by the organization. Whether the organization decides to implement a security group of one, two, or five people, one specific person with an appropriate backup should be dedicated to monitoring the security intelligence sources on a daily schedule. In some cases, if multiple people are completing the same tasks, overlaps or missed important announcements can occur because the monitoring schedule is not clearly communicated. Rotation of duties must also be implemented so that more than one employee knows how to monitor the intelligence sources should the primary not be available.

New security advisories and vulnerabilities are released frequently. Therefore, diligence on the part of security group is required at all times.

Intelligence sources will normally publish a detailed, formal announcement of a security vulnerability. These announcements usually provide a description of the vulnerability, the platform or application affected, and the steps necessary when available to eliminate the risk or even link directly to the patch that is required to be installed. In addition, employees or contractors outside the security group and even the security committee may become aware of vulnerabilities through personal sources, including hands-on experience and word-of-mouth. They should be encouraged through security awareness training and regular communications to report these to the security group.

Software vendors and advisory boards are establishing means to automate this method. As discussed, vendors offer services that will alert the organization when a patch is released that affects systems within the environment. Some vendors' alerting systems often not only e-mail notifications but also assign tasks to other individuals, track the progress of the patch on a Web site, and forward the notifications to other individuals within the organization. If the organization is small or is lacking the dedicated resources to monitor for patches, to stay on top of the latest activity regarding vulnerabilities, and to carry out their normal day-to-day operations, this may be a viable solution. The security group should take this option into consideration when designing the patch management process to see if it can incorporate this into its standard operating procedures.

Initial Assessment Phase

Once the organization has identified a potential patch that affects the organization, an initial assessment must be completed to make an accurate determination. While this step is brief, and should be completed in a short period of time, it is necessary to determine whether the patch even applies to the organization's environment. There are only three major steps in the initial assessment phase; the fourth is the result itself. The following steps are completed in the initial assessment phase:

1. Initially review the patch.
2. Analyze the vulnerability.
3. Start documentation.
4. Determine result.

Once a vulnerability that affects a platform or application in use within the environment has been identified, the security group should perform an initial review to establish the resources required to perform adequate analysis of the vulnerability and to establish an initial level of exposure. This should be completed within 48 hours of the vulnerability being released. The security committee is also informed of the vulnerability so that appropriate actions can begin to take place, including the coordination of meetings to discuss the issue in more detail.

If a vulnerability is released that drastically affects business-critical systems within the organization, a lead analyzer from the security committee may be called in to assess the vulnerability immediately for these systems. In other cases, the security committee would assess the vulnerability and make a determination on whether the organization is impacted. The vulnerability needs to be thoroughly analyzed to decide if the organization is susceptible. For example, it may impact only an older version of software that the company has since migrated from, therefore leaving the organization unaffected by the newly released vulnerability.

The *initial assessment phase* is a task headed by the security group with involvement from the security committee, including updates from the security group on the progress of the initial assessment. However, additional resources may be used to assist in the process, including members of the security committee and additional resources from the operations group, if necessary. The initial assessment phase also begins the documenting process that the patch management process should engage. This includes a spreadsheet or other tracking mechanism that details which vulnerabilities were released and which vulnerabilities the organization is and is not susceptible to. In some cases, the initial assessment may prove that the company does not run that version of software; therefore, it is not affected by the new vulnerability. However, the vulnerability announcement and the conclusion would be tracked in this tracking mechanism, whether it is a database or a spreadsheet.

Impact Assessment Phase

Once the initial assessment is complete, the security group, with guidance from the security committee, assesses the impact of the vulnerability on the environment. The operations group is also included in this phase of the process because it has product engineering responsibility and a detailed technical understanding of the product. An important step in the impact assessment phase is to complete a cost–benefit analysis, which immediately analyzes whether the cost of implementing the remediation plan is less than the asset itself. An in-depth and detailed analysis may not be feasible for each patch released. However, from a high level, the organization should be able to determine whether the cost of deploying the patch on the vulnerable systems is worth the cost of addressing an exploit should it choose not to patch.

Typically, the following steps are completed in the impact assessment phase:

1. Assess the need for remediation.
2. Hold internal discussions.
3. Conduct more in-depth analysis, if needed.
4. Document the results of the analysis.
5. Rate the relevance and significance or severity of the vulnerability.

Assessing the need for remediation requires developing a risk profile, including the population of hosts that are vulnerable, the conditions that need to be satisfied to exploit the vulnerability, and the repercussions to the company if it were to be exploited. This is where the security committee provides its most valuable knowledge share. The security committee is responsible for holding internal discussions to discuss the vulnerability and its impact on the organization. The security committee, which consists of members from previously mentioned groups, works together to remediate the vulnerability at hand. In some cases, further in-depth analysis needs to be completed; some factors to consider in the impact assessment include the following:

- Type and delivery of attack
- Exploit complexity
- Vulnerability severity
- System criticality

- System location
- Patch availability

The factors taken into consideration can be addressed in the form of a question. To determine the type and delivery of an attack, the security committee must answer whether an exploit has been published for the vulnerability. Another more detailed question regarding the type and delivery of attack that the security committee must answer is whether the vulnerability is at risk of exploitation by self-replicating malicious code. In other words, if one system is vulnerable, will it propagate throughout the entire network, and what is the impact of this? The first question obviously holds the most weight. If there is an exploit in the wild at the time of patch release, then the organization must prioritize this patch appropriately to ensure that it is protected in the shortest period of time possible.

Another factor is the complexity of the exploit itself. The level of difficulty in exploiting the vulnerability can affect the security committee's level of priority applied to the patch. If a high level of difficulty is required, the chances of an exploit being released in the short term are lower versus a low level of difficulty, which could result in the exploit being released within days following the release of the vulnerability. The number of conditions that must be met to exploit the vulnerability also has an impact on the priority level assigned. This, along with the infrastructure and technical elements that must be in place for the exploit itself to be successful, must be examined by the security committee. While some of this information may be difficult for the security committee to determine on its own, most of it is provided by the vendor or by the group publishing the vulnerability and the appropriate patch.

In some cases, exploited vulnerabilities can be more of a nuisance than having devastating effects on the system affected. The severity of the vulnerability must be identified to determine what effect the exploit will have on the vulnerable system. In the past, organizations have been fortunate, in that most exploits do not cause serious danger but instead are just an inconvenience. Over time, exploits may not be as kind and will be able to result in lost data, revenue, and even production. Determining the severity of the vulnerability will assist the organization in prioritizing the patch and patching the vulnerable systems in the appropriate time frame to avoid the chance of severe consequences.

During the design phase of putting the patch management process in place, which is discussed in a future chapter, mapping systems to criticality is performed to ensure that they are patched in the appropriate order. This is a required step to immediately determine what systems are at risk during the impact assessment phase. The security committee must be able to understand what systems are at risk and the level of damage that would be caused if these systems were compromised. Understanding the systems' criticality also controls which systems will be patched first and which will need to make certain that the patch has been thoroughly tested prior to being installed. Understanding not only the criticality of the systems but also their location is important during the impact assessment phase. Finally, the impact assessment should answer the question of whether a patch is available to remediate the vulnerability. The vendor's responsibility includes issuing patches when the vulnerabilities are released; however, this is not always the case. Another workaround may have to be implemented by the vendor who will then create and distribute the appropriate patch to its customers. The organization may wish to wait prior to fixing the vulnerable systems until the vendor has issued this patch. The security committee will have the ultimate responsibility of making this determination.

Once the impact assessment has been completed, the results of the analysis are documented in the same manner as was done during the initial assessment phase. To conclude, the vulnerability is rated based on relevance, significance, and severity, taking into consideration the results of the cost–benefit analysis. If the security committee concludes that the security vulnerability has no impact on the environment, no further action is needed. A record of all information gathered to date would be stored by the security group for future reference.

Remediation Phase of Patch Management

Once the analysis phase of the patch management process is complete, the organization moves into the remediation phase. The main emphasis in the remediation phase is the development of the course of action plan. This is what drives the actions throughout the rest of process because this is how the organization will address the patch and mitigate the risk within the organization.

While testing is included in the remediation phase, an entire chapter is dedicated to the subject of testing. This is an important piece of the patch management process and one with which a lot of organizations have the most difficulty, mainly because of the complexity that goes along with the testing. The next step within the remediation phase concerns critical vulnerabilities. This is where critical vulnerabilities are addressed as needed to be certain that processes are in place to help an organization react quickly if necessary. The final step in the remediation phase is the standard build. This is included in this phase of the patch management process because once the patch has gone through testing it can be incorporated into the standard build that the organization uses for desktops and servers. In most cases, an organization will use a standard build for all desktops. It is important to include the patch in this build to prevent the vulnerability from being in production while the rest of the systems have been patched appropriately. The same holds true for servers, given that the organization enforces the use of a standard build on all its servers, regardless of the operating systems. Figure 9.4 shows the remediation phase of the patch management process, which is derived from the detailed process flow diagram in Figure 9.2.

Patch Course of Action

Once the impact assessment phase is complete and the risk or exposure is known and documented, the operations group then develops a course of action for the vulnerability to be remediated on every platform or application affected, which will be performed with the involvement of the security group, along with reporting to the security committee to provide periodic updates.

A suitable response (security advisory) to the persons responsible for the vulnerable systems is designed and developed and details the vulnerability and how it impacts the organization along with the importance of eliminating the vulnerability, which is based on the results of the impact analysis. These are usually sent out via e-mail but also at times in an attached document. Each organization can

From Analysis Phase

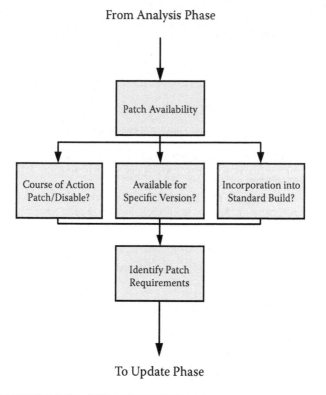

Figure 9.4 Remediation process flow.

tailor the response to fit its specific needs; the example response provided is included as a guideline (Table 9.2). The security committee, which includes members of the operations group, security group, and NOC, should build the course of action plan to be used to remediate the vulnerability from within the organization's environment.

The course of action phase consists of the following steps:

1. Select the desired defense measures.
2. Identify, develop, and test defense measures.
3. Test availability of security-related patches or influence vendors in developing needed patches.
4. Develop and test back-out procedure.
5. Apply a vendor-supplied patch, either specific to the vulnerability or addressing multiple issues.

Table 9.2   Sample Security Advisory Template

Sample Patch Security Advisory

<*TITLE OF ADVISORY*>

Internal Advisory Version and Date: <used to track advisories and subsequent updates>

Release Date: <date of source release>

Risk Level: <emergency I critical I urgent I important I informational>

Deployment Time Frame: <based on priority level assigned to vulnerability>

Vulnerability Description:
<Describe in five sentences or less what the problem is, using common terms such as worm or virus, remote exploit, buffer overflow, and local exploit. Describe in direct terms why the receiver of this advisory should be concerned.>

Impact:
<Describe the potential conditions that exist until such time as this advisory is acted upon.>

Systems Affected:
<List the systems—including version numbers—that need attention.>

Required Actions: <actions that are expected>

Implementation Plan:
<Detail the steps necessary to mitigate the situation.>

Back-out plan:
<Detail the back-out plan to address any issues the patch may cause on the vulnerable systems.>

---

6. Modify the functionality in some way, perhaps by disabling a service or changing the configuration.
7. Prepare documentation to support the implementation of selected measures.

The desired defense measure is usually in the form of a patch or a hot fix from the vendor and is a manual configuration change. It is usually selected, or chosen, based on the release of the vulnerability. When a vulnerability affects a vendor-supplied product and the vendor has not supplied an appropriate patch or workaround, the operations group can work with the vendor to develop an appropriate mitigation strategy. Regardless of the vendor's recommendation, the operations group needs to determine and document the best course of action to take.

When a vendor-supplied patch is to be used, the operations group will be responsible for retrieving all relevant material from the vendor.

Once the defense measure is chosen, it must be tested to ensure that it will function properly in the organization's current environment. Usually, this is done in a development environment, where implementing, testing, and creating back-out procedures can all be accomplished. This ensures a smooth transition when implementing the defense measure on all the systems affected. A procedural document is created to assist in this smooth implementation, which is then provided to the operations group to follow when implementing the fix. However, the operations group should be involved in the testing of the patch, or configuration change, to make certain that what is being documented can accurately be used on the systems in production. In most cases, the operations group not only will be involved in the testing but also will be doing the actual testing.

Patch Security Advisory

Once an appropriate course of action has been agreed upon, the security group will release an internal patch security advisory to the persons responsible for the systems, whether it is within the operations group or members of the organization impacted by the vulnerability. The advisory is always issued using the template provided to show consistency and to reduce confusion. Each advisory contains the following information:

- Vulnerability description
- Risk level
- Implementation plan
- Back-out plan
- Deployment time frame

The vulnerability description will provide the reader with the type of vulnerability that has been identified—that is, whether it was a buffer overflow, denial of service, or potential worm or virus-based attack. The affected applications and operating systems version would also be included in the vulnerability description section. A sample security advisory template is included at the end of this section (Table 9.2) to provide guidance on how the template should be established. Finally, within this section, the method used to exploit the vulnerability is included. Depending on the audience receiving these security advisories, they can be either nontechnical or technical but must provide a clear description of how the vulnerability is exploited.

Included within the advisory is the risk level that the security committee assigned to the vulnerability. This level is a result of the impact assessment phase and is a combination of the vendor recommendation and knowledge of the infrastructure. There are typically five different risk levels applied to a given vulnerability: emergency, critical, urgent, important, or informational. A vulnerability assigned with a risk level of emergency means the conditions warrant *immediate* action. In such cases, the organization's incident response plan will likely need activation. A vulnerability should be given this rating only on rare occasions, perhaps for a zero-day exploit. A critical vulnerability results from conditions such as a vulnerable externally facing system, remote buffer overflow, denial of service, or a direct threat (exploit in the wild or actual compromise of an organization's systems) and warrants an immediate response. An urgent vulnerability results from conditions such as vulnerabilities with no reported exploit and may be held as the change management procedures allow and after some testing has been completed. An important vulnerability is a theoretical vulnerability that can wait until the next patching or change management cycle, when other patches are applied. An informational vulnerability is another theoretical vulnerability and has a low likelihood of affecting the organization. It may have a low credibility rating; however, it is still considered a threat. This can also be used to inform the organization about worm or virus propagation or other threats that do not necessarily require direct action.

The next section in the advisory is the implementation plan. This section is part of the course of action plan. It contains detailed instructions on how to mitigate the vulnerability on the affected systems, the location, whether it is a direct link or repository, and where the patch is stored if personnel are required to install the patch themselves. In most cases, the operations group, system or application owners, or NOC would have the patch and would be responsible for scheduling the installation of the patch on the vulnerable systems. However, if a certain department is responsible for patching its own systems, this is not recommended, and then the security committee must ensure that the department installs the proper patch by providing a centrally located repository. The detailed instructions are provided mainly for the installers to follow; however, the department would also be provided with the course of action plan to guarantee that all the steps have been completed accurately.

The back-out plan regarding the patch is also included in the security advisory. This encompasses the details on how the patch would be removed from the system and how to address any unexpected problems caused by the implementation of the patch on the vulnerable systems. While the testing should uncover any issues with installation of the patch, a detailed back-out plan is also required as part of the course of action. The NOC and the operations group must be in agreement with how the back-out plan has been established, because they will be responsible for removing the patch from any system that has a negative result due to the patch being installed.

The final section in the advisory, which ironically is located at the top of it, contains the time frame for deploying the patch on the vulnerable systems. This is based not only on the risk level of the patch but also on the criticality of the systems. Locations can also play a role in this. The security committee makes the decision on what time frame is required for the patch to be deployed on all the vulnerable systems and then includes these time frames in the advisory. Putting the time frame at the top of the advisory enables readers to immediately identify how long before the patch will be installed on the systems for which they are responsible. If a patch must be installed on desktops, the users will need to be notified as to what their responsibilities are to make certain that their desktop is patched appropriately.

The item of informing the desktop users of a patch being deployed onto their system has its pros and cons. In the best-case scenario, the user should not even know the patch is being installed. If any reboots need to occur, they should be performed after hours or when they are not at their desks working. Having a policy in place that users must leave their desktops on at night when they leave with no critical applications running should be documented. This way, if the NOC is deploying patches to desktops during the change management window and the desktop needs to be rebooted, the user will not know about it, and no critical data would be lost. If there is no method of completing this without informing the desktop users, then part of the training on patch management must include an agreement form that states what users must comply with when a patch is installed on their system that requires a reboot. For this reason alone, having an agent installed on the system as part of the patch deployment tool will allow the NOC and the security group to track what desktops have been patched appropriately. If users have not rebooted their system (and it is not automatic), then the NOC or the security group must communicate with them, further conveying what the patch management process entails and what their role is in that process.

The audience that receives the security advisory will depend not only on the vulnerability but also on how the roles and responsibilities have been established within the organization. The security committee will not want to send all security advisories to the entire organization, because some users will disregard them or will not take them seriously. Only the personnel responsible for completing tasks within the patch management process should be sent the advisory. The only instance when the general user population should receive a security advisory is when the vulnerability itself affects all users within the organization and they all have a task to complete. This ties back to the desktops and the users' responsibilities in ensuring they are patched appropriately.

One additional item that has not been discussed is record keeping regarding the security advisories. The security advisories that are sent must be maintained for a period of time determined by the organization. The organization may choose to keep a yearly record of all security advisories sent out to track the number of instances of the patch management process. The number of advisories sent (meaning number of patch releases) can be used to demonstrate to management that the investment in patch management is paying off. A formal method for numbering the advisories should be established. This will eliminate any confusion, or duplication in advisories, and it incorporates an overall best practice.

Table 9.2 shows a sample security advisory template that can be used by an organization to inform the defined individuals regarding the patch and the appropriate course of action.

Testing the Patch

While an entire chapter has been dedicated to testing the patches prior to deploying them on the vulnerable systems, it is important to note where the testing phase of the patch management process fits in. Testing is typically coordinated through the operations group and the NOC and includes services from appropriate business units or departments and access to necessary resources (e.g., test labs). The operations group, along with guidance from the security committee, is responsible for preparing a detailed implementation plan and performing appropriate testing in a representative lab environment. A formal plan and documentation to govern the testing will be generated based on the type of system and vulnerability. Formal testing is conducted, and documented test results are provided to the security committee. A back-out plan would also be developed and tested to ensure that if the patch adversely affects a production system it can be quickly reversed and the system restored to its original state. The back-out procedures would include vendor specific procedures to remove the patch or fix or other backup and restore procedures to bring a disrupted system to its original state.

The security committee is responsible for granting final approval of the implementation plan for production systems based on the test results and recommendations from the operations group. The operations group must validate that the patch is protected from malicious activity before it is installed on the system.

The chapter on testing should be referenced for details surrounding the steps to follow when conducting testing of the patches in the organization's environment. However, patches do not exist in a vacuum, so detailed testing of all patches must be included in the overall process. As part of the testing, the following conditions—at a minimum— must be met before proceeding to the next step:

- The testing environment simulates a majority of the targeted platforms.
- The patch installs on the target platform without significant issues.
- The software delivery process succeeds on the targeted test platform.

- Previously functioning operations on the target platform continue to operate after installation of the patch.
- The patch can be successfully backed out in case of problems.

"Critical" Vulnerabilities

In some situations, a vulnerability introduces a significant threat to the organization. This can be magnified if the vulnerability identified affects a large number of systems within the environment. These are identified as critical vulnerabilities and should be treated in an escalated manner throughout the patch management process. A critical vulnerability can be classified as such if an exploit has been released prior to or in tandem with the patch release. If an exploit is released in this manner, it is called a zero-day exploit. While such vulnerabilities are a rare occurrence, organizations must prepare to address vulnerabilities that result in zero-day exploits.

Some organizations are protecting their infrastructure against these types of exploits by introducing additional technologies into the environment. Technologies such as intrusion detection systems (IDSs) and intrusion prevention systems (IPSs) can be used to protect companies from these types of threats. IDSs offer protection through either host-based or network-based products. While an entire book can be dedicated to IDSs and IPSs, they warrant mention in this section because they can add another level of protection to an organization that wishes to ensure that it is not susceptible to the threat of a zero-day exploit.

With some critical vulnerabilities, vendors will inform their customers of the immediate remediation plans that must occur to protect themselves from the vulnerability and from the exploit. They would include which operating system or application is susceptible as well as the appropriate method to alleviate this risk. Vendors must provide a great deal of communication to their clients regarding these types of vulnerabilities to guarantee that they, the customers, have the methods to protect themselves.

Within the organization itself, awareness of critical vulnerabilities must be promoted to individuals who are part of the patch management process. This would include the communication of any additional procedures that must be followed when a critical vulnerability has been released. While not necessary, a different patch security advisory template could be used for these types of vulnerabilities. It would be similar to the standard template but would contain the expedited process for ensuring that all vulnerable systems are patched within the organization. For example, the time frame for installing the patch for a critical vulnerability is different from an urgent, important, or informational vulnerability. The course of action would also be established appropriate to the vulnerability, making certain that the patch can be tested properly and installed quickly.

The security committee would be responsible for making the ultimate decision on what constitutes a critical vulnerability. Even an urgent vulnerability can be considered by the organization, especially when there are a large number of vulnerable systems in the infrastructure. For critical vulnerabilities, the security committee must ensure that the time frame, course of action, and testing are all paramount to the vulnerability itself.

Use of a Standard Build

The use of a standard build is often overlooked or is not associated with patch management. The opposite should be the case with any organization. Typically, the use of standard builds, or operating system images, is often overlooked when it comes to patch management. If a standard build is deployed on the desktops and a vulnerability is released that impacts that standard build, it must be updated to protect additional desktops implemented in the environment. This confirms that any future implementation of a platform or application has the modifications necessary to eliminate the vulnerability.

A time frame for deploying the updates into the build must be determined in the remediation phase. It must be carefully set to make sure that a build is not updated too frequently, thereby risking the validity of appropriate testing, and not too infrequently, such that new implementations are installed without the fix or update to address the security vulnerability.

The security committee is responsible for ensuring that the standard build has been updated with the appropriate patch to avoid replication. This group is also responsible for monitoring the frequency of the updates to the standard build, through working with the operations group or group responsible for the standard builds themselves, to establish that a proper procedure is put in place for updating them.

In some cases, one standard build for the desktops may not be a feasible solution. Instead, the organization will issue multiple standard builds, one for each of the various departments, locations, or even countries. The number of standard builds issued in the organization can lead to more confusion or more inconsistency in their updates. It is important to limit the number of standard builds to ensure that they can be updated as needed and to avoid confusion not only as patches are released but also as new desktops are issued to end users. Another option to this is to issue a baseline build that is standard for all additional standard builds. Then, options to include specific applications or functions based upon department or location can be added, thus providing more centralized control over the standard build.

Regardless of how the organization maintains, issues, or updates standard builds within the environment, it is important that, as patches are released that affect them, they need to be updated via a regularly documented process to ensure that the organization is protected against future threats.

Updating the Operational Environment

Updating the operational environment is no easy task. There are many steps involved, and the security committee must make sure that all processes and procedures are adhered to when making updates to the organization's environment. In the security advisory, the steps for implementation are included at a high level, which kicks off the implementation of the remediation plan. In the security advisory, a timetable is defined, which dictates how long the operations group and the NOC have before the patch or fix is implemented. To guarantee that the operations group and NOC can meet the timetable, the security committee must have the material available that supports remediation of the vulnerability before the security advisory is sent. The security-related patches are usually stored in a repository provided by the NOC or within the operations group, once it has received them from the appropriate vendor (or source).

The security committee may choose to send out a more general notification regarding the vulnerability to the general user population, depending on the severity of the vulnerability. This is done only as needed and is determined during the impact assessment phase. However, the notification would go out *after* the security advisory is sent because the security committee and operations group must know how to fix the vulnerability and must develop an implementation plan prior to causing concern with the general user population. The operations group and the NOC, both of which may be responsible for making the updates, must follow all corporate change and configuration management procedures during the update. This is coordinated through the NOC with updates provided to the security committee. This includes not only patching the vulnerable systems but also conducting any additional testing.

There are also instances in which the operations group or a subset of the operations group, perhaps a specific business unit or department, may choose not to implement a patch. In these cases, an exception request can be completed, which is used to process requests for exemptions. If the waiver request is not agreed upon by the security committee, a dispute escalation process can be followed to resolve it. Included in the security advisory is a reporting structure. Each responsible party and the operations group must provide progress reports to the security group on the status of implementing the required fix. This ensures that the timetable is followed and that the security advisory is adhered to. Once the security group has received all of the status reports, a summary is then formulated and presented to the security committee. Figure 9.5 depicts the update operational environment process flow, which has been taken from the detailed patch management process flow diagram.

Distributing the Patch

During the planning phase of putting the patch management process in place, which is discussed in a previous chapter, the organization will determine what its requirements are for distributing the patches to the vulnerable systems. It is within the design phase, however, that the organization will analyze how it will complete this today and how it can complete it with the new, or modified, process. The method for

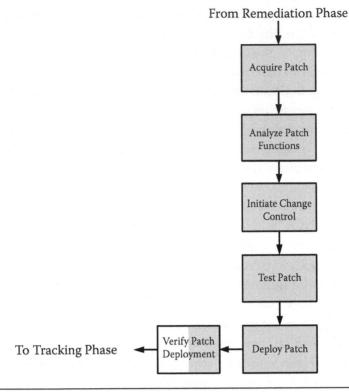

Figure 9.5 Update operational environmental process flow.

distribution relies heavily on whether a tool will be used to distribute the patches or if it will be done manually. Regardless of how the patch management process is designed, the method for distribution of patches must be clearly and accurately documented to avoid confusion and to ensure that all systems are patched appropriately. This can ultimately affect the success of the patch management process. If all vulnerable systems are not patched appropriately, the threat of an exploit still has a significant chance of occurring.

In most cases, the operations group will distribute all files, executable programs, patches, or other materials necessary to implement the mitigation strategy to the appropriate operations personnel or the NOC, using an internal File Transfer Protocol (FTP) server, internal document portal, or a general internal security Web site. The operations group is responsible for ensuring that the data are transmitted via a secure method that meets integrity requirements. Because the NOC will most likely be responsible for implementing the patch, it must make certain that the patch it has received has not been tampered with.

The decision regarding whether to use an agent-based or agentless patch deployment tool can affect the integrity of the patch being deployed to the vulnerable system. As discussed in a previous chapter, the organization will evaluate various tools and determine which one will meet the requirements it has defined. Whether the use of an agent is one of these requirements resides with the organization. The issue of integrity when deploying the patch must be included in the evaluation, because the organization must be able to establish that the patch has not been tampered with in transit to the vulnerable system.

Regardless of the method chosen to distribute the patch, this is a key step in the update operational environment phase of the patch management process. If the patch or patches are not distributed accurately, the success of the patch management process will be in question. While the implementation of the patch itself is an even more important step, ensuring that the personnel responsible for implementing the patch have distributed it accurately can still affect the success of the overall process.

Implementation of Patches

When the security advisory is released, it prepares the NOC and the operations group that a patch has been released that needs to be deployed onto the vulnerable systems. At this point, the NOC can begin to take the proper steps to guarantee that the patch is deployed accurately once the NOC receives it. The security advisory will also dictate the time frame in which the patch must be deployed. Depending on the criticality of the patch, the NOC may need to escalate its standard operating procedures to ensure that the timeframes dictated can be achieved.

The actions that the NOC and operations group follow are based on the course of action that has been defined for that patch. During the development of the course of action plan, the specific step-by-step instructions for deploying the patch are defined. The NOC will then take this information and apply it to its standard operating procedures. The NOC will also provide input into the course of action plan so that when it is received the NOC will agree with and understand the procedures that it must follow.

If a tool is being used to deploy the patches, the NOC will have the procedures necessary to operate the tool to ensure that the patch is deployed to the pertinent systems. The staging of the deployment is also considered. Not all systems can be patched at once. Therefore, the NOC will coordinate the staging phases of the patch deployment, making certain in the long run that all have been patched within the defined time frame. Some systems may not be able to be patched immediately. Instead, the patch may need to go through additional testing before it is deployed on business-critical systems. The NOC will be informed as to when the patch has been tested appropriately and will then deploy it onto those critical systems by following the standard operating procedures.

The operations group or the NOC, depending on the makeup of the organization, will apply patches in accordance with established change management procedures. The NOC has the change management procedures defined, which must be followed when implementing the patch. The NOC also maintains the configuration management procedure, which must also be updated once the patch has been implemented. Following the implementation, the operations group is responsible for testing production systems to ensure stability. Production systems may experience disruption after a security patch has been applied. If this occurs, the defined back-out procedures should be implemented.

Time Frame of Deployment

The results of the impact assessment phase of the patch management process will dictate the time frame in which the patch must be deployed onto the vulnerable systems within the environment. The time frame can be different for different systems, based upon the location, criticality, and method of updating required. The security committee will determine the time frame and will include this in the security advisory that is sent to the selected individuals. Because the security committee consists of various members of the security group, operations group, and NOC, they all have a voice in the time determined to ensure that the organization is protected against the vulnerability.

Table 9.3 Release Schedule Based on Security Priority

PRIORITY	RECOMMENDED TIME FRAME	MAXIMUM RECOMMENDED TIME FRAME
1: Emergency	Within 12 hrs	Within 12 to 24 hrs
2: Critical	Within 48 hours	Within 2 weeks
3: Urgent	Within 1 week	Within 2 weeks
4: Important	Depending on availability, deploy a new service pack or update rollup that includes a fix for this vulnerability within 1 month	Deploy the software update within 1 month
5: Informational	Depending on availability, deploy a new service pack or update rollup that includes a fix for this vulnerability within 3 months	Deploy the software update within 2 months or may choose not to deploy at all

The change management and configuration management procedures defined within the organization will also dictate the speed with which the patch can be installed. Table 9.3 shows recommended and maximum time frames that should be established based on the priority of the patch.

While the priority patches labeled emergency, critical, and urgent show the shortest time frames for completion, the security committee must make this determination during the design of the patch management process. Each organization can set its own time frame based on what it can achieve given the staff, resources, and tools at its disposal. The number of vulnerable systems within the organization's environment will influence the release schedule and should be taken into consideration when assigning these time frames, which should be static in nature and not change when a new patch is released. Instead, the priority level given to the vulnerability will change, depending on the stance the security committee chooses to take. It is important to note that if the time frames change then understanding how patching is completed within the organization can be confusing to readers of the security advisory and to those individuals responsible for patching the systems. It is important for the organization to be consistent in the time frames established for each vulnerability according to its priority. This is why the impact assessment phase is important—so that the security committee can determine the priority level given to the vulnerability that aligns with the time required to make sure that all systems are patched appropriately.

Exceptions to the Rule

Organizations must keep in mind that not all patches can be implemented all the time, and this is not feasible for an organization to believe going into the patch management process. There will be cases when a patch cannot be installed on the vulnerable systems for one reason or another. It may not even be all vulnerable systems; instead, it may be one system or a group of systems that cannot have the patch installed. These situations must be taken into consideration during the design of the patch management process. A question the security committee must ask itself is what is the organization's stance on patches that cannot be installed on the required systems? Typically, this is answered through an exception process.

In an exception case, the security committee may determine that the organization is unable or unwilling to implement mitigating measures within the required time frame, or at all, for the following reasons:

1. A system or group of systems is not vulnerable to the threat due to other factors.
2. The vulnerability is considered a limited threat to the business.
3. The patch is determined to be incompatible with other applications.

In the first instance, the operations group or a department within the organization may bring it to the attention of the security committee that specific systems are not vulnerable to the threat the patch incurs. This can be due to other factors that prohibit the threat from being exploited if the system is not patched. For example, if the patch pertains to the Oracle database and requires a Web-based front or back end to successfully complete the attack, the system or group of systems may not use the Web-based front end. In this example, the Oracle database server is not vulnerable to the threat because the second piece, which is required to exploit it, is not present in the organization. To take this one step further, while the organization may be using Web servers throughout the environment, if it does not communicate with the Oracle database in any fashion then this patch may not need to be implemented.

The second reason pertains more to the amount of risk the organization is willing to accept. If a group brings a patch to the security committee and states that it is not applicable to that group's systems because the level of risk is very low, then the security committee must make a decision. While hearing the business reasons from the group on why the patch should not be installed, the security committee must determine what level of risk the organization would be accepting if it chooses not to deploy the patch on those systems. The group determining that the patch is not required because of the low level of threat must have a strong business case to support this decision. While the security committee will most likely disagree with the group, the business case must be heard and discussed. In this instance, the chief information risk officer (CIRO) or CIO of the organization may need to get involved to resolve the dispute.

The third reason might be a result of testing the patch. This is why ensuring that the patches are tested properly prior to installing them on the vulnerable systems is a required part of the process. If during testing it has been determined that the patch will break another application on a system or that another application on the system will not function properly, this needs to be brought to the attention of the security committee. Once the security committee has reviewed the testing procedures and results, it may agree with the decision that the patch cannot be installed on systems that are running the combination of applications. For example, if Internet Explorer does not function properly after a patch for FrontPage is installed, then systems running the vulnerable version of FrontPage, in combination with the version of Internet Explorer that was tested, the patch would then not be installed on those systems. These three cases are all extreme and very rarely occur. This reason for the extremity is to ensure that only a limited number of patches are not deployed on vulnerable systems.

The security committee may not be the driving force behind issuing this exception. Instead, a department, or business unit, within the organization may be providing the push-back on installation of the patch onto its system. In such cases, the aforementioned group can submit an action plan to the security committee to pursue alternate mitigation strategies. If that department wants to delay the implementation of the patch, it must complete a risk acceptance form that details any risks resulting from the failure to deploy the patch. The risk acceptance form is then presented to the security committee for approval.

In some instances, the security committee may not be able to agree on whether the organization is susceptible to the vulnerability or the criticality of the vulnerability itself. This can become a common occurrence within any organization; therefore, a distinct dispute resolution path must be defined to clearly dictate how such vulnerabilities will be resolved. This is also known as an *escalation path*. When a dispute cannot be resolved properly within the security committee, the committee should escalate the dispute to the organization's CIRO, or CIO if no CIRO exists. The CIO would then consult with the committee, hearing both sides of the impact assessment phase before resolving the dispute.

Updating Remote Users

In many organizations, the growing number of mobile users is causing pain in ensuring that they are patched appropriately. There are more mobile, remote, or virtual users today than in years past. In some cases, the users may be traveling or working remotely or at client sites. While there are various scenarios to accomplish this task, a few examples are provided herein to explain some possible solutions. While a lot of how to deal with remote users depends on the tool used to deploy patches, this will be taken into consideration when providing the examples.

If the patch deployment tool uses an agent installed on the client, monitoring these systems can be easy. Of course, they need to be connected to the internal network for this to occur, but it is a source for gathering the current patch status. If the organization requires that a VPN connection be established for remote users, this can provide the ability to quarantine users until they have been validated. For example, if a mobile user is working off-site, he would establish a VPN connection over the Internet to the organization's internal network. Once connected, the user would be put into a network that is separated from the rest of the internal network. Once on this network, the user's system would be validated to ensure that it has been updated with the appropriate patches. After the system has been validated, the user would receive access to the internal network but still reside on this segmented network because the user is coming in over the VPN connection. Establishing this type of scenario for remote users will assist an organization in ensuring that the mobile user's systems are patched appropriately. This also provides the organization with the tracking required to maintain a report on the frequency that each mobile system has been updated to make certain that none are overlooked.

If the organization has decided to implement an agentless tool on the client systems, a method to validate the systems prior to granting them access to the internal network will be more difficult. In some instances, the organization might rely on a software program such as Windows Update to alert users when a new patch is available for their laptops. It will then be up to the users to install the patch. If Windows Update is not a viable solution, the operations group could e-mail the patch to the users with the step-by-step instructions on how to install it. Of course, this and other options can have negative consequences. If mobile users connect to the Internet over dial-up, or a slow link, then the process of downloading e-mails can be a cumbersome task. If it takes a long time to obtain the patch through the specified method, the chance that users will stop the download to accomplish work-related tasks will increase. As a result, their system will be susceptible to an exploit if it has not been patched appropriately.

Whatever option the organization chooses to use for patching a remote user's system, the process must document how it will be addressed. These users may also be required to attend an additional training class that outlines their responsibilities regarding protecting that system. Typically, organizations also establish a remote access policy, which users must read and agree to comply with. In this policy, a high-level process for obtaining remote access is defined as well as what users must do while having remote access. This policy can include a reference to the patch management process that states how remote users' systems will be updated. Remote users' systems should be treated no differently from a stationary desktop on location. They both should have a standard build implemented and the appropriate access controls enforced to establish that users cannot make changes that affect the integrity of the build.

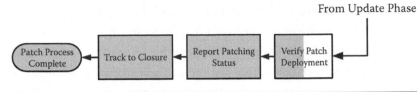

Figure 9.6 Tracking process flow.

Tracking Patches

The final phase of the patch management process is tracking the patch. It is important to ensure that all vulnerable systems have been patched appropriately. The operations group, in conjunction with the NOC, is responsible for tracking the progress in updating the operational environment during the patch management process. However, the NOC's change and configuration management procedures will track this information according to the predefined process.

The tracking process includes detailing each vulnerable system, taking the steps to eliminate the risk, and confirming that the system is no longer vulnerable. Any exception made to a vulnerable system must also be included in the tracking process. A standardized form will be specified to record when a system has been patched. The tracking results will be reported to the security group in accordance with the timetable set out in the security advisory.

Included in the tracking process, typically in a comments section, are the lessons learned and recommendations to improve the process. This allows for feedback from the security committee on the patch management process itself, and it gives constant feedback on how to update or improve the process. The patch management process should be reviewed and updated on a biannual basis or at existing, predefined procedural review intervals. The security committee is responsible for taking the feedback into consideration when making changes to the overall process. Figure 9.6 shows the tracking portion of the patch management process taken from the detailed patch management process flow diagram.

Patch Reporting

The security group will maintain the reporting information from the NOC and operations group in a central repository. The security group will then provide the security committee with a summary report that outlines the percentage of systems patched on an updated basis. For each vulnerability, the following documentation will be maintained by the security group:

- Vulnerability overview with appropriate references to supporting documentation
- Test plan and results for relevant security-related patches or other remedial measures
- Detailed implementation and back-out plans for all affected systems
- Progress reports and scorecards to track systems that have been patched

All supporting documentation for a processed security vulnerability is stored in a database maintained by the security group. If no database is available, another tracking mechanism can and should be used.

The security group publishes a list of security-related patches that have been determined to be necessary to protect the organization. This list is reissued whenever a new security-related patch is sanctioned by the security group. An online system is used to report status. System owners are required to report progress when deploying required remedial measures. When feasible, the security group monitors vulnerable systems to make certain that all required remedial measures have been successfully implemented. A scorecard is used in the reporting process to ensure that any vulnerable system is, in fact, fixed. The security group is responsible for creating and maintaining the accuracy of the scorecard for each system affected by the vulnerability. The scorecard must be monitored and kept up to date to establish that there are no outstanding issues.

10
PUTTING THE PROCESS IN PLACE

Implementing the process can be as difficult as defining it, especially if the organization does not currently have a patch management process in place. If an organization is just revamping the process, implementing the recently modified process can be an easier task to accomplish. Regardless of the state the organization is in, the standard steps—plan, design, implement, operate, and maintain—should be completed. Organizations will be dealing with patch management on an ongoing basis for the unforeseen future. It is important to define a patch management process not only that can grow with an organization but also one that can be well integrated into the organization's standard operating procedures. It is important for organizations to do their due diligence when it comes to planning, designing, implementing, and maintaining a patch management process.

Once the patch management process has been clearly defined and documented, it is time to implement it within the organization's environment. Of course, the current state of the organization should be considered during the planning and designing phases; otherwise, the process will not be successful. This also holds true if the organization tries to implement a cookie-cutter patch management process. All organizations are different, and each process defined within them will be similar in goals but different in process. Carefully walking through the next steps will result in a patch management process that not only is easily integrated into the organization but also can operate smoothly and be maintained for the long-term with minimal revisions as the organization grows.

For the process to be successful, before it is defined and documented, executive or upper management within the organization should be briefed prior to starting to ensure that it agrees with and

217

will support the process from an organizational perspective. If this is not done, a major roadblock could occur.

The group responsible for defining and documenting the patch management process or the group performing patch management today should provide upper management with a snapshot including statistics on how patch management is addressed now, and how it will be addressed once the process has been revamped. This snapshot is to provide upper management with a clear understanding of how the organization's risks will be reduced. Management needs to clearly understand the importance of supporting the patch management process. Because management has the ability to force change throughout an organization, gaining its support somewhat forces the entire organization to participate in this task. One way to show members of executive management the benefits of going through this exercise, thereby gaining their support, is by providing them with a return on investment (ROI) or business value (BV) through analyzing costs, trade-offs, and system impact, and customers.

Preparing for the Process

In many cases, organizations are too busy fighting fires to step back and look at the whole picture and how to improve it. Planning must be completed thoroughly to make the rest of the integration run smoothly and accurately. It is the first step in newly implementing or modifying an existing patch management process. The organization may have a patch management process in place today, and it may very well be a well-executed patch management process. Only a few modifications may be necessary to get it where it needs to be to mitigate the associated risks with the lack of patched systems. Regardless of the state of the organization, if a new or updated patch management process is required, planning must commence.

The tasks within the planning phase of putting the patch management process in place entail completing an assessment of how patch management is currently being completed, what the requirements are moving forward, and performing a gap analysis on the systems to determine what state they are all in today.

Assessing Current State

The first task within the planning phase is to assess how the organization is currently doing things. This can help determine whether the organization has a patch management process documented and what the issues are presently regarding the process. If the current patch management process is not documented, then part of the assessment is to put what is being done today on paper to clearly evaluate its existence. This will take a certain level of effort from the group performing the assessment, but the existing process must be clearly understood. A group of individuals should be responsible for gathering all pertinent data. This can be done through group interviews by meeting with various departments within the organization to see how they are patching their systems. It can also be done through a self-assessment questionnaire. If a self-assessment questionnaire is used, the information provided would still need to be validated for accuracy. This method often does not work well, since it results in inaccurate data or different answers from individuals when they should be the same. Self-assessment questionnaires should be very used sparingly, and not throughout the entire organization to gather the pertinent data. The department heads or pertinent information technology (IT) staff are required to answer a list of questions pertaining to how patching is being done within the organization on all relevant systems. Data may also come in the form of an inventory of systems within the organization that have been patched or a list of those that cannot be patched due to various reasons. If patching is being completed, any documented records of what is being patched must be included in the assessment. Some departments or business units may have implemented their own tools, depending on how IT is established throughout the organization. These tools should be considered in the design phase.

Once the data have been collected, they should be compiled into one simple report, which is used as the baseline not only for setting the requirements but also for designing the process efficiently. The report should be broken down, at a minimum, into three sections: (1) findings; (2) analysis; and (3) gaps. The findings will include a summary of all interviews and meetings that occurred to discuss how patching is being completed today as well as a list of systems being patched on a regular basis and their details. It can also include a list of systems (or list of departments whose systems) are not being patched on a regular basis. For example, perhaps IT is performing patching in its internal IT systems on a regular basis through a defined process. This would be included in the report. If vendors are used throughout the environment and they are responsible for their systems and the patching of those systems, they would be included in the report as well. Whether it is listed by vendor or is system specific, being able to identify which systems are not being patched regularly will help in designing a new or modified patch management process. An analysis section then summarizes the findings and how patching is being completed today. A gap analysis shows, if possible, where gaps exist in the process today and even identifies areas where improvements or requirements must be defined. This assessment report will be key moving forward—not only through the rest of the planning phase and in the design phase but also to compare with another assessment once the patch management process has been fully integrated.

Determine Requirements

Once the current state of the patch management process has been assessed or established, it is time for the organization to determine what the requirements are moving forward. The second task within the planning phase is to document the requirements that the organization must meet to consider the patch management process a success. Gathering the requirements during the planning phase is typically accomplished through the following means:

- Gather the process stakeholders together to document what the patch management process needs to include.
- List the importance of the requirements, by need, want, and nice-to-have.
- Document the requirements that will be used later in the process creation and implementation.

Depending on the size of the organization, this step can be completed in one meeting, or it may take several meetings. Sometimes, just identifying the process stakeholders can be a daunting task. The stakeholders should include anyone that will own a piece of the process or will be affected by the process. Executive management can also be considered a stakeholder, especially if it is supporting the process or driving the individual groups to develop one collaboratively. Therefore, the stakeholders should consist of a group of individuals not only responsible for planning, designing, and implementing the process but also for operating and maintaining the process. Department managers or heads of business units should also have a say because, chances are, their systems will be patched using this same process. All should have the option to voice their opinions and requirements for the upcoming process. Of course, gathering all these individuals in the same room to conduct the meeting can be just as difficult as defining them. Separate meetings can be held for department managers and IT staff to get a clear understanding of what is required for the organization moving forward.

During these meetings, the stakeholders should first document what they feel is a requirement for the patch management process. Of course, once the brainstorming is complete, the ideas should be formulated into a more structured manner and can fall into three categories: (1) need; (2) want; and (3) nice to have. Some requirements may not be appropriate for the organization, or they may be long-term goals; depending on where they fit into the needs of the organization at that time, the requirements should be divided into these groups. Once the initial discussions have been completed and the requirements have been broken down into the three groups, they should then be compiled into one requirements document. This document is used not only in the design phase but also in the operating and maintaining phase to ensure that the organization has achieved what it set out to do with the patch management process. The documented set of requirements is used to measure the level of progress from the current process, the requirements set forth by the participating members, and the final process to be implemented. It may not be possible to implement all the requirements for various reasons such as budgeting constraints and interoperability; however, a road map can be established to meet those requirements in the short- and long-term.

At this point, the organization should begin to think about the mechanism that will be used to identify all its systems or, at a minimum, those that will be part of the patch management process. The process may look to include only the desktops within the patch management process; therefore, all desktops within the organization should be inventoried, including operating systems, applications, and services required for the individuals using them. Depending on what was identified during the assessment of the current patching process, there may be a tool or mechanism in use today that can be leveraged either for the short- or long-term. The actual task of gathering the inventory is not completed at this point; instead, it will be completed during the implementation phase. However, the organization should keep this in mind while planning and designing the patch management process because asset management plays an integral part in ensuring that all the systems affected by the vulnerability are patched appropriately.

Performing the Gap Analysis

Once an assessment has been completed to determine what state the organization is in today and the requirements have been documented on what the organization is trying to achieve, the final task in the planning phase is to perform a gap analysis against the systems included in the patch management process. The purpose of this task is to determine what state each system is in and to plan for bringing them up to the minimum state required. If patch management has been done ad hoc throughout the organization, then the systems may be at different patch levels. In most cases, there are patch dependencies to evaluate prior to the installation of a new patch. For this reason, every system included in the patch management process must be brought up to a minimum level.

Standard builds and baseline configurations were discussed in a previous chapter and are the result of the gap analysis completed against the systems. The patches to be installed on the systems prior to including them in the patch management process should be determined with a road map in place to update them. This can be done in tandem with putting the rest of the patch management process in place. However, the systems should be separated from the overall process until they have been brought up to speed. This can make for a management nightmare, and one solution to address this issue is to go back a certain number of patches to ensure that they can all be updated prior to moving forward. For example, Microsoft issues its patches the second Tuesday of every month. If July's patches have just been released, the organization may wish to start the patch management process with March's patches to guarantee that all the affected systems have been updated appropriately. It is recommended to start with patches that were released a few months prior to build up to where they should be today. While the organization will be a few months behind, once the process is in place it will take only a short while to bring all systems up to date.

The tracking used during the patch management process will make certain that all vulnerable systems have been patched appropriately and all are at the same patch level. This will avoid the risk of an exploit having an impact on the organization once the patch management process is in place. The ability to report on the status of systems and the patches to be installed on them will provide the security committee with the status of each system and how the threat has been mitigated against it. One of the key factors in the success of the patch management process is the ability to track and report on the status of installation of all patches across, at a minimum, all mission-critical systems.

Once the assessment of the current process has been completed and the requirements for the new process have been clearly defined and documented, the organization can begin the design phase of implementing the patch management process into its environment.

Designing the Process

Once the organization has gone through the proper planning phase steps, it can begin to design a patch management process tailored to fit its needs and requirements. Designing the "perfect" patch management process is different from designing one that can be well integrated into the organization as it exists today. A surplus of resources is available that defines patch management processes and provides great examples on how it should work in an organization. While these are all great examples, the organization must look at itself and ensure that the process it wants to integrate will actually work within the boundaries of the organization's environment. That is not to say that an organization should not look at all of its options and guarantee due diligence by trying to analyze all the recommended implementations. It just means that an organization should not think of a patch management process as a "cut-and-paste" from a Web site—it must be tailored appropriately to the organization's specific environment.

By this stage, the patch management security committee or, at a minimum, a small team of individuals who will be an integral part of the patch management process should be established. This group should be the same individuals who were responsible for the planning phase or at least who were involved in it. To take a step back, one group of individuals drives this project, whether it is from the perspective of a project sponsor, of budgeting, or even of the group responsible for implementing it. It may also be an outside consulting company that has come in to establish the patch management process in house for the organization. Regardless of the case, the identified group of individuals is responsible for designing the patch management process—that is, putting it down on paper—and also for all phases of putting the process in place, unless of course it would turn it over to operations personnel to implement and operate.

The previous chapters discussed what should be included in the design of a patch management process. To avoid repetition, it is recommended that organizations review the previous sections carefully to determine how the process should be designed to fit their environments appropriately. As previously stated, industry best practices should also be considered when designing the process. However, the details of the process should be carefully analyzed to ensure it will fit well into the organization's environment.

One additional step should be considered in the design phase. The following section details how an organization should assess the network devices and the systems within the environment to map them according to importance. In some instances, this may have been completed during a risk analysis or compliance requirements or for a disaster recovery or business continuity plan. If an organization has not completed it, the following section outlines how it should be done prior to moving to the next phase in implementing the process in the organization.

Assessing Network Devices and Systems

During the design phase, the organization must assess its network devices and systems that will be included in the patch management process. This is an important step that must not be overlooked. The organization must take a close look at its inventory and map all devices and systems according to their importance or criticality. The security committee should complete the following steps in this task within the design phase:

1. Determine operating systems that exist within the organization's environment.
2. Determine patch levels currently installed on all network devices and systems that will be included in the patch management process.
3. Determine the baseline at which all network devices and systems need to be for a minimum level.
4. Accurately identify all assets that will be part of the patch management process and a procedure for adding additional network devices and systems into the process as they are rolled out within the organization.

Typically, a baseline is the configuration of a product or system that is established at a specific point in time. An application or software baseline, for example, provides the ability to rebuild a computer to a specific state. It might be necessary to set up baselines for different software applications, hardware vendors, or types of computers. In the patch management process, a baseline is referred to as the minimum number of patches required to be installed on a specific device or system.

Before an organization can set a baseline requirement, an inventory of the network devices and systems must be completed. Depending on the patch management process the organization had in place, patches may have been applied inconsistently throughout the organization. There may also be little or no documentation to support the reasoning behind the inconsistency or the method to which the patches were applied in the first place. To create an accurate baseline, the organization must answer the following questions accurately:

- *Operating systems:* Which operating systems and which versions are present in the environment?
- *Software:* Which specific software programs and related versions are in use in the environment?
- *Compatibility:* Are there any limitations regarding the software and which operating system versions it will function on?

- *Patches:* Which service pack versions, software updates, and configuration changes, such as registry modifications, are present in the environment?
- *Contact information:* How can the persons involved in the patch management process contact the individuals or groups who are responsible for maintaining each system in the environment?
- *Countermeasures:* Which countermeasures to address security vulnerabilities have been deployed in the environment?
- *Assets:* Which hardware and software assets exist in the environment, and what is their relative value?

The organization will need to map the patch management process to the systems based on their category or value. To assist organizations in determining which patches are relevant as well as which systems should be updated first, the organization can create categories for its devices and systems based on their function and criticality. Once the categories have been determined and the systems placed in their appropriate category, monitoring and implementation can occur at a smooth pace. The number of categories an organization chooses to implement is not relevant; whether it is 5 or 20, the proper categorization will assist the organization in testing and deploying the patches to each category.

Implementation Phase

Of course, things always look better on paper than in real life. Now is when the truth comes out because it is time to implement the process into the environment. At this point, it should come as no surprise that this is a requirement for the organization moving forward. Completing the implementation phase should be a matter of publishing the documented process, implementing the tool of choice, beginning a pilot within the organization, and then rolling out the process into full production. While not mentioned, this also includes publishing and training the operations personnel on the standard operating procedures that have been created to support the process.

It is at this stage where having an accurate and up-to-date inventory of the organization's environment is most critical. Once the organization has properly defined and documented the patch management process, no systems that are vulnerable can be overlooked when it comes to patching them. This is why having the inventory in place and leveraging it to track the installation of the patches is so important. If one system is missed because it was not included in the inventory and a virus, worm, or other malicious activity spawns because of this, the process will be seen as flawed, or lacking, and less likely to be followed.

In this section, the following tasks to be completed in the implementation phase are discussed in detail:

- Standard build
- Implementing the tool
- Piloting the process
- Moving the process into production
- Updating the design

Of all the phases of putting the patch management process in place, actually implementing the process is the most complex and time-consuming task. However, if the planning and design phases are not done thoroughly, then the organization might not get through the implementation phase without having to go back and make major updates to the design of the process. This step often has to be performed, but it is better to make an update based on fine-tuning requirements than on a major flaw in the process itself.

Standard Build

One item to note and one that might be overlooked by the organization is whether it deploys and enforces a standard build within its environment. Standard builds are most common on desktops and thus are less common for servers, because servers tend to accomplish various tasks, making a standard build more difficult to implement and enforce.

This is an important aspect to consider prior to implementing a patch management process within the organization, more so when it comes to patching desktops. If no standard build is in place for all its desktops and various operating systems are using multiple applications, an organization might choose to complete this task first prior to implementing the process on the desktops. Therefore, the first step before even implementing the patch management process might be to develop a road map for the desktops so that these systems can be brought up to the baseline level and then to tie them into the patch management process. While this can be a major setback for the organization, it will make the inventory, success, and effectiveness of the patch management process that much better once a standard build has been deployed on all desktops.

The reason for this is that desktops may not be able to comply with the patch management process if they are not at a minimum (baseline) level. There are instances where previous patches must be installed before a later patch can be put on an operating system. While this holds true for servers, it also applies to desktops, especially when it comes to service packs and application updates that are used by the desktops. Organizations have many options to address the lack of a standard build for their desktops. In some cases, they may be in the process of rolling out a standard build. In addition, if the tool of choice requires that an agent be installed on the desktop, this may be the driving force for implementing a standard build throughout the organization. Therefore, organizations may choose a phased approach to roll out not only the patch management process but also the standard build. While this item should have been discovered in the planning phase of implementing the patch management process, it should be addressed prior to implementing it.

In the case of servers and standard builds, this may take more time and consideration prior to implementing them throughout the environment. In certain cases, the organization may have a minimum build requirement for each server prior to placing it into production. In other cases, the organization may require that the server be thoroughly tested prior to placing it into production, thus ensuring that it does not impose any risks on the organization. In either case, some form of standard build requirements should be set for servers, regardless of the operating systems running on them. While some modifications may be required depending on the business purpose, some restrictions and minimum baseline requirements should be established. If the organization plans to deploy an agent on the servers to install the patches, each server would need to be evaluated to determine whether it meets the minimum baseline requirements. If the server does not, a road map for bringing them up to the baseline minimum can be set up as an ongoing task, again implementing the patch management process on the servers in a more phased approach.

Implement the Tool

There has been a lot of discussion up to this point about issuing a tool into the environment to assist both in inventory management and in patch deployment onto the vulnerable systems. By the implementation phase, the chosen tool should have been determined with plans in place not only to purchase it but also to begin to implement it within the environment. There are three different instances of using a tool: the organization will purchase a new tool, leverage an existing tool, or leverage an existing tool with the purchase of an additional module for the product suite already in use.

In the case where the organization has chosen to purchase a new tool to assist in the deployment of patches, steps must be taken to ensure that it meets the organization's needs. Prior to purchasing the tools, most vendors will permit an organization to determine its feasibility through either a pilot phase or a trial version of a software license. These precautions should be taken to guarantee that the tool chosen will actually meet the requirements defined in the planning phase of implementing the patch management process. Having determined that the tool does fit its needs and requirements, it is recommended that the organization take the necessary steps to purchase the tool and to begin to implement the appropriate infrastructure to support it. The group responsible for the day-to-day operations of the tool or piece of software and corresponding hardware needs to be trained. In many cases, vendors offer training on their software to ensure that it can be supported appropriately. If it is determined that the tool does not meet the requirements, then the organization must go back and evaluate other software products to find a more suitable tool for its environment. The process for testing and acquiring the tool then restarts from the beginning.

In the case where the organization has chosen to leverage an existing tool, fewer pre-piloting tasks are required. The organization will already have purchased the tool and the supporting infrastructure to operate the tool already in place. This also cuts down on the training of the group to operate the tool on a daily basis because it is already integrated into the environment. Minor modifications may need to be made to the configuration of the tool compared with how it is used today, but these should be only minor, with no impact on business operations. Once the piloting begins, the organization may determine that it cannot leverage an existing tool due to incompatibility or to the lack of the ability for the tool to deploy the patches in the manner required. If this is the case, the organization must go back to the design phase and, based on the requirements, evaluate other tools to see which would be the best fit for the organization.

In the case where the organization has chosen to leverage an existing tool but needs to purchase an additional module for the product suite, the same would apply as if the organization was purchasing a new tool. While most of the costs would be absorbed through the main license agreement, a separate purchasing requirement may be needed to get the functionality required from the additional module. The same would hold true with this option as with the new tool in which the organization must ensure that it will meet the requirements defined in the planning phase on what it must accomplish for it to be deemed appropriate to the organization's needs. Prior to purchasing this module, the vendor may give the organization a chance to pilot the tool, thus ensuring that it meets the requirements prior to purchase. Once the organization has determined that it does, the organization should take the appropriate steps to purchase the tool and to establish the appropriate infrastructure to run it accordingly. The operations staff must also be trained on the additional module; while overall knowledge of the tool is understood, it will be necessary to be aware of additional features to support it appropriately on a day-to-day basis.

Regardless of which case the organization has chosen to follow, once the tool has been put in place, with the appropriate infrastructure and trained personnel, the following steps will apply. Implementing the tool can be a daunting task because it must meet certain requirements determined by the organization. The first choice in the tool selection may not be the right one; therefore, due diligence should be taken when evaluating which tools to use. In the chapter dedicated to discussing tools, the criteria for determining which tool is best should be followed by the organization to make the right choice the first time. If the organization must reevaluate tools and retrace their purchasing and testing steps, it can affect the time frame needed to implement the patch management process within the organization or can halt the process if the process is already in place before it is realized the right tool was not implemented.

Piloting the Process

Now that the tool is in place, it is time to start a pilot phase of the process itself. As with a planned implementation, it is considered best practice to do a pilot to ensure that the process functions are defined within the organization. Also during the piloting phase, the organization will notice any discrepancies between the documented process and how the process actually functions and can pinpoint any modifications that need to be made the process itself.

The organization should plan to pilot the process in small, manageable-sized pieces. For example, on the desktop side, the pilot should include 10% of the total desktops within the organization. This is only a small amount, but if the first 10% goes through the process with no issues, then an additional 10% of the desktops can be included in the piloting phase. This would make a total of 20% of the desktops included in the piloting phase. This number is kept relatively small to make certain that if any issues arise the piloting can be backed out with minimal disruption to the desktops until such issues can be resolved. Completing the pilot in small chunks allows the new process to be more easily managed and ensures that desktop users are not disrupted by the implementation of the new process. Tools that use an agent on the desktops should be installed on the pilot systems in a phased approach. If there is no standard desktop build and the organization chooses to not implement a standard build, then there is no accurate way to test the agent to guarantee that it will function properly with the various desktop configurations within the organization's environment. This is why it is important to incorporate a standard build within the organization, as it will also aid in the success and timeliness of the piloting phase.

On servers, piloting will take a different approach. Within the organization, systems are typically rating-protected depending on their business purpose. Obviously, the piloting phase would not include testing the process on mission-critical systems unless the process has been tested in a lab environment and then on nonbusiness-critical systems. If the organization decides to pilot the patch management process in a lab environment, it must ensure that the servers in the lab are configured in the exact same manner as those in production. Typically, weaker security controls are implemented on lab servers than on ones in production, which can have a drastic effect on the production server once it has been incorporated into the patch management process. The organization should pilot the process on nonbusiness-critical servers in production only after having done so on the lab systems. Once these nonbusiness-critical servers have been piloted, then a small sampling of business-critical systems should be piloted. Again, the total number of servers included in the piloting phase should be 10%, ranging from lab to nonbusiness critical and then moving to business critical. This will give the organization an accurate summary of how well the patch management process can be integrated into the entire organization's infrastructure.

Another task in the piloting of the process that warrants note is the level of collaboration required from individuals not only in the security committee and in the predefined responsible groups but also extending out to users and system administrators. Since the patch management process covers all devices and systems within an organization, it must be carefully executed to make sure that service is not disrupted, not only during piloting but also when the process is rolled out to full production. All kinks should have been worked out during piloting so that when the process goes into full-blown production no speed bumps hinder progress.

In the planning phase, as part of the requirements defined, a measure to determine how the piloting phase will be considered successful should be established. The security committee will have the ultimate decision of determining whether the pilot is a success or if it needs to go back to the design phase and undergo some changes. This can also result in another pilot being required. The measures by which the piloting phase is deemed successful can be based on specific metrics or just through a final piloting phase report that outlines the steps completed and the results of each. If there is an 85% or higher success rate with the piloting phase, the security committee can then make the decision to move the process into production.

Moving the Process into Production

The patch management process has been documented, the tool has been implemented, and the piloting phase has been deemed a success. The security committee now must make the decision to move the process into production, incorporating all systems previously defined as being included in the patch management process. As the process affects all users from a desktop perspective and various administrators from a server perspective, communication regarding the process must be provided in a clear, concise manner. In some instances, the organization may have a thorough and well-executed security awareness and training program, in which case a module on patch management and how the organization will address this moving forward should be provided to the entire user population. It is very important to communicate to the user population, mainly from a desktop perspective, what the organization is doing to address the implementation of patches on the desktops and what the users' responsibilities are in regard to complying with the process. In some instances, users may not have any influence, and in some cases they may be required to interact or even reboot their desktops once the patch is installed. Whatever the situation is, they must clearly understand and agree to the process, assuming accountability if they make any changes to their desktops that negatively affect the patch management process. If the organization does not have a standard security awareness and training program in place, communication regarding the patch management process can take other forms, such as an e-mail, a newsletter, or even posters positioned throughout the facility. The method of communication is not relevant; instead, the point must get across what the organization is doing and what users' responsibilities are. The organization can even go a step further and require all users to read and agree to the patch management policy stating that they understand the process, that they agree to comply with the process, and, if appropriate, that they assume accountability.

Once the patch management process has been communicated to the general user population and all those responsible for the process itself, the organization can formally "kick off" the process into production. While this still should be done in a phased approach, the communication should be completed at once. The piloting phase showed that

20% of the desktops were able to adhere and follow the patch management process with no issues, including the use of the tool. Now it is time to roll out the process to another 20% of the desktops, based on a predefined schedule, to ensure that if any issues arise only a small number of desktops are affected at any one time. The same holds true for the servers: they should slowly be migrated into the patch management process, especially if an agent-based tool has been implemented on them. This allows for careful planning to occur prior to installing the agent on the system and also when the patches are being deployed onto the server, as they are required.

In instances where the organization has decided to implement a standard desktop build throughout its environment, the phased approach can be aligned with the roll-out of the standard builds. This would force the phased approach to be taken because only a percentage of systems would be updated in a week's time, thus ensuring they are established in the process appropriately and then moving on to the next set of desktops to be updated. While this will take longer to put the process in place throughout the organization—depending on the size and number of desktops—this is a more cautious approach and will result in a successful implementation of the patch management process on the desktops.

The security group is responsible for monitoring the process as it moves into production. While not responsible for all the steps of putting it into production, this group should be provided with regular updates from the operations group to track its progress. Then, on a weekly or even biweekly basis, depending on the speed at which the process is moving into production, the security group would roll up the progress into one report and present this information to the security committee. While the members of the security committee are part of team of individuals implementing the process into the environment, having one status report of the progress coming from the security group makes the success of the implementation easier to track. During the requirements gathering that occurred in the planning phase, the security committee would again need to set parameters stating when they would determine the process is in full production and the organization can go into operate mode. These can be simple matrices, such as the percentage of systems complete after a certain period of time.

There are many steps in the implementation of the patch management process and even within putting the process in place, including pre- and postimplementation steps. This is not a process that can be implemented on an ad hoc or short-term basis. Organizations must follow all steps to guarantee not only that the process is successful and accurate but also that it can be scaled as necessary as the organization grows in size and systems. It is very difficult to estimate how long it would take for an organization to follow through on all the steps required to put the process in place. There are too many variances as far as size of organizations and where they are currently regarding completing patch management to accurately state how long it will take in days, weeks, or months to go through all of these steps. It is estimated that a successful patch management process can be implemented within 3–6 months' time. Again, this is dependent on the size of the organization, and what tasks in the creation process are already in place. As with any project or task the organization is trying to achieve, a standard project plan should be developed identifying milestones throughout to track how the project is flowing and whether it is meeting the estimated dates for completion. This is another task that should be completed during the planning phase, or even prior to getting started, to assist the organization in measuring the success of the project and then the success of the patch management process.

Update Design Based on Implementation

Once the security committee has accepted the patch management process as being in full production mode, some clean-up activities should take place prior to moving into operating mode. One of the main clean-up tasks that the security committee must complete involves updating the patch management process design to accurately reflect what was implemented. In some situations, once the organization begins implementing the process it realizes, for various reasons, that it cannot achieve this according to how it was designed. This commonly occurs because things look better on paper than in real life. The final task within the implementation phase must be to go back and update the design document, as well as all supporting patch management process documentation, to ensure that what is documented matches accurately with what has been put in place within the organization.

The updates of all the patch management process supporting documentation is a task for the security committee to complete. Updates and information from all individuals involved in putting the patch management process in place should be taken into consideration for the updates. Also, all documentation that is submitted to the security group and operations group in the operate phase must accurately reflect what is in place today and not what was planned for. This is a short task and should not consume a large amount of time. It is only a matter of documenting the changes in design during implementation and the updating of all the supporting documentation pertaining to the process. It should really take no longer than 2–3 weeks to complete this task.

When the documentation is updated, it also provides the security committee with the opportunity to go back to the requirements document that was defined, noting the gaps on what was determined to be a requirement and what was actually implemented. These will be reviewed in more detail during the maintaining phase but should be analyzed at this phase of the process implementation as well.

Operating the Process

Now that the organization has established the process throughout the environment, it needs to operate as it is been designed. This can be the most daunting task of the process. Planning, designing, and implementing may seem like a struggle, but it is during the operate phase that push comes to shove and the patch management process must function accurately.

It is during the operate phase that the responsibilities of the patch management process must be clearly defined and documented. While the roles and responsibilities were discussed in a previous chapter, these must be explicitly defined not only to achieve accountability but also to ensure the effectiveness of the process itself. Within the operate phase of the patch management process, the security committee as well as the security group, operations group, and any other groups involved or included hold responsibility. An organization's infrastructure can change rapidly, and patch releases occur frequently; therefore, all groups must remain up to date on the occurrences both internal and external to the organization. When a patch is released and the process needs to be initiated, there should be a clear level of communication and understanding of how the process flows through each phase, making certain that patches are installed on the vulnerable systems in the time frame determined. Issues with the flow of the process in the organization should be documented and addressed in the next phase—maintaining the process.

Another item to keep in mind is how the organization will track the successfulness of the process. In some situations it may be measured in terms of the time it takes to implement the patches on the affected systems. In other cases, it may be measured by whether a virus or worm can still make it into the organization's network. Regardless of what the organization will use to track the successfulness of the patch management process, a mechanism for doing so must be implemented during this phase. These results will also be used in the next phase, the maintenance phase, to assist in determining what needs to be changed (or improved) in the process to remediate any issues that have been defined with the successfulness of the process.

Several tasks occur during the operate phase of putting the process in place. Of course, this will be an ongoing phase and is considered one of the organization's standard operating procedures. However, the tasks can be broken down into the following high-level areas:

- Integration into existing processes
- Updating standard builds
- Implementation of new servers into the environment
- Day-to-day operations with the tool
- Deployment of patches

Integration into Existing Processes

Depending on the security and vulnerability management processes in place within the organization, integration of the patch management process into these may need to occur. Processes such as change, configuration, release, and vulnerability management may exist. This can be a difficult task to complete because it depends on what state the organization is in when it has established the patch management process.

As an example, assume that, at a minimum, the organization has a change and vulnerability management process already in place. While asset management is very important to ensure success of the patches actually being deployed on all vulnerable systems, this process is left out for the purpose of this example. The assumption will be that the organization has a method in place to collect the inventory and to accurately determine which systems are vulnerable. During the design of the patch management process, the standard operating procedures must be considered to guarantee that the process fits into other processes while it is put into production. If a network operating center (NOC) maintains the change and configuration management processes, then its input into the design would be required. Because patch management will initialize these other two processes, minimal actual integration is required. A standard operating procedure for determining at which stage these processes are called out would need to be documented in the patch management process itself, but no major changes to the other two should occur as a result.

Asset management would require similar integration. When the patch is released, the organization must be able to determine in a short time frame whether it is susceptible (i.e., if any systems are vulnerable). This would require access to the asset management database or tool to be able to search for the operating system or application to which that patch applies. Therefore, a method for calling the asset management process should be incorporated into the patch management process documentation. No major changes to the asset management process would be required—just the fact that patch management may spawn this other process when a patch is released.

When it comes to security management and vulnerability management, more modifications or adjustments should be established when patch management is put into production. Because vulnerability management is a much larger process—of which patch management is a part—establishment of the two can be done either in conjunction with one another or separately. Whether vulnerability management is in place, the organization must take its existence into consideration during the design of the patch management process.

Updating Standard Builds

While the topic of standard builds was discussed in previous sections, it does not stop once the process has been implemented. Depending on the organization's stance on this topic, the ongoing deployment of standard builds may roll into the operate phase of the overall patch management process. If the organization needs to begin a separate project that entails deploying standard builds on the desktops throughout the environment, then as they are updated the NOC will need to be informed to ensure that these new desktops are included in the patch management process, namely, that they would get the patches deployed on them as needed.

It is necessary to have in place a mechanism for the security group to inform the operations group when a newly released patch should be integrated into the upcoming standard build release. This will make certain that as patches are released it ties back to the standard build and is updated appropriately. Another chapter discusses standard builds from this perspective and should be referenced for more detailed information.

Any new desktops added to the environment must also get the standard build; if the standard build has not been updated with all the new patches released since its existence, then those desktops should be updated with those patches prior to placing it in production. This is an effort taken on by the operations group, or the desktop group if such exists, in conjunction with the security group to make certain that it has been added to the patch management process properly.

Implementation of New Servers

When new servers are added to the environment, they too must go through the formal process for deploying a new system but must also be added to the company's inventory management and patch management programs. This ensures that new servers are not overlooked as they are added and are patched appropriately as needed. Depending on the tool used for inventory management, the applications running on the server must be included in the inventory management database to guarantee that as patches are released this system is taken into consideration while completing the initial assessment of the patch and determination on whether the organization is susceptible to it.

A member of the security committee should be on the team that monitors and approves all new servers being implemented in the organization's environment. If the organization does not have a formal review process for implementing new servers, then the new server must go through the security committee to ensure that it will be included in the process and protected from vulnerabilities.

Day-to-Day Tool Operations

There are also day-to-day operational tasks within the tool used to do inventory management and patch management. For the purpose of the operate phase, the tool used to deploy the patches will be discussed. It is not relevant whether the organization purchased a new tool, leveraged an existing tool, or added an additional module to an existing software suite; day-to-day operations still exist for any software tool integrated into the organization's infrastructure, especially from a support perspective.

Simple operating procedures will need to take place on the system that deploys the patches to the vulnerable systems. This includes daily backups of the system that align with the organization's overall backup procedures. The software on the system must also be upgraded as appropriate with the new release of updated software. This needs to be not only scheduled within the NOC but also approved by the security committee, because it has the potential to affect the organization's overall patch management process. There are also the security controls surrounding the system itself. One example would be the establishment of access controls. The controls implemented on this tool should align with the organization's security policy and overall access control policy. Only individuals who require access to the system to accomplish a legitimate task should have access rights. This should be no different from any other support system within the organization. Finally, the final approval for the deployment of patches onto the vulnerable systems needs to be determined. A procedure for pushing out the patches must be enforced to make sure that not just any individual can walk up to the system and begin pushing out patches without obtaining formal approval.

The actual patch deployment and scheduling of such must comply with the organization's overall change management procedures. A change management window must be established so that business operations are not disrupted due to pushing out patches that have not been tested thoroughly. All of these items should be documented and communicated to the NOC personnel and the security committee to make sure the tool itself is protected properly and does not introduce any additional risk into the environment.

Deployment of Patches

The final task within the operate phase is the actual deployment of patches to the vulnerable systems. This is not completed just by pressing a button on the systems containing the patch deployment tool and walking away. As much due diligence should be taken when patches are deployed as was taken throughout the entire process. This step can also affect the success of the process moving forward. If a patch is deployed on a server that has an ill effect, causing an interruption of business operations, then the chance that the security committee will lose its executive management support runs high. Once executive management ceases to support the process, the chances of it being successful within the organization drastically decrease.

It is for this reason that the deployment of patches is performed in a staged manner, complying with the organization's change management process along the way. Due diligence should be taken for patching both the desktops and the servers. The desktops should be approached in a group manner, updating one group at a time, ensuring that no issues surface because of the patch. This also reduces the load on the organization's help desk. If all the desktops are patched at once, chances are that the help desk will be swamped with calls from various users with no way to efficiently remediate all of their issues. Although patching in a staged manner lengthens the time for deployment, it elevates many issues that can surface due to the patch. Once one group of desktops has been completed, the NOC can deploy patches to another group of desktops and then repeat this until all desktops have been patched appropriately. A method for tracking and reporting the success of the patch deployment would be to send a report to the NOC that it has been completed, which would be passed along to the security group for further analysis.

The patching of the servers takes on a slightly different method. While the desktops will be patched according to department (e.g., IT first, then help desk personnel, then human resources), the servers are patched according to their criticality. Within the inventory management database, the NOC should have a list of servers within the environment and their level of criticality. This is then sorted by vulnerable systems to ensure that the least critical servers are patched first, moving up the line until the most critical servers are patched. This is also where the testing aspect comes into play, because the business-critical systems should have the patch thoroughly tested prior to it being applied. In addition, the NOC's change management process must be followed because most, if not all, of the servers would not be able to be rebooted (if required) until after hours or during the change management window.

How the systems, regardless whether they are desktops or servers, are patched is determined and documented in the design of the patch management process. There should be a clear understanding of the process to be followed when it is time for the NOC to deploy a patch. Of course, the NOC does not maintain all the responsibility for deploying the patches. The operations group must be closely involved in this process because if the patch causes an issue on the systems the operations group must be able to remediate it in a very short time frame. Through proper documentation and a clear understanding of roles and responsibilities, the patch management process can function smoothly, regardless of the size of the organization and the number of desktops and servers within its environment.

Maintain

The maintain phase of implementing the patch management process is not a one-time occurrence; it is similar to the operate phase in that it is ongoing. As with any successful process, it must be maintained on a regular basis. This includes a review of the process and how it is functioning, along with any supporting documentation. These aspects must be regularly reviewed and revised not only as necessary but also on a regularly scheduled basis. Review includes the patch management process, including documentation, any supporting procedures, and the patch management policy. The security committee is responsible for conducting the annual review, noting any changes to what is actually occurring and how the documentation states it should be occurring. The security committee would then request the appropriate changes, vote on them, and make them as agreed upon. All groups responsible for the process would then be reeducated on the updates that were made—not only to the process but also to the supporting documentation. Each time a change or modification is made to the process, those responsible for operating against the patch management process must be told what is expected of them now.

The patch management process should be reviewed when the following incidents occur:

- Organizational structure changes
- Operational changes
- Purchase of new or additional tool
- Annual basis

This is also where the requirements defined during the planning phase can be matched against what was actually put in place. As discussed, there are instances where a requirement cannot be met due to a budget or interoperability constraint. A process in the maintain phase is to document the gaps between the requirements and the actual process. A road map for bridging the gaps should also be established so that the organization can plan for the future. This can be based on short- and long-term goals, depending on the complexity of each, and the needs of the organization. Not all requirements can be implemented within the organization; for example, with the nice-to-haves, these may not be feasible for the organization in the short- and long-term. Additional requirements may also surface that need to be considered for the patch management process as the process goes through its life cycle and over a period of time. These requirements would be added to the original requirements document as an appendix, with each one being revisited each time the process is reviewed.

Organizational Structure Changes

There are instances where the organizational structure of a company changes, due to a merger, acquisition, or even downsizing or growth within the company. If the roles defined in the patch management process change, the process must be refined to take these changes into consideration. Names of individuals should not be explicitly stated in any of the patch management process documentation. This makes updates more frequent and difficult to track. The responsibilities defined within the patch management process should be based on the role, or title, of the position responsible for accomplishing the tasks and not the name of the specific person involved.

If there is a major change in the way the organization is structured (perhaps the operations group is divided into three separate groups as discussed: server, desktop, and network infrastructure), then the process should be reevaluated, defining these responsibilities at a more granular level.

Operational Changes

The patch management process may need to be reevaluated if there are any operational changes in the company, including a network infrastructure modification, such as the addition of a demilitarized zone (DMZ), or an entirely new network addition to the existing one. An operational change can also include any type of Internet Protocol (IP) address restructuring or modification or anything that would affect the deployment of patches to the defined systems. While these may not be changes that affect the patch management process directly, they do warrant a review of the process to ensure that it will still function as defined once the changes have been made.

Other operational changes can include the introduction of a new process within the organization or even new compliance requirements. These operational changes are provided as examples, and the organization should use its best judgment to determine what is and is not an operational change that warrants a review of the patch management process. In some cases, the operational change will not affect the process; however, the security committee should make that determination once it has received the relevant details. While these changes should not result in any major revisions to the patch management process, it makes certain that once these operational changes are put in place the process will continue to function accurately, efficiently, and effectively.

Purchase of New or Additional Tool

During the planning phase of putting the process in place, an organization might determine that a tool to assist in deploying patches is not necessary or required. It might attempt to put the process into production and operate it manually until a tool can be thoroughly tested and evaluated. Once the process has been in existence for a period of time, the organization may come to realize that a tool is required to deploy the patches to the vulnerable systems in a timely manner and to assist in ensuring that all vulnerable systems have been patched appropriately. Once the tool is implemented into the organization, the patch management process must be reevaluated and updated to incorporate the use of the tool for the deployment of patches. Another option, which is not recommended, is that the organization may have used a trial version of software to get the process in place and then may have decided not to purchase it right away. To emphasize, this is not recommended, and an organization should not put a formal process in place using a trial or evaluation version of software. If, however, this has been done, then once the organization purchases the software the process should be reexamined to guarantee that it still functions as planned with the licensed version of software.

If during any reevaluation of the patch management process the organization determines that the tool in use is not feasible, a decision may have to be made to replace it. This, of course, would require an entire reevaluation of the process itself, including a possible redesign based on the new tool and how it will function. The organization may also be using the existing tool to do only patch deployment, requiring that inventory be done manually through the use of scanning and spreadsheets. At some point, the organization may decide to implement an inventory management tool to automate the inventory process and assist in maintaining an accurate and up-to-date inventory. Once this new tool has been implemented, the security committee should go back once again and reevaluate the process to ensure that any changes that must be made are implemented with the appropriate and updated supporting documentation.

Annual Basis

Finally, if none of the aforementioned changes are made within the organization, the patch management process should be reviewed on an annual basis. Although there have been no organizational, operational, or tool changes, it is still considered a best practice to review all processes annually to confirm their accuracy. During this review process, it may surface that certain steps within the process are not being performed or are not being performed accurately due to interoperability issues or just a lack of communication. Whichever the case may be, this is the time when the security committee can and should review the process and make determinations on what needs modification. The security committee is responsible for scheduling and overseeing the review process while it is occurring.

The review process should be incorporated into the patch management policy established for the organization. The following section discusses the patch management policy that includes incorporating a review schedule.

Patch Management Policy

As with any new process or procedure, a policy should be created to support it. This should be similar to other policies the organization has in place. For example, the organization should have not only an organizational security policy but also specific policies such as a firewall policy, e-mail retention policy, and acceptable use policy. Just as with any of these policies, a patch management policy should be created to state the organization's stance on patch management and what is enforced in its regard.

An organization should include the following attributes in its patch management policy:

- What the organization is trying to achieve
- The roles and responsibilities that have been defined in the process, including:

- The roles and groups, and what is expected of them
- High-level steps within the process
- The patch management process review schedule, including revisions and updates

A sample patch management policy is included in this section. Generally, an organization has a standard template or format that it uses when publishing a new policy. This same template should be used in creating the patch management policy. If an organization has a dedicated group responsible for all organizational security policies and procedures, a member from this group should work with the security committee to draft the patch management policy to ensure it adheres to the organization's standard format, approval process, and publishing procedures.

Various attributes are included in a policy and based on the organization's style and templates; the patch management policy should not deviate from the company standard. In the beginning of the policy, usually within the first paragraph, a few sentences should state what the organization is trying to achieve with patch management and why the integration of patch management into the organization assists in reducing the threats and risks to the organization's assets. This can be accomplished in only a few sentences and summarizes the objectives the organization is trying to achieve with this new process.

Once the process itself has been defined and documented, then the policy can be created. The roles and responsibilities defined within the process itself are stated in the policy. This will include the security committee's responsibilities and who makes up the security committee. No individual's names should be included in the policy; instead, titles or groups should be cited. The responsibilities of the security group, operations group, and NOC should be included in the policy, defining what their tasks are in the process to provide accountability for all roles involved in the process.

Because the policy is based on the process itself, the high-level steps of the patch management process should be included. Details regarding the process should not be completed, but from a high level the policy should reflect the process installed to provide compliance to the policy as the process is followed through each iteration. Because policies are typically two- to three-page documents or part of a larger document, no great detail should be provided; processes and procedures should instead be referenced.

Finally, at end of the policy, the process review schedule should be stated, dictating how frequently the process should be reviewed. This would also include the various changes that may occur within the organization that would call for a process review. Typically, the organization's overall security policy dictates the frequency with which all policies are reviewed and revised as necessary. If this is not the case, the policy should also state the frequency with which it is reviewed and revised as necessary. This should correspond with the review of the process itself. If the process requires a revision, then changes in the policy that support it will need to be reviewed and revised as well.

In the standard policy template, a section should include approval sign-off and the date it was approved. This allows for proper tracking of the policy and a method for retaining the documentation for the period of time determined by the organization. In some cases, regulations require an organization to maintain documentation for a period of time; to accurately track versions of policies, the date of approval and posting should be included in each revision. At the end of the policy, there is typically space allocated for definitions. The definitions section typically includes important terms used throughout the policy to make it clearer to the reader in case some topics are not known to all individuals. In some cases, the organization may have a central definition document that is used for all of its policies, or it may choose to include the applicable definitions in each policy. This, of course, is by preference of the organization and not a requirement.

What follows is a sample patch management policy that an organization may choose to implement when the patch management process is ready to go into full production.

PATCH MANAGEMENT POLICY

Overview of Policy

The patch management policy is a reflection of <COMPANY NAME>'s commitment to ensure the confidentiality, integrity, and availability of its information technology assets. <COMPANY NAME> will educate its workforce members about the patch management policy and the applicable supporting process to <COMPANY NAME> generally and to them in their individual roles. <COMPANY NAME> will implement the patch management process in accordance with its organizational process for policy development and review.

SCOPE

The patch management policy applies to <COMPANY NAME>'s employees who have a role and responsibility as it pertains to the patch management process. The patch management policy also pertains to <COMPANY NAME> systems that have been predefined in the patch management process.

PURPOSE

The purpose of this policy is to provide standards and guidelines for compliance and adherence to <COMPANY NAME>'s patch management process. These standards and guidelines are designed to minimize the potential exposure to <COMPANY NAME> from damages, which may result from unpatched systems. Damages include the loss of company confidential data, intellectual property, damage to public image, or damage to critical <COMPANY NAME> internal systems.

POLICY: PATCH MANAGEMENT

1. <COMPANY NAME> establishes and implements a patch management process to address the predefined requirements defined to protect <COMPANY NAME> from exploits due to vulnerabilities within unpatched systems.
2. <COMPANY NAME> designs its patch management process to take reasonable and appropriate steps to ensure the confidentiality, integrity, and availability of its information technology assets.
3. <COMPANY NAME> informs its workforce members about the patch management process and their responsibilities that apply to <COMPANY NAME> generally and to them in their individual roles.
4. <COMPANY NAME>'s patch management process takes into consideration:
   a. Size, complexity, and capabilities of <COMPANY NAME >
   b. <COMPANY NAME>'s technical infrastructure, hardware, and software capabilities
   c. Cost of implementing additional resources and tools
   d. Probability and criticality of risks to <COMPANY NAME>'s assets
5. <COMPANY NAME> performs periodic reviews of its patch management process and revises it as necessary.
6. <COMPANY NAME>'s security committee oversees and maintains the patch management process.

ENFORCEMENT

<COMPANY NAME> workforce members found to have violated this policy will be subject to disciplinary action, up to and including termination of employment and possible legal action.

Anyone who knows or has reason to believe that another person has violated this policy should report the matter promptly to his or her supervisor. All reported matters will be investigated, and, where appropriate, steps will be taken to remedy the situation. Where possible, <COMPANY NAME> will make every effort to handle the reported matter confidentially. Any attempt to retaliate against a person for reporting a violation of this policy will itself be considered a violation of this policy that may result in disciplinary action up to and including termination of employment or contract with <COMPANY NAME>.

REVIEW OF POLICY

In the event that a significant change occurs, the policy will be reviewed and updated as needed. The policy will be reviewed annually to determine its effectiveness in complying with the patch management process as it is defined and documented.

REVISION HISTORY

This document was created on 11-07-2003 and has been last updated on 06-15-2010.

Approved By:

Date:

DEFINITIONS

Availability: That data or information is accessible and usable upon demand by an authorized person.

Confidentiality: That data or information is not made available or disclosed to unauthorized persons or processes.

Information system: An interconnected set of information resources under the same direct management control that shares common functionality. A system normally includes hardware, software, information, data, applications, communications, and people.

Workforce member: Employees, volunteers, and other persons whose conduct, in the performance of work for a company, is under the direct control of such company, whether they are paid by said company. This includes full- and part-time employees, affiliates, associates, students, volunteers, and staff from third-party companies that provide service to the company.

11
CONCLUSION

Unfortunately, for all organizations, patch management is not going anywhere. It has been around since the release of the operating system and the use of applications. No release is ever the final release. Patch management has been getting publicity for a few years now. Organizations still are not prepared, and there is still a lack of implemented patches on systems. Attempts have been made to rely on a tool for all patch management needs, but this reliance is futile. Now organizations are again looking to update, modify, or implement a patch management process to protect its environment from the threat of an ever growing number of exploits. Sometimes, the most difficult hurdle is determining how to approach a patch management process.

Understanding that patch management is just a process, and nothing more should ease an organization's mind-set. It is not a complete rearchitecture of the environment, nor does it require a major organizational change. It does not require a separate budget to keep it functioning on an annual basis. However, it does require communication, collaboration, and a sense of understanding of what is expected from everyone in the organization to protect them from the vulnerabilities and exploits that result in the lack of patched systems. With the release of vulnerabilities today occurring at a rapid rate, it is better to address the vulnerability before an exploit is executed within the infrastructure. The patch management process will reduce the risk of a successful exploit. It should be looked at as a proactive measure instead of a reactive one. On the other hand, it is a security measure that an organization implements to improve its overall security posture.

When the organization decides to modify or implement a new patch management process, a substantial amount of time and dedication must be devoted in the planning and design phase to ensure a solid process has been defined and documented. This is why putting a security committee in place to oversee and maintain the process transfers the accountability of the process from one individual to a group of individuals to guarantee that no items are overlooked or systems unpatched. Of course, in smaller organizations, the security committee may actually be a single individual instead of a team, and the tasks may also be broken down and assigned to specific individuals instead of in a team atmosphere. While this is not a recommended practice, due to the size of the organization, this may be the only option. It is also important to remember that the security group maintains overall ownership of the process. This group has the responsibility of ensuring that the process is adhered to when each patch is released. Some other responsibilities include making certain that it is updated on a regular basis. If there is a break in the process, the security group must establish that with the next revision these issues are identified in the process and it is updated appropriately. The security group also has the responsibility of communicating the process to all individuals involved in the process as well as the general user community. The patch management policy will state what the organization is trying to achieve with patch management and that information needs to be communicated to the entire organization so that they understand what their part in the process entails.

Once the process has been put into production, the process cycle will begin to take on a smoother existence with each release of a security vulnerability (each time the process is gone through). Therefore, the organization may not see immediate gratification with the process in production, but over the course of the first 6 months a noticeable difference should be recognized in regard to getting each vulnerable system patched in the required time frame. The organization should be able to notice the reduction in manpower to get all systems patched appropriately, through the use not only of the process but also of the patch deployment tool. The underlying statement here is *patience*. Not all of an organization's patch management woes are going to be eliminated once a process has been documented. As with any new process or function being implemented, it takes time to get to an appropriate level of comfort. If the tasks are completed properly in the beginning (e.g., communication, training), then the transition time will be reduced. It is a common perception that implementing a tool is easier than implementing a process. Whether that is true depends on what is being put in place along with the tool. If it is a stand-alone tool that one person will manage, then, yes, that can be easier than completing all the tasks necessary in establishing a process. Processes are more difficult to implement than tools because people and technology are involved. Getting these three aspects aligned properly (*properly* is the key word here) is what takes time in getting the process to a state of smooth existence.

The common saying, "Use what works and what you can support," should be the driving force during the design of the patch management process. This book was developed to provide a guide to organizations on what a patch management process entails. This is from the perspective not only of the process itself but also of putting one in place and all the various aspects surrounding it. Organizations must consider and evaluate what they have in place to combat patch management and then what they are able to support moving forward. Implementing a complex patch management process in an organization that is small or lacking manpower can result in a process that is not performed accurately or efficiently. This can result in vulnerabilities continuing to rear their ugly heads throughout the infrastructure. The organization must consider what parts of the process it can do, what it can automate, and how it divides the responsibilities across various individuals to not overtask an already overworked individual or group of individuals. There are various degrees of patch management, and the organization must determine the degree to which it wishes to implement it to protect the environment.

The bottom line is that patch management is not going anywhere; organizations must learn to adapt to it and take care of it now, thus ensuring a vulnerability-free future. Patch management should be a standard operating procedure within the organization now and moving forward. There is no way around it, nor should it be avoided unless grave repercussions can be accepted by the organization. Just as there are security-focused individuals protecting organizations from threats, vulnerabilities, and risk, there are other individuals who thrive on releasing the next exploit that attacks an unpatched system.

Challenges

When trying to implement a patch management process, an organization will face numerous challenges. Some of the most common ones are explained in this section. Organizations will also encounter organization-specific challenges on their own, especially in an environment that is extremely political or decentralized.

The biggest challenge for any large, distributed organization is the basic discovery, identification, and standardization of operating systems and application images. This topic was raised in various sections of this book, stating the importance not only of having an accurate and up-to-date inventory of all the systems in the organization's environment but also of incorporating the use of standard builds for both the desktops and servers. Tackling this challenge in the early stages of planning in putting the patch management process in place will assist the organization in the long-term. While the initiative to create the process should not be stalled because of these roadblocks, instead, road maps for addressing these issues should be developed and worked in tandem. It is important to note that it is not the security committee's responsibility to implement these standard builds as part of putting the patch management process in place; the security committee holds the responsibility of overseeing and maintaining the patch management process. While some individuals that are part of the security committee may branch out and address this as well, it does not fall solely on the shoulders of the security committee.

Another more political challenge is gaining executive management support to install the patch management process. The executive management of an organization ultimately dictates the security posture that organization wishes to take. Security is communicated and enforced from the top down to the lower levels in an organization. Without their approval, support, and involvement, the patch management process will not be successful. Providing a clear and concise return on investment (ROI) on how the patch management process not only will save the organization money but also will protect its reputation and business operations is one way to gain executive management support. The security committee must provide executive management with a business plan, or case study, on why this initiative needs to occur, a high-level time frame for completion, and then a follow-up report once the process is in place, further providing business value justification.

Collaboration among various teams of individuals can also be a challenge for the organization. Implementing a patch management process is not a simple task, especially because some groups and people involved in the process may not currently collaborate on such items. Providing communication to the various groups with frequent updates and status will convey to the organization how the patch management process is proceeding and will further define what their responsibilities are as users. A clear understanding that the patch management process is part of the vulnerability management process enables the company to address not only security-related patches but also those that pose a risk to the security posture of the company. Through frequent meetings and communication sessions in the early phases of putting the patch management process in place, collaboration can begin to build, resulting in a security committee that has established a team-like atmosphere even with the differences of opinions.

The following set of challenges relates to assessing the vulnerability and the course of action taken against the patches as they are released. Even during the initial assessment phase, determining whether a patch applies to the organization can be a challenge (again, unless there is an inventory of all systems in place). When a patch is released, the security group, and the security committee, must be able to immediately determine whether the patch applies to the organization's environment. This is a critical piece in allowing the process to move through the various stages quickly and efficiently. If it takes a week to determine whether the vulnerable application is installed in the environment, the exploit may be released prior to even finishing the first step in the process. Through the impact assessment phase, determining when and when not to patch can be a challenge and can also cause other slowdowns in the process. The security committee must determine whether to implement a patch after the results of the impact assessment are compiled. If they cannot gain a consensus, executive management must be brought in to assist in making the right choice.

When deploying patches to the vulnerable systems, other challenges can arise. Patch dependencies seem to be the biggest cause of these issues. In many cases, a patch will require that a previous patch be installed on a system. If this step is overlooked in the testing phase, deploying the patch to the production environment can have ill effects and ultimately cause a back-out to occur. This emphasizes why the testing phase is so important—to make sure these items are not overlooked or missed altogether. This also touches on the subject of standard builds and maintaining a baseline requirement on all systems. When a patch is ready to be deployed into production, no system should need to have a previous patch installed before the later version is installed. This can slow down the deployment of the patches, again leaving the organization vulnerable to an exploit if it is not completed in the time frame assigned to that patch.

Typically, documentation is looked at as a meaningless step and something that is put off until the very end, if ever completed at all. However, as with any process that an organization implements, accurate documentation must be available to support it. This includes not only the process itself but also any supporting procedures and the overall patch management policy. This documentation must also be reviewed on a regular basis and revised as needed. If the documentation is not followed, perhaps it is because the process is unachievable or not functioning properly. If this is the case, the security committee must go back and review the process, determining where the gaps lie between the process and what is being done, and then must update the process and the documentation appropriately. Keeping the documentation in a centralized location ensures that each individual or group involved in the process can obtain the documentation on an as-needed basis without having to worry that it is outdated.

Holding people accountable for their actions poses a challenge to any organization, regardless of its security posture. Within the patch management process, the security committee addresses the issues of accountability because it is placed on a group of individuals to oversee and maintain the process instead of just one person. Of course, the users are a different matter, and ensuring that they understand their responsibilities as it pertains to the process is important for them to be held accountable. Because the security committee is derived from individuals from various other departments within the organization, each plays a major role in the patch management process; they must all work together to guarantee that the vulnerability is addressed throughout the organization. In the end, they are all held accountable for the success of the patch management process.

Next Steps

Now it is time to take the knowledge gained from all the previous chapters and apply it to the organization. This is easier said than done. As has been mentioned numerous times, each organization is different, and each will approach patch management in a different manner. Every organization must take from this book what is relevant to its environment and may apply it equally to what it can support daily. Patch management is not a one-time effort; it must be continuously followed because vulnerabilities are released at various times and intervals. Patch management is not a cookie-cutter solution. Each and every aspect and piece of the process can be applied to every organization. Thus, this book should be used to provide guidance to the organization regarding what needs to be done in a patch management process to cure the patch management headache many are facing today.

The first step in mapping the organization to the recommended patch management process is to go back and complete the first steps in the planning phase of putting the process in place. This would entail completing an assessment of how patch management is being addressed internally. As part of the assessment, the organization should document its findings to evaluate them accurately. This will show the organization where it stands with patch management and how it differs from what is recommended. The organization should also document what its requirements are with regard to a patch management process. The requirements can then be compared with what is being accomplished to determine where the gaps reside, and then a road map for bridging these gaps can be put in place with plans to implement them. These are the most important steps in establishing the patch management process. If these steps are done properly, the rest of the steps will follow suit.

Two key next steps for any organization include the inventory management and standard build recommendations discussed throughout the book. The first, inventory management, is absolutely necessary for the patch management process to be successful within the organization. If the organization does not know what is in the environment, it cannot be patched accurately. Regardless of the size of the infrastructure, number of locations, or even span of the network itself, each and every device and system on the network should be contained in a centrally located database, establishing that each is tracked throughout its life cycle. If this is not being completed, the organization should consider creating inventory management in conjunction with planning for starting the patch management process. A common problem organizations are facing is that they think they have patched every vulnerable system in their environment. Then, they come to find out when a virus is identified in the infrastructure they have, in fact, missed one system or a group of systems. Unless inventory management is being performed to some degree, the chance of this problem reoccurring will be high.

The step that includes implementing a standard build is probably the most intense and time-consuming one to address. However, it needs to be implemented to ensure that the process is a success. Again, each desktop within the organization's infrastructure should be running on the same standard build, or at least a variation of one. Having variations of standard builds is also feasible because a location, or department, may require a specific application, whereas other departments would not. Keeping the standard builds down to a reasonable level is appropriate, although the more standard builds on the desktops the more difficult these can be to track. One option might be that the organization will have one baseline standard build for the entire organization, and then, depending on the department or function, additional applications can be installed as needed as long as they are included in the centralized database. A standard build for the servers applies to this situation as well. If departments are putting servers into production without any formally defined server hardening guidelines, the organization may not realize what applications or services are running on those servers. This can make patching them more difficult, because they will not have an accurate inventory of what needs to be patched in the first place.

Each organization must approach patch management with the mind-set that it is not going away anytime soon. It is not the latest fad or greatest technology. It is a process that protects an organization from vulnerabilities, exploits, and malicious activity. These three items will always be in the information technology (IT) world as long as there are people out there who wish to bring these vulnerabilities to light, resulting in business-interrupting exploits. Organizations must protect their assets from such threats. Therefore, patch management must be considered a standard operating procedure moving forward within the organization. Taking the time and due diligence up front when implementing the process will ensure that the organization is protected for years to come, even with the changes that occur within an organization.

Index